HOW TO BE INVISIBLE

THOMAS DUNNE BOOKS
ST. MARTIN'S PRESS
NEW YORK

HOW TO BE INVISIBLE

THE ESSENTIAL GUIDE TO PROTECTING YOUR PERSONAL PRIVACY, YOUR ASSETS, AND YOUR LIFE

J. J. LUNA

This publication is for informational purposes only and should not be used as a substitute for legal or other professional advice. If professional advice or other expert assistance is required, the services of a competent professional should be sought to address the particular circumstances involved.

THOMAS DUNNE BOOKS.
An imprint of St. Martin's Press.

www.stmartins.com

Library of Congress Cataloging-in-Publication Data

Luna, J. J.
     How to be invisible : the essential guide to protecting your personal privacy, your assets, and your life / J. J. Luna.—Rev. and updated.
          p. cm.
     Includes index (p. 279).
     ISBN 0-312-31906-1
     EAN 978-0312-31906-9
     1. Privacy, Right of—United States. 2. Identification—United States.
   3. Computer security—United States. I. Title.

JC596.2.U5L86 2004
323.44'8'0973—dc22

                                                                2003058770

10 9 8 7 6 5 4 3 2

A NOTE TO READERS

This book is dedicated to an anonymous member of Spain's Secret Police. On January 27, 1960, during a brief encounter on a quiet back street in Santa Cruz de Tenerife, I asked him for advice on how best to avoid any problems in the land of Generalissimo Francisco Franco. The advice he gave me has served me well for more than forty years. He said there was only one way to avoid troubles with the authorities:

"Make yourself invisible."
And so I did.

CONTENTS

PREFACE

Some things change slowly, some things change quickly, and some things never change at all. This certainly applies to those of us who, despite having "nothing to hide," are deeply concerned with keeping our private lives private.

The first edition of *How to Be Invisible* was published in July 2000. On September 11, 2001, my advice about anonymous air travel was suddenly as useless as a telephone directory for offices in the Twin Towers. The anthrax scare produced another change, and, ten weeks later, with the passing of the USA Patriot Act, yet more changes were in order. The results of that law—and of the U.S. Attorney General John Ashcroft's interpretation of it—are still being disputed in the press and in the courts.

More than 30 percent of the information in this second edition is new, thanks in part to feedback from thousands of readers who purchased the first edition. Some wrote to me in the Canary Islands. Many more posted comments on my Web site, *www.howtobeinvisible.com*. A common refrain was, "Your book has changed my life!"

Here are some of the changes from the first edition:

TRAVEL

You can still travel anonymously, as long as you do not—within the U.S. boundaries—travel by plane or, to a lesser extent, by bus or train. I discuss vehicle ownership and tips about travel, including updates on what the police can or cannot do if they stop your vehicle.

BORDER CROSSINGS

A survey showed that this information was the only section of the book that readers felt could be eliminated. The only remaining information—that of precautions when crossing into Canada or Mexico—has been incorporated into Chapter 21.

E-MAIL, COMPUTERS, AND THE INTERNET

Two readers were kind enough to contact me last year and offer their services. One is a forensic computer investigator for the Seattle Police Department and the other is an international expert on computer privacy. The results are scary, but if you value your privacy on the Internet, these are the things that you *must* know.

The original chapter covering this subject has now been expanded into two chapters. The first has a series of suggestions for protecting information on a computer that is not connected to the Internet by either a wireless connection or a land line. The second chapter outlines the additional dangers from an Internet connection. *Both chapters now stress the laptop's superiority to a desktop computer, even if you never travel.*

ALTERNATE ADDRESSES

Next to questions about limited liability companies, this was the topic that generated the most questions from readers. As a result, I have eliminated some of the more exotic suggestions and have also clarified the way a post office box can be used in conjunction with a commercial mail-receiving agency. Most important, I now list many true experiences from readers who successfully obtained alternate addresses in new and interesting ways. Using these true examples, readers will now find practical, easy-to-copy examples for setting up new "ghost" addresses.

LEGAL ENTITIES

Among the thousands of questions and comments from my readers, only five were about corporations or trusts. I have, therefore, limited myself to a few brief comments about these two categories. The overwhelming interest from all other readers was in the use of limited liability companies, especially for titling vehicles and real estate. Many questions had to do with insurance, and some asked about using the LLCs for business and/or banking. As a result, I've doubled the amount of information about the proper use of limited liability companies.

RECOMMENDATIONS

Originally, it seemed proper to give multiple recommendations for forming legal entities, buying books or magazines, seeking help from private investigators, or finding household help among groups that are known to be of total confidence and trust. In practice, however, this left many readers confused. For example, if you seek the best doctor in the country for an extremely delicate operation, you don't want someone to hand you a "preferred list." You want the name of the *very best man or woman in the field*, do you not? For that reason, you will find a single recommendation in each category. This is based not only on the opinions of others but on my own personal experience. Although this limits the number of recommendations and they remain, of course, a matter of opinion, I stand firmly behind the ones that I do make.

LEGALITY

Again and again, reviewers of *How to Be Invisible* have had words of praise for my emphasis on doing everything according to the law. Once again, I stress that, with a few minor exceptions, there is no reason not to follow the laws and regulations of the land.

HOW TO BE INVISIBLE

HOW THIS BOOK CAN MAKE YOU INVISIBLE

Fear of jail is the beginning of wisdom.

—SEEN ON A BRIGHTLY PAINTED
CHAMBER POT IN NIGERIA

Even though all may be well with you at the present moment, don't be complacent. Danger can strike at any time, at any place, and from any direction. For example, while I was editing this chapter, the following e-mail came in from William Farrell, an investigator for the Department of Defense and a reader of the first edition of *How to Be Invisible:*

> I recently filed a vehicle-fire loss claim with my insurance company (State Farm). I was immediately telephoned by an accusatory and demanding insurance adjuster. Although the local police and fire department have investigated and found the fire cause to be 'undetermined,' the insurance company has put my spouse and I through two interviews and have requested a third! I have also been asked to sign a general release form that would

allow the bearer access to such information as retail buying records, utility records, phone records, financial records, etc. The adjuster also requested copies of telephone (including cell phone) records, and copies of income tax returns. A lesson learned: YOU NEVER KNOW WHAT CIRCUMSTANCES MAY SUDDENLY PUT YOU UNDER A NOSEY INVESTIGATOR'S MICRO-SCOPE! BE PREPARED, BE PREPARED, BE PREPARED!

Fortunately for Farrell, he had previously put into practice many of the suggestions from my book. As a result, he managed to keep his true home address and other personal information from the troublesome investigator. (Also, he crossed out some sections of the form before signing.)

The above is just one of a countless number of sudden emergencies my readers tell me about, leaving their stories at the COMMENT link on my Web site, *www.howtobeinvisible.com*. Some readers—not yet organized—send me unhappy stories as a warning to others. More frequently, however, the readers have prepared beforehand and wish to share their happy experiences. The purpose of this book is to assist *you* in being prepared.

Think of this book as flood insurance. If the river near you has not yet started to rise, I can show you how to move to higher ground. If the river is already rising, I hope at least to show you how to build a raft. And just because the river has never flooded before does not mean it will never flood in the future. Unexpected torrential downpours can come in many forms.

PHYSICAL HARM

In Europe, rapes and murders are just a fraction of those in the United States. No nation on earth has more guns per capita, and few if any have a larger percentage of the population in prison. Besides the muggers, the robbers, and the serial killers, you may suddenly be confronted by

- an irate neighbor, a fellow worker, or a disgruntled client
- an ex-spouse, an ex-lover, or an ex-employee
- in-laws, outlaws, or someone mentally deranged
- a kidnapper, a burglar, or a con man.

MENTAL HARM

The mental damage from worry and fear can be more devastating than a physical attack. This may come from

- stalkers, investigators, or anonymous phone calls in the night
- telephone conversations secretly taped, then passed around
- "confidential" medical records released to your employer, your clients, or your insurance company (this might include mental problems, impotence, abortion, alcohol/drug abuse, a sexual disease, or [fill in the blanks]).

In one recent case, Herbert Goldberg (not his real name) arranged to move east, to Atlanta, to work at the Yerkes Primate Research Center at Emory. *Before he even left California*, a local animal-rights activist group obtained the address of his newly purchased home in Georgia. By the time he arrived, the animal-rights protesters were going from door to door in his neighborhood, distributing leaflets with gruesome pictures and captions like "Look what your new neighbor, Herbert Goldberg, does to animals in the laboratory!"

FINANCIAL HARM

Make a random list of twenty people you know. On the average, six of them have already been sued, or will be in the future. Lawsuits are not filed only because of accidents, negligence, separations, divorces, or contract disputes. In the United States, anyone can sue anyone else.

One of Wiley Miller's *Non Sequitur* cartoons is titled "Legal Mugging." It shows a businessman on the sidewalk of a dark street with his hands in the air. A sign on a post reads: "CAUTION: Watch for Trial Attorneys." Stepping from a narrow alley is a lawyer wearing a stocking cap and dark glasses and holding out a legal document.

"This is a frivolous lawsuit," says the attorney to his victim. "You can either spend years and thousands of dollars defending yourself, or we can settle out of court right now."

Although this was in a cartoon, what it portrays is not comical. More than one million lawsuits are filed each year in this country. How many of those do you think are frivolous but are nevertheless settled out of court?

TOTALLY UNFORESEEN TIDAL WAVES

You peek out your window. Look! Reporters, photographers, and trucks with big satellite dishes! If you think this cannot happen to *you*, then kindly allow me to give you a homework assignment. From this day forward, when you read your newspaper or watch the news on TV, start searching for cases where an unknown person is suddenly thrust into the national spotlight. Then ask yourself, *Could this possibly happen to me?*

Here are just a few of the many things that could bring the media, or worse, to your home address:

- A bomb goes off, you were in the area, the FBI thinks you fit the profile.
- You win the lottery. (More tears have been shed over winning a lottery than not winning one.)
- An Ident-A-Kit of the person who robbed the convenience store at 11:45 last night is flashed on TV, and it looks just

like you! And you don't have a plausible excuse for that time that anyone's going to believe.

• You were innocently involved with the wrong people, and the 60 *Minutes* crew is within minutes of tracking you down.

• Someone faked your e-mail address when searching for "young virgins" on the Internet, and the postal inspectors (yes, the 'Net is in their jurisdiction) are about to confiscate your computer.

Do not think for a moment that the information to follow is of mere academic interest—it may be useful beyond your wildest imagination. An article in *Newsweek*, titled "Getting the Wrong Man," gave a chilling example of something that occurs more often than we care to think about.

"Tom Kennedy found the body of his wife, Irene, who had been strangled and stabbed 29 times while on her daily stroll through a park in the Boston suburb of Walpole. Then, a few hours later, the police called at a nearby dilapidated bungalow where Eddie Burke, a 48-year-old handyman, lived with his mother . . . He was practically a textbook match for police profilers: a loner who knew the victim and was clearly eccentric."

[What on earth does "eccentric" mean? My best friends—with a smile—call *me* eccentric. Do I therefore fit a certain profile?]

"Burke was visibly nervous and gave contradictory answers when questioned by investigators."

[Wouldn't you be nervous, too?]

"There was blood on his clothes and hands. And forensic dentists would soon match his teeth with bite marks left on Mrs. Kennedy's breast."

Burke was arrested for murder. Within twenty-four hours, the police learned that the DNA from the saliva on Mrs. Kennedy's chest could not have come from Burke. Did they then release him?

"Incredulous, they ran more tests, which again exonerated him. In addition, blood found on Burke turned out to be feline; he had been tending to injured cats. A palm print left on Mrs. Kennedy's thigh didn't match Burke's hand, while the bite-mark evidence proved inconclusive . . . Yet for six weeks, police kept insisting they had the right man in jail . . . While he was locked away, Burke's life was put under a microscope. He was demonized in newspapers and on TV. . . . The sociopathic profiles were fueled by details of his home's contents—X-rated videotapes, kitchen knives, the book *Men Who Hate Women and the Women Who Love Them*. 'They didn't mention the three Bibles in my room,' Burke says. 'They could just as easily have said I was a religious fanatic.' "

The police claim they followed a logical course and "had the backing of reputed scientific experts." Let us assume that is correct. The point is that even though Burke was the wrong man, *the contents of his house were published by the media.*

Suppose *you* are suddenly arrested, even though innocent, and the contents of your home are made public? Would anything on the following list—if found in your house—give you cause for concern?

- Excess cash?
- Guns and ammunition?
- Telephone records of all long-distance calls?
- Books, magazines, brochures, correspondence?
- Empty whiskey bottles or evidence of substance abuse?
- Statements from your bank, your broker, your credit card company?
- The contents on your computer's hard drive, including so-called deleted files, along with a list of sites you once entered on the World Wide Web?

If the police are after you, whether you are guilty or not, what is your first priority? Is it not *time?*

You need time to think, time to get certain items out of the house, time to locate your attorney, or—heaven forbid—time to pick up some cash, arrange transportation, and flee. This book is designed to give you that time, and to help you keep your private information private.

Before we continue, let me say that if someone with *unlimited funds* is after you, you will eventually be found. If you doubt this, contact a competent (repeat: competent) private investigator and say, "I wish to disappear so completely that even you couldn't find me. Can you help me?" The six-word answer will be, "No, because I can find anyone!"

And I agree. Repeatedly, private investigators (PIs) make this point in their books, articles, and personal interviews. And if the police are truly after you, *their* record isn't bad, either. Captain Robert L. Snow, a police officer for more than twenty-five years, says in his book *Protecting Your Life, Home, and Property* that the Indianapolis Police Department finds 98 or 99 percent of all persons reported to them as missing.

But in the Private Investigator section of my home library, I find no PIs anywhere who will admit defeat under any circumstances, *as long as payment is forthcoming.* The closest I can come to a failure is a certain PI who says he successfully tracked down 298 of the 299 targets he was given over his lifetime. As for the one he missed, he eventually concluded that he was given false information, that no such person ever existed.

The fuel that runs a private investigator's engine is M-O-N-E-Y. In your present situation, a PI may come up with your home address with a single phone call, and with a list of your assets the next day. What this knowledge can help you to do, then, is to:

1. Plug the immediate loopholes in your security.

2. Put you on guard before you ever again give out your Social Security number, home address, or correct date of birth, to anyone other than a government agency.

3. Make it so expensive to trace you and/or your assets that the bad guys or gals will give up before achieving their goals.

The direct correlation between money and results cannot be overemphasized. In the sections to come, I'll be referring to various levels of security, with a general outline as follows. However, there may be no clear-cut divisions between one level and the next—it depends on who is after you, why, and the price he or she is willing to pay.

Level One Very basic, economical moves that will give you more privacy than 98 percent of the general population. The opposition might have to pay a private investigator several hundred dollars to track you down.

Level Two At this point, your utilities and your telephone will be in alternate names. The license plates on your vehicles will not reveal your true name and address. Your trash will be shredded. The PI may now require several thousand dollars in order to track you down.

Level Three Welcome to my level! Both your home (or rental property) and your vehicles will be in the name of a limited liability company (LLC). Your home address will now be hidden from your banker, your dentist, and your doctor. It will no longer appear on your annual tax returns. The black-hat boys and/or the law firms may have to pay a PI some serious money to track you down. Are you worth that much to them? If not, sleep well.

Level Four At this level, you are duplicating the federal Witness Security Program (incorrectly called the Witness "Protection" Program in the media) for criminals protected by the U.S. government. When the Feds do it for a felon, it's legal. When you do it for yourself, it's illegal. Your bridges are now ashes, your friends and relatives just a distant memory. You've canceled all magazine and newsletter subscriptions, cut all ties with clubs, hobbies, and religion, no longer file tax returns, and will never again work for an employer. You may feel this is necessary if there's a bounty on your head or a contract on your life, but at this point, is life still worth living?

If so, keep running, because you can *still* be found. The PI, however, must now have unlimited funds at his disposal, and will call for help. Just as pinned-down soldiers on a battlefield call in air strikes, PIs call in investigative reporters. These are the men who dig up celebrity skeletons for tabloids such as the *National Enquirer*, the *Globe*, and the *Star*. Don't underestimate them. These guys are good—the best in the business.

I recommend you start working on Level One even before you finish reading this book. In the weeks and months to come, raise yourself to Level Two. After that, decide whether or not you wish to ease up to Level Three. It may look difficult at first, but countless others have done it, and so can you. Not only may it be easier than you think, but it can be fun as well, and lead you to a more stress-free life.

However, you must first ask yourself the following question:

"WHOM SHALL I TRUST?"

In 1978, a short, balding man named Stanley Mark Rifkin worked at the Security Pacific National Bank in Los Angeles. Security Pacific thought of him as a computer programmer, but Rifkin thought of himself as a consummate thief.

On October 25, he entered the bank, crossed the lobby, and took the elevator up to the wire transfer room. From this room, hundreds of millions of dollars passed each day from Security Pacific through the Federal Reserve system and on to international banks. Rifkin, who identified himself as the bank's computer consultant, was not challenged as he walked into the heavily guarded room. By interviewing one of the workers, he learned the routing instructions, transfer routines, and the day's security code. Before he left, he memorized an employee access code from an information board on the wall. Later that day, posing as a branch manager, he called the wire room.

"This is Mike Hansen on International."

"Okay, and the office number?" came the response.

"It's 286."

"And the code?"

"Code is 4739."

"Okay."

Now came the moment Rifkin had been living for.

"The bank," he said, speaking in a calm voice, "is Irving Trust in New York City. Payment is to Wozchod Bank, Zurich, Switzerland. The amount is ten million two hundred thousand even."

"Okay, and what's the interoffice settlement number?"

"Let me check. I'll call you right back." Rifkin then called a different number at the bank. Posing as someone working in the wire room, he requested the settlement number—and he got it. When he called the wire room back, his order was accepted. Rifkin had just managed to pull off one of the biggest bank thefts in history. Before the day was out, he was high above the Atlantic, bound for Europe.

In Switzerland, he purchased 250,000 raw diamonds, weighing nearly four pounds. (Raw diamonds are easy to sell and cannot be traced.) At this point, it appeared that Rifkin had pulled off the perfect crime. No one at Security Pacific even knew the money was gone! There are conflicting stories as to what happened next.

Some say he had an ego problem, and couldn't help showing the diamonds to his friends. Others say he bragged about the heist to his lawyer and "trusted friend," assuming he was protected by the attorney-client privilege. Whatever the case, *someone* told the FBI. They chased him, they caught him, and he went to prison.

My original choice for a quote at the beginning of this chapter was from *Poor Richard's Almanac*. There, Benjamin Franklin wrote, "Three may keep a secret, if two of them are dead." Stanley should have followed Ben's advice.

However, you and I have not stolen any money, nor are we on the run for murder, so there will be few if any instances where if three know our secret, two must be dead. I cite the Rifkin case not out of admiration for his cunning but as an example of stupidity.

Francis Beaumont, one of England's most popular playwrights in the Age of Shakespeare, had this to say about secrets: "All confidence which is not absolute and entire is dangerous. There are few occasions but where a man ought either to say all, or conceal all, for, how little ever you have revealed of your secret to a friend, you have already said too much if you think it not safe to make him privy to all particulars."

Allow me to rephrase his comment, boiled down to plain language of the present day: *Do not trust your attorney, CPA, private detective, banker, doctor, dentist, school authorities, relatives, family, friends, or anyone else unless you would trust them with your life.*

Here is my own short list of whom I do and do not trust:

- *Family* I trust my wife. I always trusted my parents, but they are dead. I see no reason to share confidential matters with our grown children or their spouses, nor our grandchildren. I love my millionaire kid sister in Hollywood, but I do not tell her my secrets. (Sorry, Sis!)

- *Attorneys* I did trust one in the Canary Islands, but he died before this book went to press. (Another one in said islands took money from my enemies to give me incorrect advice!) I still trust an attorney in San Francisco whom I used for many years. When tested, he was not found wanting. Another one, in Oakland, has worked out well so far.

- *CPAs, bankers, doctors, dentists* One CPA in Texas. None of the others.

- *Private investigators* Some of my clients are PIs and look to me for advice. There are a few good PIs, a number of mediocre PIs, and a sizeable number that are badly bent. To date, I have never had to trust a PI. Should the need arise in the future, I would choose the one listed in the Appendix, because he has a reputation too valuable to risk with a betrayal.

In the list above, perhaps the most innocent-appearing category is that of dentists. "Surely," you might say, "our friendly family dentist will cause us no pain."

That is what Holly LaFontaine of Everett, Washington, used to think. That was before Holly's ten-year old son missed a dental appointment to take care of very serious cavities. According to an article in the *Seattle Post-Intelligencer*, the dentist called Child Protection Services and reported her! The article goes on to say the mother was "furious" with the charge of possible neglect or abuse. That must have been the understatement of the week.

"Professionals who have contact with children," says the last paragraph, "are required by law to report cases of suspected abuse or neglect. . . ."

PRIVACY

This book has a single theme: *How to keep your private life private*. It is not about avoiding taxes (see the first question at the end of this chapter) nor about protecting your assets, although the latter may be an added benefit. Nor is it a call to disobey the law. I consider myself a law-abiding, tax-paying citizen of the world. True, I may not be accurate when called upon to give my home address, and I do confess that I am allergic to business permits when working from home. However, if I mention any procedure which I suspect might be construed as illegal in some states or provinces, I will warn you of that fact beforehand and let you make your own decision. (Although I've made privacy my business for more than forty years, I am not a lawyer. So, to repeat, don't take any unusual measures without the advice and counsel of a trained legal professional.)

For example, you may wish to operate a legitimate but anonymous business from your home. This means you may ignore the requirements for a business license and also the resale tax permit (assuming you live in a sales-tax state). The city will lose a small fee when you don't pay for a license. On the other hand, the state will gain when you pay sales taxes for supplies that might otherwise be exempt. Other small pluses and minuses will enter into consideration. Depending upon the community, there may or may not be any penalty if you are caught, other than catching up on some payment you failed to make. So then, please note:

- My job is to explain the options.
- Your job is to make the decisions.

WHAT MAKES THIS BOOK UNIQUE?

- *Author's qualifications* Other than searching out odd ways to make money in niche markets, my only business is privacy. I live, eat, sleep, and breathe privacy. I have been living a private life since 1959.

- *Anti-offshore* I do not suggest you leave the country, nor do I recommend foreign corporations, trusts, or tax-haven bank accounts. You can accomplish your goals right here—cheaper, better, and safer.

- *Alternative to Delaware and Nevada corporations* I will recommend a legal entity in a certain state—one that I have never seen discussed in print—that, formed correctly, can never be traced back to you. No managers, no directors, no annual report.

- *No ranting or raving* Well, a little ranting maybe, but definitely no raving about Big Brother, jack-booted government thugs, or the Internal Revenue Service. This is a book about

Life in the Real World, not a treatise about the Constitution, the Bill of Rights, or Common Law.

• *Up-to-date advice for the year 2004 and beyond* Any book written prior to this time will be out of date when it comes to police powers, e-mail accounts, ChoicePoint, limited liability companies, commercial mail-receiving agencies, and the increasing danger in giving out the last four digits of your Social Security number or your true date of birth. Although no book can be completely up-to-the-minute, since laws and procedures are constantly changing, I maintain a Web site, *www.howtobeinvisible.com*, exclusively for you, readers. Go there for the latest information about personal and business privacy. The password for the update link is *ssndob*.

HOW TO USE THIS BOOK

Each chapter offers basic information, step-by-step. Although I explain new terms when they are first introduced, if you run across a word or acronym you do not understand, please consult the Glossary.

You will find questions and answers at the end of each chapter. Many of these questions have been sent to me via my Web site, and I have included them in this book as something extra. If you wish to have more information about the subject of a given chapter, do review them. Otherwise, feel free to jump ahead to the chapter that follows. (You can always come back to the Q & A sections later.)

Also, you may choose to skip some chapters—such as those about radios and computers—that you feel do not apply to you. However:

Do not skip—repeat, DO NOT skip—the next chapter. Your journey to invisibility must begin with the way in which you receive your mail.

QUESTIONS & ANSWERS

Why don't you admit that income taxes are voluntary?

From time to time I get "tips" from readers about how to avoid paying taxes. (Since I pay my taxes and advise others to do the same, one reader called me "morally bankrupt.") A typical scam making the rounds on the Internet is headlined "Untax Yourself for $49.95." You wouldn't think anyone would be ignorant enough to believe this, but many people continue to be taken in. The ads may say that paying taxes is "voluntary," but that is absolutely wrong. The U.S. courts have continuously rejected this and other similar arguments. If you follow the advice contained in these scams, you can end up with civil and/or criminal tax penalties being assessed. Numerous sellers of these bogus packages have been convicted on criminal tax-fraud charges. For more information, go to *http://usgovinfo.about.com/library/ weekly/aa021701a.htm.*

Why are you against offshore trusts, when this is recommended by attorneys and promoters at so many seminars?

Despite all the books, Internet advertising, and island-based seminars, I cannot recommend them. (Those that do are, of course, often selling a product.) Many seem to overlook the Small Business Protection Act of 1996. The code provision (IRC Section 6048-c) says a taxpayer who receives a distribution from a foreign trust shall "make a return," which includes the name of the trust, the amount of the distribution, and "such other information as the Secretary [of the Treasury] may prescribe." At least one of the authors who writes about hiding your money offshore has recently been indicted, along with his lawyer-partner. According to the charges, they allegedly played host to "offshore wealth summits" that were advertised in in-flight magazines, such as *American Way* and *Sky Mall*. Would you like to see *your* name on a seminar list, when the authorities examine their books?

What about offshore corporations?

Same answer, even though I once used them myself. Every year the risk of trouble increases, as reporting requirements are amplified and tax-haven governments are subjected to increasing pressure from the U.S. government—especially since the events of September 11, 2001. If you fill out the required reports, you compromise your privacy. If you don't fill them out and are caught, you can go to jail.

How about banks in tax-haven lands?

You mean, to maintain secrecy? If there is one common denominator in all the reports I receive about tax havens, it is about the increasing likelihood of offshore banks being forced by U.S. authorities into revealing confidential information.

I buy all the latest books on privacy and security, and I pay out thousands of dollars for magazines and newsletters in this field. Not a month goes by without my reading a warning that in such-and-such tax haven, privacy and secrecy are being whittled away. Here's just one example, this one from CNN.com:

> "The Justice Dept. and the Internal Revenue Service are nearing an agreement with American Express to turn over the names of its credit card customers who pay bills through offshore tax havens, a newspaper reported Friday. The IRS, which declined to comment, is attempting to identify people who are cheating on their taxes by paying bills through offshore accounts in places such as the Bahamas and the Cayman Islands, the *Wall Street Journal* reported."

Why go offshore when you can better accomplish your goals in the USA?

How about keeping offshore communications private?

Unless you use snail mail, forget about privacy. Your e-mails, radio signals, and telephone conversations will be monitored by Echelon, as indicated in this article in *Business Week:*

> "You think the Internet brings grave new threats to privacy? Then you probably don't know about Echelon. Run by the super-secret National Security Agency, it's the granddaddy of all snooping operations . . . it eavesdrops on just about every electronic communication that crosses a national border—phone calls, faxes, telexes, and E-mail—plus all radio signals, including short-wave, airline, and maritime frequencies."

Echelon can also listen in on both local cell-phone calls and long-distance telecom traffic *within* countries, as can the FBI's DCS1000. DCS1000 (originally called "Carnivore") is specialized software installed by the agency on an Internet service provider's network under federal wiretap authority. It is capable of keeping tabs on your e-mail, instant messages, and Web-surfing activities, watching for key words that include all known slang words for drugs, cash, smuggling, bombs, etc. The system is ripe for abuse, because of the secrecy surrounding the way it scans passing data to find its targets.

2

U.S. MAIL—
SERIOUS DANGERS

Do not, as long as you live, ever again allow your real name to be coupled with your home address.

—J. J. LUNA

Washington state resident Elizabeth Reed, 28, dated Anthony Nitsch Jr., 32, for about two months in the fall of 1996. Then, concerned about his drinking, Elizabeth told Anthony the relationship was over. When she stopped taking his calls, he became angry and began stalking and harassing her.

She continued to live at the same address.

Anonymous packages arrived at her home, one with a dead skunk, another with a sex toy and an obscene message. Strange items began to appear in her yard. Someone disconnected her heat pump fuse box and defecated on it. Her new fiancé came to visit her and, when he returned to his car, he discovered the tires had been slashed.

Two years passed. Elizabeth Reed continued to live at the same address. She went to a judge and sought a restraining order against Anthony Nitsch Jr. The judge refused to grant it, because Elizabeth could not prove Anthony was the person who was harassing her.

On a warm Monday night in early June, Anthony cut the telephone line that led into her home. Then he broke in, threatened her, and fired one shot at her from a .40 handgun.

The ending of this story is not as sad as might normally be the case. I have before me the Tacoma, Washington, *News Tribune* dated June 5, 1998. The headline on page 3 reads: "Intruder Who Was Shot Held for $500,000 Bail." Although Elizabeth Reed had failed to move away, she was armed and ready. Nitsch missed. She did not. "Nitsch remained in serious condition Wednesday," says the article, "at Harborview Medical Center with five gunshot wounds to his chest."

TO MOVE OR NOT TO MOVE

Mexican journalist Fernando Balderas and his wife, Yolanda Figueroa, wrote a book called *The Boss of the Gulf: The Life and Capture of Juan Garcia Abrego*, which was published in August 1996. The book was dedicated to Mexico's federal attorney general, Antonio Lozano Gracia. At that time, Fernando and Yolanda lived with their children Patricia, Paul, and Fernando in an attractive home in an upscale neighborhood in Mexico City. Although nothing in the book appeared to warrant retribution, it did discuss Mexico's drug lords and revealed bribery in high circles. What follows is from the December 9, 1996, edition of *USA Today*:

MEXICO CITY—Police found journalist Fernando Balderas, his author wife, Yolanda Figueroa, and their three children, ages 18, 13, and 8, bludgeoned to death in their beds last week . . . a brutal murder that shocked even hardened residents. Adding to the intrigue: Police say the family was probably murdered Tuesday night, a day after President Ernesto Zedillo fired Mexico's federal

attorney general Antonia Lozano Gracia, to whom Figueroa's
book was dedicated.

They should have fled their home the very day when President
Zedillo fired the guy their book was dedicated to. Some say that
if the bad guys are out to get you, there's nothing you can do,
but I disagree. You can be seen in public but still keep your home
address *private*.

I suspect that the Balderas family did indeed think about
moving, but then decided it would be too much trouble. Trust
me on this one: trouble or not, moving is better. However, even if
all is quiet and you are unable or unwilling to move at this time,
I urge you to take the steps recommended in this and succeeding
chapters. As you will see when you come to the section about a
"ghost address" in chapter 5, there are legitimate ways to disconnect your name from your property, your telephone, your utilities, your licenses and yes—even from your tax returns. The place
to start is with home deliveries, be that by mail, by UPS, by
FedEx, or by your local pizza parlor.

If you plan to move within the year, perhaps you will stall on
some of the other suggestions. Do not, however, delay on this
one. If there is only one lesson you carry away from this book, let
it be the one listed at the beginning of this chapter.

*Do not, as long as you live, ever again allow your real name to be
coupled with your home address.*

NEVER GIVE YOUR ADDRESS TO STRANGERS

Consider the case of George Joseph Cvek, as presented in the
book *Diary of a D.A.* by Martin M. Frank, formerly an assistant
district attorney in the Bronx. Frank writes:

> When the doorbell rang on that January afternoon, a young
> housewife opened her apartment door to find a slim, ordinary-

looking man of about twenty-eight standing at the threshold. He
was a stranger to her.

"Are you Mrs. Allen?" he asked.

"Yes, I am."

"Is your husband home?"

"No," she replied, "he isn't here now."

"Gee, I'm sorry," he said. "I know him from Norwalk, Connecticut. I thought this was his early day. Maybe I'll come back
tonight." He seemed rather well acquainted with her husband, a
route salesman in Connecticut for a bakery company.

The caller half-turned to go, then stopped and apologetically
asked, "Could I have a drink of water?"

"Sure," she said, "wait here a second." Leaving him at the door,
Mrs. Allen went into the kitchen. When she returned, she found
that he had walked through the foyer into the living room and
was seated on the sofa. . . .

The caller continued to deceive Mrs. Allen and then suddenly
struck her down and prepared to rape her. At that moment, the
telephone rang. He jumped up and ran from the apartment, slam-
ming the door behind him. But in the years to come, more than
two hundred women were not so fortunate. Their telephones did
not ring. In each case, the caller gained entrance by telling the
wife he knew her husband, and, after gaining entrance through
subterfuge, he raped and killed her, then burglarized the home. In
each case, the husbands themselves were the ones who had unwit-
tingly made the crime possible. They had picked up a neatly
dressed hitchhiker—George Joseph Cvek—who said he was from
Boys Town, Nebraska, and given him a ride. When Cvek was
dropped off, he asked the drivers for their *home address,* so he
could show his appreciation for the ride by mailing a small gift. At
that instant, *each husband sealed his wife's death warrant.*

This is but one of many chilling examples of allowing mail to
come to your home address. In fact, there are dangers not only in
receiving mail but in sending it, as we shall see.

MAIL THEFT

The *Seattle Post-Intelligencer* runs a "Rant & Rave" section each Sunday. Readers can call in during the week with whatever they wish to praise or condemn. The following complaint comes from the January 5, 2003, edition:

> A big rant to the felon who stole our outgoing U.S. mail, forcing several people to close bank accounts and depriving friends and relatives of holiday greetings and children and grandchildren of their Christmas checks.

Does anything about this rant sound a little strange to you? What if the reader's message had started out like this?

> A big rant to the person who saw us park our car on the street, loaded with Christmas packages, and walk away. Although we did leave the doors open and the key in the ignition, he had no right to get in and drive away. . . .

When you walk out to the curb, place your mail in the box, and raise the red flag, your mail is as vulnerable to theft as your car would be if you left the key in it and the doors open.

Every day more than one hundred thousand residential mailboxes in the United States are burglarized. This applies to mail being received both in the city and in the country, both in private homes and in apartment complexes. In Hammond, Indiana, before they were finally arrested, two men and a woman went from door to door but did not knock or ring any bells. The neighbors saw nothing more suspicious than each person depositing an advertising brochure in each mailbox. What they didn't see was the sleight of hand when the person traded the brochure for whatever mail was in the box.

More than a year prior to the rant about theft from a mailbox, the *Seattle Post-Intelligencer* had run a series of articles warning of mail theft not only from home mailboxes but from mail collection boxes on the street, plus the boxes used at thousands of apartments, condominiums, and commercial buildings in the Pacific Northwest. For months, thieves had been using counterfeit "arrow keys." Each arrow key provides access to about twenty-five hundred mail collection boxes, more than ten thousand apartments and condominiums, and virtually all office and commercial buildings in the region. (The keys give postal workers easy access to the mailboxes, making it easier for them to pick up and deliver letters and packages.)

Readers were urged to stop using outside mailboxes to deposit mail, including their own home mailboxes. Instead, they were to deposit mail only inside a post office.

In addition to professional thieves, it was said that many others have been stealing mail: drug addicts, to support their habit; teenagers looking for cash; petty thieves looking for any number of things.

In the article headlined "THEFT OF MAIL A PROBLEM AT OUR DOORSTEP," U.S. Postal Inspector Jim Bordenet voiced his mail-security concerns:

> "Thieves rifle outgoing mail for checks written to pay bills. They then alter the checks so they can cash them for large amounts." He suggests people not put outgoing mail into their own boxes, and especially advises against using the red flag, which is a signal to thieves. "Thieves sometimes follow carriers around and steal incoming mail," he said. "They're typically looking for boxes of checks and credit-card offers."

I will spare you the flurry of articles and letters to the editor that followed publication of the article just quoted. Some of the questions raised were:

- Why didn't the Postal Service warn the public about such thefts years ago?

- Why was nothing said until the thefts were exposed by the local newspapers?
- Why—even now—is the problem not being solved?

Another article, this one from the McClatchey Newspapers, is titled "Post Office Fights Mailbox Theft." It reports that hundreds of pieces of mail are stolen *daily* in the Sacramento, California, area. In rural areas, the criminals watch for raised red flags, the signal that outgoing mail is inside. Others pry open "cluster boxes" at apartment complexes or housing developments and steal everybody's mail at the same time. In some cases, they even pry open the standard blue U.S. mail collection boxes. The article quotes Tom Hall, a postal inspector who investigates mail theft from Sacramento to the Oregon border:

> "Today, thanks to chemicals and computers, thieves can use almost any kind of financial information to commit a variety of financial crimes. If you write a check to a utility and a bad guy gets it, he can 'wash' the utility's name off and make the check out to himself in a higher amount. With that one check, he can also make himself a whole new set of checks under your name."

Even worse, continues the article, "some criminals 'assume' the victim's identity and apply for credit cards in the victim's name."

In Chattanooga, Tennessee, U.S. Postal Inspector Dianne Bracken, who investigates criminal cases in the metro area, says, "Unfortunately, in the United States, mail theft is becoming more common. It's getting to be a bigger problem. I was looking back over some statistics, and in the year 2000 the U.S. Postal Inspections Service arrested almost five thousand people for mail theft."

In an upscale neighborhood in Campbell, California, mail was being stolen on a regular basis. The thief was an elegant-appearing woman who dressed in expensive clothing so that she would not attract attention when she walked up to houses and stole the mail.

Remember, all these thieves need is your name, address, account number, and credit information. They then get on the phone and order merchandise through catalogues. If your home is vacant during the day, they may even have the products sent to your home. They'll just park on your street and wait for FedEx or UPS to swing by! My advice, therefore, is to deposit all outgoing mail inside a building.

Not just any building, however, as Juanita Yvette Lozano discovered. She was indicted by a grand jury in Austin, Texas, after mailing a package inside a post office. (She later pleaded guilty for mailing a video of George W. Bush's confidential debate-prep material to an Al Gore adviser.) Ms. Lozano's problem was that the Austin, Texas, post office has a surveillance camera that takes a video of everyone mailing packages and letters inside the post office. What is the lesson here?

Assume you mail a letter to order a subscription to *Family Circle* magazine. What if, about the same time, someone else mails a letter that contains a white powder or a threat on someone's life? If there are tapes of the event, you may be one of the persons— even though innocent—to receive a scary visit from the FBI.

The next time you are in your local post office, glance around. If you spot a video camera, you may wish to find a different place to mail your letters and packages in the future. Try a smaller post office, or a pickup station inside another business, such as in a strip mall or a supermarket.

By using only boxes inside a building, you will protect your outgoing mail not only from random theft but from having it surreptitiously read. (If you have been targeted for any reason, an investigator might be illegally "borrowing" the mail from your home mailbox, reading it, and returning it the next day, apparently unopened. If no mail ever comes to your home, he will have nothing to read.)

Alternatives If dropping your mail off at the post office is not practical, perhaps you could drop it off at work. (Check first, of course, to see where *that* mail is dropped off.) Or, if you are home all day, you could put the mail out just as the mailman comes by. A third choice—albeit the poorest—is to drop it in one of those big blue mailboxes at shopping centers and other public places. Even here, however, it is best to do it just before the listed pickup time.

If you are still in doubt about the dangers of mail theft, do this: Bring *www.google.com* up on your computer screen and search for "mail theft." (Enclose the two words in quotation marks, as shown). Allow two hours minimum to read the scary stories.

RECEIVING MAIL AT YOUR PRESENT HOME ADDRESS

If you are presently receiving mail at home, you can stop this immediately by turning in a forwarding address. But where should this mail go? Certainly not to any permanent address you will use in the future. Here are some options:

1. If you presently have a P.O. Box that was rented in your own name, and you gave your present address, then forward your mail to that box. Then, when forwarding is no longer needed, close the P.O. Box.

2. If you still receive mail at a commercial mail-receiving agency (CMRA), forward the mail there temporarily. Once again, close your account there as soon as convenient.

3. Have your mail sent on to your place of business if you have one, or perhaps to a friend who is in business.

4. Forward your mail to a friend or relative, preferably across the country. Tell him or her to keep the magazines, toss out the junk mail, and to remail the rest back to you at your new (alternate) address. You haven't got one yet but be patient. It's coming, it's coming.

MAIL FORWARDING

With the exception listed below, I suggest you not check the little box marked "Permanent." If you do, your name will go into the Postal Service's National Change of Address list, and this list of persons that have moved is sold to the commercial mail-list folks, and thus your name and new address will go into countless computers.

Instead, check the "Temporary" box and give a date when this is to end. When that date arrives, notify the post office that you are moving away and do not wish to have any mail forwarded. Mail will then be returned to sender.

Exception If you wish to throw others far off the trail, then do file a Permanent Change of Address. I suggest the actual street address of a mail drop in northern Alaska or—if you already live up there—a mail drop in Florida or Hawaii. Here is an easy way to do it:

1. If you have access to the Internet, go to *www.mbe.com*, the home page of Mail Boxes Etc., or to *www.postnet.net*, the home page of PostNet. Look up the location you want. Or look up one of their locations in the phone book, call them, and ask them to give you the address at such-and-such a location.

2. On your forwarding-address card, fill out your name, the street address, an apartment number, city, state, and ZIP. Example: Your name is Jane Winner and you want your ex to think you moved to Florida.

   If the address you pull up on the Internet is

   MBE#0955
   9970 E. Osceola Pkwy.
   Kissimmee, FL 34743

Forward your mail to

> Jane Winner
> 9970 E. Osceola Pkwy.
> Kissimmee, FL 34743

Here, then, is what will happen. Your mail will be forwarded to the address shown, but because this is a commercial mail receiving agency, and no "#" sign followed by a number is included after the word "Pkwy," the envelope will be stamped with a message similar to the one that follows and will then be returned to the sender.

UNDELIVERABLE
COMMERCIAL MAIL RECEIVING AGENCY
NO AUTHORIZATION
TO RECEIVE MAIL
FOR THIS ADDRESSEE

Will your local post office, the one forwarding the mail to Florida, know what is happening? No, because the mail does not come back to them.

Will the person you are trying to avoid realize you didn't go there, after all? Not necessarily. The stamp on the envelope does not say "No Such Person." It merely says the CMRA is not currently accepting mail for you.

ADDITIONAL FAMILY BENEFIT

If you have young children, you may find this Web site to be of interest: *www.escapeschool.com*. On the subject of incoming mail, it has this to say:

"Do you want your kids to open the mail before you are home? Or should it all wait? If you have a post office box, then you can be the one to pick it up. Otherwise, should they bring it in? Where should they put it? Should they open it or not? What about parcels?"

The obvious answer to those questions is to never receive anything at your home, no mail, no packages, no courier deliveries. Nada.

AN OPTION FOR NONPERSONAL MAIL

Although we ourselves never receive mail at a home address, two of my clients currently receive nonpersonal mail at home for specific reasons:

Rolland H——— recently moved to a rural area. He arranged to receive all personal mail at the home of a widow who lives in the nearest small town, seventeen miles away. (She rents several rooms in her large home to single men, and there is a frequent turnover, so new names at her address are not unusual.) Rolland is a voracious reader and subscribes to more than thirty weekly and monthly magazines. Rather than burden the widow with this volume, however, he orders each new subscription in what appears to be a business name, R & R Services, and has them come to his rural mailbox (where he actually lives). He never uses "R & R" for any other purpose whatsoever. Therefore, if his name is run through a national database of magazine subscribers, there will be no trace back to him.

Janet S——— is a single mother with a six-month-old baby. She recently fled from Washington, DC, to a southern state to escape an ex-lover who was threatening to kill her. She is establishing herself at the new location under another name. She has a new (alternative) address at which she receives mail in a business name from her mother and sister, as well as bank statements, telephone bills, and other personal mail. However, she *wants* to make her new name known, so she receives *Good Housekeeping* and *Reader's Digest*, as well as small shipments of mail-order vitamins, at her home. The orders and the subscriptions have automatically put her new name into various databases and she receives Sweepstakes offers and other junk mail in the new name.

"If someone wishes to look at this mail," she says, "or even steal it, be my guest!"

I have been referring to your "new" or "alternate" address, but from this point forward, it will be called your *ghost* address. A ghost address is a street address that has no connection with your actual place of residence. How this address is obtained will be explained in the following chapter.

Because the secure sending and receiving of mail has become so complicated, the question-and-answer section that follows is one of the largest in this book. If you are in a hurry, however, jump to the next chapter. You can always come back.

QUESTIONS & ANSWERS

What is a "mail cover"?

This is a system used by a number of governments to check your mail without a court order. Your mailman, or the clerk that "boxes" your mail, will be instructed to note the return addresses and country of origin of your incoming mail. If you live a squeaky-clean life, you may say to yourself, imitating *Mad* magazine's Alfred E. Neuman, "What? Me worry?" Read on:

Suppose you send mail *to* a person or company that is the subject of a mail cover? If you list your name and return address, you yourself could end up on a suspect list. There are at least two obvious solutions:

1. copy the British, eliminate a return address; or

2. use some other return address, far, far away.

Recently, the postal authorities have been getting more cautious, e.g., the current requirement makes you take any parcel weighing a pound or more to the counter, in person. For such parcels, they will insist that you include a return address. The day may soon be here when a return address will be required on letters as well.

I send out large volumes of mail, so I use a postage meter. Any danger there?

I don't know how large a volume you refer to, but with one of my previous businesses, my wife and I used to mail two thousand letters a week. We had a regular system, using self-adhesive stamps. First, we stuck one stamp on each of four fingers, then we put them on four envelopes, one, two, three, four, and repeat.

Why didn't we use a postage meter? Because each postage meter has an identification number that ties it to a renter and to a specific location, that's why.

Does it matter if, unsure of the exact postage, I put on more than enough stamps?

Judge for yourself. I know of a case in Missouri where a man put $38 postage on a small package that weighed less than two pounds. Destination was Los Angeles, but it didn't arrive. In view of the excessive postage, the DEA (Drug Enforcement Administration) was called in, and the package turned out to contain $10,000 in cash. Although I do not know if the source of the money was legal, I do know that the DEA "arrests" and keeps most confiscated cash, even though the owner may never be convicted of anything. Actually, cash can be mailed most anywhere using many envelopes and small sums per envelope. With $38, the Missourian could have bought 102 first-class stamps. Had he then put just three $100 bills in each envelope, wrapping the money with a page or two from a magazine, he could have mailed out not $10,000, but $30,600. And if mailed on different days from various post offices, and with a variety of fictitious return addresses, would anyone even have a clue?

This was not the first time I heard of incorrect postage alerting the authorities. One of the telltale signs postal inspectors look for, in the case of letter bombs, is "excess postage." I use an unusually accurate electronic scale and double check all outgoing mail.

At present, I receive a daily newspaper in my own name. It goes into its own box alongside my rural mailbox. Is there some way to at least continue to receive my daily paper, both at my present home, and at the new one when I move?

At one time we had a Canadian newspaper delivered directly to a holiday home under another name. No longer. Too many cases like the one cited in Carson City's *Nevada Appeal*, headed, "Minden Teen Appears in Court, May Face 15 Charges." The charges were that three teenagers burglarized houses in the Carson Valley *while the occupants were away*. And how did they know the occupants were away? From "information allegedly obtained through his job as a newspaper carrier." Nevertheless, if you cannot live without your daily newspaper being delivered to your home, then at least heed this advice:

- Cancel the newspaper you now receive. A month later, order a new subscription under another name. Avoid paying the newspaper carrier in person.

- When you leave on a trip, do not have the newspapers held. Get a friend or neighbor to pick them up. (Nevertheless, the best way is still to have the newspaper delivered to your ghost address.)

How secure is my incoming mail?

That depends on where it's coming from, what it looks like, and who your enemies are. Under normal circumstances, I have far more confidence in regular mail (often referred to as snail mail) than in most electronic mail, because there is no possible way to scan the interiors of *all* letters in the U.S. postal system at any one time. Contrast this with electronic mail, which can be computer-searched at every junction along the way, red-flagging messages with any of hundreds or thousands of key words, such as *bomb, gas, gun, rifle, money, cash,* or with any specific name, including yours.

Note, however, that certain government officials *do* monitor mail from tax-haven countries, especially those on the following list:

Andorra	Germany	Netherlands
Antigua	Great Britain	Nigeria
Aruba	Guernsey	Pakistan
Austria	Hong Kong	Panama
Bahamas	Hungary	Russia
Belize	Iran	Saudi Arabia
Bermuda	Isle of Man	Singapore
British Virgin Islands	Latvia	Switzerland
	Liberia	Thailand
Cayman Islands	Liechtenstein	Turks and Caicos Islands
Channel Islands	Lithuania	
Columbia	Luxembourg	United Arab Emirates
Cook Islands	Marshall Islands	Uruguay
Ecuador	Nauru	Vanuatu
Estonia	Nevis	Venezuela
Gibraltar		

Also, what do your incoming letters look like? If you are in my age bracket, you may remember when your mother dripped hot red wax on the flap of an envelope, then pressed a seal into the wax before it cooled. The more modern method is to seal the flaps with clear tape. Neither is secure, and both methods (especially the red wax seal!) draw unwanted attention to the envelope, saying "Something valuable in here."

Further, anyone with a spray can of freon gas—sold under various trade names in spy shops—can read what's inside without opening the envelope at all. When hit with the spray, the envelope becomes transparent. Thirty seconds later, as the gas evaporates, it returns to its normal condition, with no evidence of this intrusion. (One way to check this is to ask the sender to address a test envelope by hand with a felt-tip pen, or with a fountain pen that uses regular ink. The ink will run when carbon tetrachloride is used—thus tipping you off that the contents have been read.)

Methods once confined to the CIA are now common knowledge, thanks to Paladin Press. They publish the "CIA Flaps and Seals Manual" that carefully details "surreptitious entries of highly protected items of mail," and removing and replacing seals and using carbon tetrachloride on tape is at the elementary level. What worries the CIA and other surreptitious readers of secret mail is not the sealed or taped envelope but the normal one.

"The most innocuous-looking envelope," says the CIA manual, "may be the one that will get the operator in the most trouble." Correct! See the following question and answer about innocuous-looking envelopes.

How I can best protect my outgoing mail?

First of all, *the envelope should appear normal.* A junk-mail appearance is best (as long as the recipient knows that in advance) and for that reason I prefer a standard #10 envelope with a laser-printed label. If a sealed, taped, or otherwise obviously protected envelope is desired, enclose and protect everything in a #9 envelope and insert that one in the #10 envelope. If you are not familiar with envelope numbers, note these measurements:

> #10 envelope: $4\frac{1}{8} \times 9\frac{1}{2}$ inches
> # 9 envelope: $3\frac{7}{8} \times 8\frac{7}{8}$ inches

To counteract the envelope's transparency when sprayed with freon, wrap the contents of the #9 envelope with carbon paper, if you can still find it in this modern age.

What's the best way to have a letter remailed from some far-away place?

In the years directly following the anthrax scare, due to increased mail surveillance by the FBI, it was best not to even think about remailing a letter. However, as this book goes to press, the scare seems to have receded, so I'll suggest a method that usually works quite well.

Prepare your letter, seal it in an addressed #9 envelope (available at any office-supply store), and put on the correct postage. Enclose your letter in a #10 envelope, add a cover letter as shown below, and a $5 bill. Note that you don't use a last name, so there is no way to prove you were not a guest.

> *Sheraton El Conquistador*
> *Attention: Concierge*
> *I was a recent guest at your hotel and was most impressed with your fine service. I do, however, have a small problem, and I must ask you a favor.*
> *During my Arizona stay, I promised to write to a friend about an errand he gave me, but I neglected to do so. Would you kindly help me cover my derrière by mailing the enclosed items?*
> *I enclose $5 for your trouble, and hope to thank you in person when I return to the Sheraton El Conquistador later this year.*
> *Yours sincerely,*
> *Jim*

Mail your letter to "concierge" at one of the very best hotels in the city of your choice. (You can get the name and address from AAA, or off the Internet.) Here is a sample of how to address the envelope:

> *For the CONCIERGE:*
> Sheraton El Conquistador

10000 North Oracle Road
Tucson, AZ 85737

Note: If there is some doubt that the hotel has a concierge, just address the letter to "Reception." (If there isn't a reception desk, you've chosen too small a hotel.)

From now on, when you travel, pick up sample envelopes and letterheads from luxury hotels. Staying at them is best, but you can often just drift up to the desk when they're busy with check-ins and kindly ask for "a sheet of paper and an envelope." One of each is enough, as you'll never use a specific hotel for remailing more than once.

What's the most remote, faraway return address I could possibly put on an envelope, that would still be in the United States and have daily mail service?

A post office box in Dutch Harbor, Alaska. Since a number of readers had expressed interest in having a faraway address, I recently flew (with difficulty) to Alaska's Aleutian Islands to arrange a mail-forwarding service for those who have New Mexico limited liability companies and have need for a faraway address. If you have an LLC, details are available at my Web site. Or contact Rosie Enriquez, listed in the Appendix.

3

WHEN IS A "LIE" NOT A LIE?

I said in my haste, "All men are liars."

—PSALM 116:11

In your quest for personal privacy, again and again you will come up against questions like these:

- What is your name?
- What is your home telephone number?
- What is your street address?
- What is your date of birth?
- What is your Social Security number?

Also, if you are (for example) a husband and father who is determined to keep the family's private affairs private, be prepared for questions like these:

Wife: What? You want me to *lie?*

Child: Daddy, did you just tell a *lie?*

Parents: What do you mean, we can't tell anyone where you really live? You want us to *lie*, son?

The time to think about how you will answer such questions is *now*, before you step up to the counter at a commercial mail-receiving agency, or before you fill out your first form at the post office.

Since lying is a moral issue, and since morality is basically a religious issue, I am going to cite the exact words from a small religious magazine I read back in 1954. It was published by the International Bible Students Association, and since it answered a question I had long wondered about, I memorized this sentence word for word:

> A LIE is a false statement made by one [person] to another, who is entitled to hear and know the truth, and which false statement tends toward injury to the other.

This is the only definition of a lie I've ever read that covers false statements made by the biblical characters Abraham, Sarah, Isaac, David, Jonathan, and Rahab. Did they disgrace themselves as liars by their caution? Not according to the above definition.

You, dear reader, must make your own evaluation . . . and accept the responsibility. What I have to say here is about decisions I myself have made. Although they are presented merely as guidelines for your meditation, I recommend them. For example:

1. Where no harm will be done, and no sworn oath is involved, I often give incorrect information. So does my wife.

2. I never give incorrect information if I am to sign a sworn statement, whether or not before a notary.

3. I may *withhold* information from the police or from government representative, but I won't lie to them.

4. Under no condition whatsoever will I file a false tax return.

Here is an example of 1, above: When I open a new e-mail account, I know that the instructions call for me to enter my true name, address, etc. However, since I do not plan to defraud anyone, I list anything *but* the true facts. At other times, I am asked my date of birth. Although it is listed correctly on my driver's license and on my passport, elsewhere the date ranges from January 1, 1926, to December 31, 1935.

Here is an example of 2: I was recently in Vancouver, British Columbia, planning to buy a cell phone scanner and bring it into the United States. (They are legal in Canada but illegal in the United States.) Since I was not prepared to hide this purchase from the U.S. customs officials, I planned to ship it over the border via UPS. The manager of the electronics store brought out a form and suggested "we" could list the scanner as something else. However, when I read the customs form, I saw that I would have to sign a sworn statement that description above was true. No sale.

Example of 3: In the first edition of this book, I mentioned that one of my readers was caught doing fifty in a thirty-mile speed zone in Bellevue, Washington. Actually . . . that reader was me. My car, with Washington plates, was registered in the name of a New Mexico limited liability company based in the Canary Islands, and with a U.S. address in Wyoming. My driver's license was from another state—far away—that did not require a Social Security number. The conversation went like this:

Cop: Where do you live? [I gave the address on my driver's license. Misleading, but it was a legitimate address that I use as my legal domicile.]

Cop: Do you work for this company in Wyoming?

I: No, I own it. [Correct, although the company's sole asset is the car.]

Cop: [Writing the ticket] And your Social Security number?

I: With all due respect, Officer, I do not give my Social Security number to anyone.

Cop: That may be the case in *your* state, but here in Washington, we track all traffic fines with Social Security numbers. May I have your number, sir?

I: I never give this number out. Does Washington state law require the number?

Cop: Our *policy* is to list all Social Security numbers on traffic tickets.

I: [in humble voice] If it is not the law, then I regret to say that I cannot give you my Social Security number, Officer.

After a pause, the cop said to sign the ticket. I signed, took my copy, and was on my way. The box for the SSN was left blank. I sent in the payment via a money order.

Yes, I confess to withholding information whenever I can. If I run a small business out of my home, I neglect to get a business license. If I move, I neglect to inform the postal authorities. If asked for information when obtaining an e-mail address, I fail to list my true name and home address. You, the reader, have three choices:

1. you can follow the pattern I have set; or

2. you can tell no untruth under any circumstances; or

3. you can lie about everything and sign anything, true or not.

In the chapters to come, I will assume you have chosen option 1. From time to time, I may add a suggestion for those of you who stick with option 2. As for any who go for option 3, I'd truly appreciate it if you took this book back to the store and demanded a refund of your money. This is not your kind of book.

PIs AND TRUE LIES

Now we come to the gray area—the hiring of a private investigator (PI). The shades of gray vary from light to just a millimeter above inky black. The PIs call it "pretexting," but you and I know what it really is, and if you hire one, are you not responsible for what he does? Here is a typical example of how pretexting works:

For a brief time, Karl and Lorelei are lovers. When Karl turns violent, Lorelei walks out. Karl stalks her. She read this same book you are reading and follows the advice by moving away and changing everything. She also picks up a double barrel shotgun.

When Karl discovers Lorelei has dropped out of sight, he vows that if he cannot have her, then no one else will have her, either. He buys a used handgun, makes his plans, and then goes to a PI by the name of Guido. Guido has a reputation for tracking down anyone, anywhere, anytime.

Karl gives Guido a made-up sob story, and the PI accepts it. He takes a hefty retainer from Karl and writes down the four pieces of information that Karl gives him: her full name, Social Security number, former address, and the name of a hospital where she was once briefly admitted.

The PI promises Karl results within twenty-four hours. Actually, Guido will have Lorelei's new address in less than sixty minutes, obtained with just two short "pretext" telephone calls. The first is to Plano General Hospital.

PGH: Hello, please hold. [long pause]

PGH: Plano General Hospital, may I help you?

Guido: Yes, this is John, with Dr. Childress's office in McKinney, and I'm processing some insurance forms for Lorelei Altbusser. Could you pull that file for me? I need the date of admission.

PGH: Do you have her Social Security number?

Guido: Let's see [makes sound of papers shuffling]. Yeah, it's 987-65-4325.

PGH: OK, please hold for a minute while I get the file. [pause]

PGH: OK, got it. She was admitted 10-10-03.

Guido: What was the complaint?

PGH: Looks like persistent pains following a termination of pregnancy.

Guido: Does it indicate any treatment?

PGH: Looks like there was a prescription, was all.

Guido: Well, thanks for the help, and—oh, one more thing. On the form she filled out, does it list her mother's name as Mary Altbusser, with telephone 344-1288?

PHG: No, her admittance form lists next-of-kin as Gertrude Altbusser at 478-1991.

Guido: Molto grazie, and have a nice day.

Next, the PI calls 478-1991, because he figures Lorelei keeps in contact with her mother. Once again, he represents himself as a doctor.

Guido: Gertrude Altbusser, please.

Mother: Yes, this is she.

Guido: Mrs. Altbusser, this is Dr. Noe at the Cook County Morgue. We have a body here that's been tentatively identified as a Lorelei Altbusser. Do you have a daughter by that name?

Mother: Oh, my God! Oh no! Oh God!

Guido: Mrs. Altbusser, is your daughter an African-American?

Mother: No, no, my daughter is white!

[Guido's reason for whipsawing this poor woman back and forth is to inject her with truth serum. Now she will tell him what he wants to know.]

Guido: Mrs. Altbusser, how do you explain this dead black girl having your daughter's driver's license?

Mother: I don't know. Maybe Lorelei's purse was stolen?

Guido: Mrs. Altbusser, when's the last time you spoke with your daughter?

Mother: I talked to her last Sunday. She's a good girl, she calls me every Sunday.

Guido: Mrs. Altbusser, it's very important we speak with your daughter on this matter without delay. How can I get in touch with her immediately?

Mother: She's living in Odessa now, and doesn't have a phone in her apartment. She works at a Circle K on Central Drive. I could give you that number . . .

Guido: Yes, please give it to me now, ma'am.

Mother: It's 960-362-0464.

Guido: Thank you, Mrs. Altbusser.

Author's note: When hearing the lie about a dead body, mothers often get hysterical. One PI, writing about this routine, says, "I've heard of cases where the mother has literally dropped the phone in midsentence and raced over to the County Morgue!"

PRIVATE INVESTIGATORS—
FRIENDS OR FOES?

In the foregoing example, *from Lorelei's viewpoint*, the PI was just a miserable liar-for-hire who should have checked Karl's story out before taking the job. When Karl breaks into her home with a gun, we all hope she lets him have it with both barrels.

But now, let's change the context. Suppose the one who goes to the PI is *you*, and this time the PI is Paulo, Guido's brother. Paulo is just like Guido, except that before he takes the case, *he verifies your story*. Here it is:

Your rebellious fifteen-year-old daughter has just run away from home with some guy from Chicago named Armen Bedrosian who is at least thirty. You call the Cook County Police, but all you get is a runaround. You go to Paulo. After checking you out, he takes the case. A quick check with his database accounts on the Internet show that Armen is an ex-con who was jailed in his teens for rape and attempted murder. He's been back on the streets for only two months. The PI tracks Armen down by first locating his mother. He calls her.

"Mrs. Bedrosian, this is Dr. Noe at the Cook County Morgue. We have a body here that's been tentatively identified as Armen Bedrosian. Do you have a son by that name . . .?"

Even if the PI had to resort to pretexts in order to save your little daughter, will you not thank him to the end of your days?

4

MAILBOXES, PUBLIC
AND PRIVATE

*It's better to look ahead and prepare than to look back
and regret.*

—Bits & Pieces

By "public," I mean the boxes you can rent at a U.S. post office. By "private," I refer to commercial mail-receiving agencies (CMRAs), such as Parcel Plus, Packaging Store, Mail Boxes Etc., Associated Mail and Parcel Centers, Pak Mail Centers of America, Postal Annex, and PostNet Postal and Business Centers. This chapter will show you a fast and simple way to achieve a basic level of privacy and security.

If you do not already have a post office box, you may wish to obtain one for your personal mail. Then you could rent a private mailbox from a commercial mail-receiving agency and use a "company name" for business mail, magazine subscriptions, and deliveries from FedEx and UPS.

Until such time as you move, of course, your present street address will be in dozens—or, more likely, hundreds—of databases.

However, from this moment on, you will never again give out your street address. Then, when you move and follow the advice in the chapters to come, you will drop below the radar.

However, before you make any changes, make sure you have read *and understood* both this chapter and the one that follows.

POST OFFICE BOXES

If a choice is available, rent a box as far away from your home as is convenient for picking up mail once or twice a week. The ideal situation—often the case if you have a long commute to work— is to have the box in another town. This is sometimes possible for those who live in "twin" cities. (If you live in East Minneapolis, get a box in West St. Paul.)

ADVANTAGES OF HAVING A P.O. BOX

First and foremost, you avoid having to give out your street address. In addition:

- If you move to another location in the same area, there will be no changes to make for incoming mail.
- Your mail will be safe from thieves, no matter how long you leave it in the box.
- When you are on vacation, mail will not pile up at the mailbox at your home—a clear signal that the occupants are away.

DISADVANTAGES OF HAVING A P.O. BOX

The biggest single disadvantage of getting a P.O. box is the process you have to go through. Until the end of the 1990s, it was fairly easy to rent a P.O. box and retain your privacy. Since then, however, this changed and is no longer the case. Thus:

- You must show two forms of ID, and one of them must show your current home address. (This violates the rule of never allowing your true name to be coupled with your true home address.)
- If you list other persons who will also be receiving mail at this address, they, too, must now furnish two forms of identification.
- You must sign PS Form 1093 right next to this chilling statement:

   Warning: The furnishing of false or misleading information on this form or the omission of material information may result in criminal sanctions (including fines and imprisonment) and/or civil sanctions (including multiple damages and civil penalties). (18 U.S.C. 1001)

Fortunately, I know of no holder who has ever been jailed for fudging on the application, as long as the box was never used for any fraudulent purpose. Having said that, let's now review how an average married man might fill out the official application card, PS Form 1093. Let's say his name is Roland James Brown, his wife is Suzanne Mary Brown, née O'Donnell, and his six-year-old son is Shannon Murray Brown. He has two goals in mind: to avoid listing his first name and to have as many alternative names as possible.

Item 1. Name(s) to which box number(s) is (are) assigned.
JAMES BROWN
SUZANNE MARY O'DONNELL

Item 2. Not applicable.

Item 3. Name of person applying, title (if representing an organization), and name of organization (if different from Item 1)
JAMES BROWN

Item 4. Leave (4a) use, and (4b) E-mail address, blank, because both are optional.

Item 5. Address (Number, street, apt./ste. no., city, state and ZIP Code).
12XX BURMA ROAD
ROUGH AND READY, CA 95975

Item 6. Telephone number (include area code)
(530) 477-83XX

Items 11–13. Not applicable.

*Item 14. List name(s) and age(s) of minors or names of other persons
receiving mail in individual box. Other persons must present two forms
of valid ID. If applicant is a firm, name each member receiving mail.
Each member must have verifiable ID upon request. (Continue on
reverse side).*
SHANNON MURRAY BROWN, age 6.

*Item 15. Signature of applicant (same as item 3). I agree to comply
with all postal rules regarding post office or caller service.*
(WRITTEN SIGNATURE)

In the above illustration, the address will be where the Browns
are currently living. The telephone number will be that of a cell
phone (perhaps of the prepaid, throwaway variety). The only
possible moral issue will be the signature below the statement
agreeing to comply with all the rules. Roland Brown will sign it,
because he remembers the definition of a lie: ". . . which false
statement tends toward injury to the other . . ." For those of you
who are uncomfortable with signing on line fifteen, consider
these two options:

1. do not rent a post office box; or

2. when you move, do notify the post office of your new
    address.

For the rest of you, why not fill out the form accurately, including
your present address, and then move? As I understand it, failing

to inform the post office of a move is not a criminal offense. If they ever find out—which is unlikely—the worst they will do to you is close your box. Or, if you cannot—or do not wish to—make a permanent move, then consider renting a cheap apartment on a month-by-month basis. Live there just long enough to rent a box and have that address checked out. Then move back home.

OTHER OPTIONS FOR RECEIVING MAIL AT A P.O. BOX

Might you have a friend or relative with the same last name? If he or she is agreeable, you could receive mail in their box. Most postal employees have more important duties than to check the first names of everyone in a family.

Another suggestion is to open the box in the name of a limited liability company (see chapter 15). Example: Your name is Abraham Goldstein, but you wish to establish a new identity under the name of Robert Johnson. Form an LLC named "Robert Johnson LLC." This is the name that will go in the box for Item 1. Your present name will go in Item 3 and also in Item 14, with the title "owner" or "member." Send yourself a few letters from time to time, addressed to "Robert Johnson LLC." After that, there should be no problem in receiving mail in your new name, even without LLC at the end.

Or, for total anonymity along with a new name, find someone whose mailbox you can take over. Either they are moving away or are poor enough so that a cash contribution will allow you to take over their box. (Naturally, you will send *their* mail on to whatever address they later give you.)

Use this person's basic name—with a slight alteration—as if it were your own. For instance, if the box holder's name is José L. Hernandez, just change the first name to Joe, or the middle initial to R. Or, if you are determined to use a different name—say, Veronica Victoria, slowly work your way through the series below, sending letters to this box number and addressed to:

1. Veronica Victoria c/o José Hernandez

2. V. Victoria & J. Hernandez

3. Victoria & Hernandez

4. V. Victoria

My experience has been that after six months, mail in whatever
name will be delivered to the box. When time comes for paying
the annual fee, do not of course show up at the counter. Mail in a
money order with the name "José L. Hernandez" as the sender.

Here's one more idea: Third-class mail from the previous box
holder may still be coming to the box you've just rented.
Hmmm . . . might that be as a good a name as any for your alternate identity? (If you do, however adopt this name, make sure
you never apply for credit in that name, nor use it for any other
fraudulent activity. Also, you might check him out on the Internet, to make sure he isn't on something like a sex-offender list!)

COMMERCIAL MAIL-RECEIVING AGENCIES
(CMRAs)

ADVANTAGES OF HAVING A PRIVATE BOX

The biggest advantage of having a box number with a private
agency is that they will receive mail from private couriers and
packages from UPS and FedEx. Also:

- You will have a street address, which in some cases is necessary.

- You can often call in while traveling, to have your mail sent
on.

- They are often open longer, and/or more days, than is a
U.S. post office.

DISADVANTAGES OF HAVING A PRIVATE BOX

- First of all, you will have to sign a "Private Mailbox (PMB) Rental Agreement" that includes a sea of small print. Next, you will have to fill out and sign the official PS Form 1583, which—like the application for a P.O. box—contains a warning of the consequences of withholding or giving false information. If an agent at the CMRA does not witness your signature, then it must be notarized.

- You will be required to furnish two forms of identification. Item 9 on this form says: "A photocopy of your identification may be retained by agent for verification."

- You are required to supply your box number in addition to the street address. Prior to 1999, you were allowed to add "Suite," "Apartment," "Space," or "Unit" before the number, but not now. Here is how a CMRA address looks:

Your Name
202-A Center St. #6666
Kodiak, AK 99615
(The "#6666" is a giveaway that you are using a CMRA.)

- All major CMRA addresses are kept in commercial databases. This will block your efforts to use such an address on your driver's license or for any other official use. Also, if you order over the Internet, many firms will refuse to ship to such an address.

POSSIBLE REMEDIES FOR PRIVATE BOXES

- Rent the box, then *move*, without telling the CMRA.

- Choose a mom-and-pop operation with a single outlet. This address may not show up in national databases, and if you "forget" to add your box number once in a while, they should still—being small and thus recognizing customer names—be able to give you your mail.

SUMMARY

If you do not plan to go beyond Level One security, get a private box at one of the CMRAs and have all your mail sent there. Even if they have your home address on file, it will not be given out indiscriminately to the general public.

For advanced security, however, I strongly suggest you avoid CMRAs. Instead, if at all possible, obtain a P.O. box that does not connect you with your present home address. Use this box number for:

- personal mail from relatives and friends
- bank statements
- telephone, insurance, and utility bills
- Social Security and Medicare (if applicable)
- any other strictly personal mail.

For everything else—and especially if you receive mail in other names, use a private, alternate street address. This "ghost" address is the subject of the next chapter.

QUESTIONS & ANSWERS

Can I use a P.O. box or a CMRA street address when I open a bank account?

Although your bank statements can be mailed to either a P.O. box or a CMRA address, they will ask for your true home address. Perhaps you will be able to use the address of a close relative. Otherwise, see the next chapter about obtaining a ghost street address.

When I recently renewed my driver's license, I gave them my address at Mail Boxes Etc., but without the box number. They didn't say anything, so should I tell my friends to do the same?

Absolutely not. One of my readers went through this process. After signing an appropriate affidavit, he says, "I obtained a new driver's license using a Mail Box Etc. address." Then, however, he went to a nightclub that uses an ID scanner. "When my card was swiped, I looked to see what appeared on the screen." On the screen was his actual address, not the address on his driver's license. "I would have to guess—as you have stated—that the DMV knew that the new address I gave them was a mail drop and not an actual residence. Then, somehow, they pulled up my real address and entered it!"

Can I use a P.O. box for the address on my driver's license?

As this book is being revised, many states do still allow this. However, each state has its own laws, and the laws keep changing. It's worthwhile to make a trip to the DMV beforehand, and ask them.

Do Canadian CMRAs also require picture identification and a box number?

Although Canadian law does not require this, all the major CMRAs have started following the U.S. rules. However, an arrangement for the readers of this book has been set up in a city in Alberta. No ID is required, and you get a street address with no box number. For details, see Ghost Addresses in the Appendix.

Can I rent a P.O. box with a single visit?

The post offices are not consistent. Some of my readers report getting a box on the first visit by showing ID with their home address. Others, however, have had an experience such as this: "I went to the post office to rent a box. They told me I had to fill out the form and they would then verify the information. After that, they said they would mail me a letter. I would then have to take that letter back to the post office and only then could I obtain a box."

If I don't tell the post office my new address when I move, is there any chance they will find out?

The only problem I've ever heard of came in from a reader just as I was preparing this section. She writes, "I have rented a P.O. box for the past nine years. About two months ago, I got a notice saying they needed to update my personal information— name, address, and telephone number—or they would stop delivery." This reader tossed the notice into the garbage, and so far reports no interruption in her incoming mail. She assumes that no one is really checking that the new-information form ever got returned. "Also, I just rented a new P.O. box last week, at a different location. All I simply had to show was my driver's license."

Note that (1) there is no consistency from one post office to another, and (2) the only "threat" was that if the information was not updated, the woman's box would be closed. This is consistent with the information on PS Form 1093, which says, "Failure to update the application may result in termination of service."

Can I open a P.O. box without showing my driver's license (which is from another state)?

Normally, yes. Use your passport and—if asked for a second piece of ID, use an old credit card, an ID card from work, or from the armed forces. One senior citizen writes, "The clerk used my credit card (she did not know it was canceled) as the second ID." When the clerk began writing the credit card number on the application, another worker told her that it was illegal to use the credit card number. So the clerk crossed it out—"but said she had gotten yelled at last week by her boss for not writing down the second ID. She then commented that she had never used anything but a license before."

5

HOW TO OBTAIN YOUR OWN "GHOST" ADDRESS

Burn every bridge. You never know who might be following you.

—ENOBRIN TAIN TO GAREK,
STAR TREK: DS9

More than half the people who come to me for help, wishing to keep their various assets invisible to others, are at the time receiving both mail and packages at their home address. This is a mammoth mistake. In some cases, it's a matter of life and death.

An extreme viewpoint? Mike Ketcher of Burnsville, Minnesota, editor of *the Financial Privacy Report*, certainly doesn't think so. He hired Yon Son Moon, a divorced woman, to work in his office. Yon Son's ex-husband, Jae Choe, had been harassing her for years. When Mike hired Yon Son, Choe was furious. Eventually he went on a rampage, shooting Yon Son, their fourteen-year-old son John, and two policemen, after which he killed himself. The publisher of the newsletter, Daniel Rosenthal, sums up the two important lessons learned, as follows:

FIRST, if you think the police are there to protect you, let me tell you differently. Yon Soon had a restraining order against Choe. So did we, at our home and our office. But the police ignored our repeated requests to enforce these restraining orders, despite Choe's continual violations and threats. On several occasions, they literally laughed at our requests for enforcement.

SECOND, when the police don't work, privacy DOES work. The only person in our company that was truly safe was Mike Ketcher. He was safe because he kept his personal affairs so private that Mr. Choe couldn't find him.

Let me repeat that last part once more: Mike Ketcher was safe because he kept his personal affairs *so private* that Mr. Choe couldn't find him.

In the context of this book, a ghost address refers to a future address you will use that is not in any database as a CMRA, and has no connection to where you really live. Although I will usually speak of this new address in the singular, you may wish to have multiple ghost addresses. In my own case, I use two P.O. boxes, three ghost addresses in North America, and two more here, in Spain's Canary Islands. (If you ever happen to vacation in the Canary Islands, don't bother trying to track me down. You could grow old and die before you succeed. . . .)

A PARTIAL LIST OF PLACES WHERE ALTERNATE ADDRESSES WILL BE USED

(It is assumed you will use a P.O. box for personal mail, bank statements, and telephone, insurance, and utility bills. Some items on the following list may also be suitable for using your P.O. box number.)

1. The Internal Revenue Service.

2. Your driver's license.

3. Any real estate you own.

4. Any loans you have made to others.

5. All licenses for your pets (a PI's favorite!).

6. Hunting and fishing licenses.

7. Your library card.

8. Your voter's registration (if any).

9. Any membership records, such as with your church.

10. Your doctor, dentist, and chiropractor.

11. Your attorney and your accountant.

12. Your pilot's license and airplane registration.

13. All limited liability companies (LLCs) used to title your vehicles.

14. All purchases, especially where a warranty is involved.

15. Rental: home, storage unit, car, tools, or whatever.

HOW TO SET UP YOUR OWN GHOST ADDRESS

Shortly after the publication of the first edition of this book, questions began arriving at my Web site, *www.howtobeinvisible.com*. Although the most numerous were about how best to use a limited liability company, the toughest questions had to do with obtaining a ghost address. For that reason I've expanded this chapter by adding some of the successful experiences my readers have passed on to me. As you will see, getting your own ghost address may involve major effort. Is it worth it? I assure you that if you make the effort, you will never regret it.

ONE OF MY OWN EXAMPLES

Before moving to a new area a few years back, I first rented a P.O. box for my personal mail. (I filled out the PS Form 1093 with my middle and last name, and gave an old address that was about to become obsolete.)

After that, my first step was to find a ghost address in the area. I made a mental list of small businesses that receive mail for at least several different persons. This included but was not limited to accountants, attorneys, clinics (medical, chiropractic, etc.), real estate offices, used car dealers, barber shops, book stores, coffee shops, bars, contractors, funeral directors (!), martial arts studios, tax consultants, RV parks, day care centers, and mom-and-pop motels.

Next, dressed in a gray suit with a plain crimson tie and driving a rented Lincoln Town Car, I headed out to search the area. Within an hour, I came across a busy real estate office with three little cabins in the rear. Two of them appeared to be lived in but the third was obviously used for storage.

I entered the main office, asked for the owner of the property, and was introduced to Jim C——— who was the broker and also the owner of the property. I explained my circumstances and offered, as a reference, the name of my attorney in San Francisco. I also gave him the phone number of a business friend. (He didn't bother to check with either person.)

"I have the perfect setup," he said with a smile. "Cabin 430 back there is just for storage now, but it has its own mailbox. C'mon back, I'll show you." Unseen from the main street was a row of rural mailboxes lined up on a wooden crossbar. All were

small, old, bent, and dirty. "I get mail in this one," he said, pointing to one of the boxes, "for all seventeen of my salesmen!" I said
he probably needed a larger box, and he said he certainly did . . .

Bottom line: I said I would put up new, larger mailboxes for
everyone, and what could I do for him besides that? Jim was
fascinated with my work as a privacy consultant and expressed concern about all the things that he owned in his own
name. I am now his consultant and have helped him make some
needed changes. Here are a few details about this "ghost" street
address:

- I never receive mail at this address in my own last name. All
  magazines come in the name of a Mexican nominee, all
  boxes from Amazon.com, Barnes&Noble.com, and
  Half.com in my first and middle names only, and everything else comes in a company name R, M & S, LLC.

- Since FedEx and UPS do not leave packages in a mailbox, I
  had Jim put a prominent notice on the door of the unoc-
  cupied cabin: "Please leave all deliveries at the main office."
  His secretary signs for whatever comes in, then calls and
  leaves a code number on my pager.

- When the time came to buy some land, I had Jim act as my
  buying agent. He made sure that my name did not enter
  the county computers. (Title was taken in the name of an
  LLC, which is owned by a trust, which is administered by a
  certain someone in her maiden name.) Jim, therefore,
  knows where I live, but he understands my desire for privacy. If anyone asks for me at the front desk, they will be
  referred to Jim, and he, in turn, will stonewall them after
  first finding out who they are. Later, he'll call me with a
  heads-up. So far, however, no one has ever asked, because,
  as I said earlier, *nothing comes to this address in my own
  name.*

The following suggestions and examples come from experiences
or letters sent to me by readers of the first edition:

RURAL MAILBOX

One reader recently moved to a new town and spent a few hours
driving around the nearby countryside to check on mailboxes.
"At the end of one side road, I counted sixteen boxes, and there
was room for a couple more. I bought a similar mailbox in a sec-
ondhand store, painted a number on the door that was similar—
but not the same—as the others, and stuck it on the far end.
We've been getting mail there ever since."

REAL ESTATE

In some places, the post office will only deliver on public roads,
not private roads. In the rural areas where one reader lives, there
are often many mailboxes, "sometimes as many as twenty," where
the public road meets a private road. "At first, I thought about
just putting my own mailbox on a post and giving myself a number, which I think would have worked." The reader also considered asking permission to put up a mailbox from someone who
already lived on a private road. "However, just before I put that
plan into action, I actually came across a situation where an old
house of questionable value—on one of those private roads—had
burned down a few years ago and had never been rebuilt. It still
had a valid street address and so—even though it is now a vacant
lot—I put up a mailbox on the corner of the public road."

OLDER OFFICE BUILDING

Another reader found a ghost address by locating an older office
building that had several floors that needed renovation and had
no tenants. All the offices on those empty floors had mail slots in
the doors. Even better, the building had multiple entrances on

different streets and residential apartments on the upper floors. The owner was suspicious at first about the idea of renting an office for its mail slot, even after the reader explained that he was often away from home and didn't want neighbors picking up his mail. The owner wanted to know what was wrong with the usual solution: a post office box.

" 'Some of it's from FedEx,' I explained, 'so a P.O. box won't work.' This answer satisfied him, and I was able to rent a space on a handshake agreement for $25 per month. The office staff doesn't know my real name or address, and my rent bill comes right to my mail slot. It is on an empty floor, so it would be difficult for anyone to keep a close watch on it."

BROOM CLOSET

Another reader has been even more creative in obtaining a ghost address. He chose a commercial building near his workplace and discretely undertook an inspection, discovering that each floor had an unlocked three-foot-square closet for brooms and cleaning supplies. "I then contacted the owner and introduced myself as the operator of a small, home-based consulting business. I explained my reasons for needing a business address (frequent travel, plus envelopes from courier services such as FedEx and Airborne Express) and said I would deeply appreciate being able to lease one of those broom closets." The owner eventually went along with the idea, cleared the brooms and supplies out of the closet, and allowed our friend to install an office number on the door and a new brass mail slot. "The monthly cost is low, and I was not asked for identification. No one in the building knows my true name."

CHARITY MISSION

The Salvation Army and other charity missions provide a place to stay for many people and often accept mail for the temporary residents. One reader saw an opportunity here: "I told the supervisor that I travel a lot in and out of town and asked him if I could use the address for my personal business and gave him a $50 donation. Now, you could have someone else *say* they are you, do the same thing I did, and have a great layer of protection (no cameras in those places, either)."

PAYDAY LOAN OFFICE

Sometimes persistence—as well as imagination—is needed to create a low-cost ghost address. One reader approached the manager of a small office that handles payday and car title loans, hoping she'd accept and hold mail for a small fee. "I explained that I didn't need a box. I merely wished to have her set my mail aside in her office so I could pick it up every couple of weeks. She said come back next week, she would make a decision. I returned to this very small business two more times, until she finally said, 'No problem, just give us $10 a month, prepaid six months in advance, and we'll gladly hold your mail for you.' My success here was due probably more to focusing on establishing a personal relationship first, and then following up with my new 'contact.' It worked!"

SMALL MOTEL

Another reader has had success in obtaining ghost addresses at independently run mom-and-pop motels. "I have found that if I dress well, many of these proprietors are very sympathetic to my situation, provided I am willing to pay them something for the service. The nice thing about this method is that you have a street address with no added room number, and, of course, it's very private. (Cheapo motels often don't have cameras, either.)"

ALTERNATIVES

Check the Yellow Pages for Office Services, Bookkeeping, etc. Don't call them, go in person. Discuss whatever services they

offer, and then, as you're leaving, imitate Peter Falk in the old
Columbo shows:

"Oh, *by the way*, do you happen to accept mail here for any of
your clients?" If they do not, move on. If, however, they say,
"Well, only for three or four . . ." see if they will take you on. If
they agree, you can almost certainly be added to their list without showing ID. These small services sort mail by name alone,
without a box number added. The ideal address is one on a street
that also has private residences—the type of street address you
will need for such things as car insurance or a library card.

SHOULD YOU ALLOW ANYONE AT YOUR GHOST ADDRESS TO KNOW WHERE YOU LIVE?

Only you yourself can answer. Hopefully, when you made the
arrangements, you gave an address other than your own, and no
telephone number. However, have they gotten to know you? Do
they recognize your car? If so, might they have seen it in front of
your home? What follows is a chilling example of what unfortunately goes on every day, not only at commercial mail drops but
even at some of the ghost addresses.

Let's call her Sally Overstreet. She is a newspaper reporter
who has twice moved to avoid an ex-lover who has been stalking
her for years. Unknown to Sally, her stalker is now working with
a private investigator, aka a gumshoe or private eye.

The PI shows up at her new ghost address. He is wearing a
UPS uniform and carries a box addressed to Sally Overstreet.
The return address is that of a major New York publisher. The
"UPS man" says he must pick up a certified check for $200 before
leaving the box. The next day is a Saturday—or a holiday—and
the "UPS man" insists the box is something Ms. Overstreet has
to have TODAY. Could the folks at the new address kindly tell
him where Miss Overstreet can be reached? How about a telephone number? Where does she work, maybe the box can be

delivered there? This ruse often works, which is why it remains so popular.

The PI's uniform need not appear to be from the UPS. Perhaps it is from FedEx, Brink's Security, or Flowers "R" Us. The return address and the story that comes with it can be anything. The object is the same: to find anyone at your mailing address that knows how to locate you and make them think they'd be doing you a favor by directing him to you.

There are two ways to protect yourself from this deception. One is to make sure that no one at your new address knows anything about you. The other is to use persons who, although they know you, will positively protect you. If the latter, then make sure they know about the various scams that may be used in an attempt to deceive them.

NOW FOR THE HARD PART

The hardest part of keeping your actual home address a secret is to educate your family to never, ever give out your home address to anyone other than relatives and close friends. And *even then* . . . not always, for *they* may innocently pass on your address to others. Even judges and policemen may have problems within the family.

Geraldine Adams, a private investigator in a southern state, specializes in tracking down corporate burglaries. (A stolen notebook computer with corporate files can fetch up to $50,000.) She had recently been responsible for a police raid and two arrests, and, as a result, threats had been made on her life. Both she and her husband, Tom, a self-employed accountant, took these threats seriously, sold their home in the suburbs, and moved to a new and supposedly secret apartment in the city. They also changed banks and used a telephone answering service for receiving mail. One day Geraldine returned home and was stunned to find in the mail a box of new checks that her husband had ordered from the local bank. Imprinted on every check was the Adamses' *ghost address*. (She destroyed the checks, said some unkind words to her husband, and ordered new checks with *no* printed address from Checks in the Mail.)

Mateo, a police detective in Miami, was hated by innumerable bad guys he'd helped put away. For that reason, he was obsessive about keeping his home address secret. One day, while he was at work, his pregnant wife started to hemorrhage. When she could not locate her husband, she called 911. An ambulance took her to Emergency and, when asked, rather than give their ghost address, she gave her actual home address. (For what she should have done, see the section "Call to 911" in chapter 10.)

A month later, as a result of this indiscretion, Mateo sold their home and moved.

YOUR HOUSE NUMBER

With one exception, there is no number or mailbox at any of our homes on either side of the Atlantic. There may be some local laws about displaying house numbers, but, if so, I have never known it to be enforced. The reason we do not give anyone our house number is that eventually *someone will write it down*. Then they may use the address to send a thank-you note and the mailperson will discover (1) who lives at this address, and (2) that there is no mailbox.

A friend of ours did let both the mailbox and the number remain on a house he purchased. He neglected to warn a visiting aunt that he never received mail at home. At Christmas time, she sent him a gift subscription to *Robb Report* . . . in his real name, of course, and with his true street address!

If you delete the number on your house but still need to have others find it, here's a little trick. If guests are coming, tell them that once they pass a certain landmark or cross street, "Watch for a house on the right with a pink flamingo on the lawn." (Don't forget to go out and plant the bird before they arrive. Extract it after they leave. They may never find the place again.)

A UNIQUE SOLUTION

I have a cartoon tacked on my office wall that shows a middle-aged couple in their living room, dressed to go out. The front door is open, and four large suitcases are sitting in the entrance. The husband is pouring gasoline on the carpet. The wife, who holds a can of gasoline in her left hand, is standing along one wall, talking to their daughter on the telephone. She says, "Oh, that sounds lovely, dear, but I'm afraid your father and I have already made plans." Although arson is not recommended, the following solution is.

I learned this one from a FEMA (Federal Emergency Management Agency) agent I met while staying in a motel that was near a flooded area. Two years ago, he bought a $98,995 motor home under another name, and *did not license it*. (He thus saved not only the license fees and road tax, but an $8,513.57 sales tax as well.) For $12 he got a fifteen-day permit to move it to a rural location in another state. From time to time, he moves it, each time getting a temporary permit. Try to find out where *this* agent actually lives!

BREAKING NEWS

As this final draft was about to go to the publisher, a disturbing message came in at my Web site, *www.howtobeinvisible.com*. It was from Scott D———, who had purchased the first edition of this book as soon as it came out. Although similar messages come in to my Web site from time to time, Scott's story best conveys the urgency I have strived to convey to you in this chapter.

> Scott says that he has been "very discreet," if not "invisible," in his personal affairs. He has no particular reason to see himself as a target—no great wealth, no known enemies—but did obtain a

ghost address. Nonetheless, according to his message, he recently received an emergency voicemail from the manager of his ghost address, reporting that the "place had been forcibly entered and my mail, and *only* mine, was rifled." Scott was naturally relieved that his mail did not lead the marauders to his actual home address. His message concludes: "A word of advice to your readers: DON'T THINK IT CAN'T HAPPEN TO YOU. I was already making arrangements for a move before this happened. The incident has convinced me to elevate my degree of invisibility, and I have resolved to make some changes in my family's habits in our new place. I'll be using every legal means from your book that applies to my circumstances . . ."

QUESTIONS & ANSWERS

I am a single mother who is having a hard time setting up a ghost address. Everyone is suspicious. How can I get around this?

Arrive in a new luxury car (borrowed or rented, if necessary). Dress well, perhaps in a skirt and sweater rather than jeans, and smile. Have a good reason ready, such as that you are being stalked by some dirty old man. If that doesn't work, show up with an attorney at your side who will support your well-rehearsed story.

Tip #1: If the person you are going to see is a woman, bring a male attorney. If it's a man, bring a female attorney.

Tip #2: In some cases, where money was not available for an attorney, a friend from out of town has come along to pose as one. Don't try this one, however, unless the friend can truly dress, act, and speak like an attorney. According to some sources, anyone can *say* he or she is an attorney, as long as no fraud is involved, but try this at your own risk. Alternatives are to bring with you a banker, a doctor, or your tax accountant.

We do use our home address on our tax returns, but isn't that information confidential?

Louis Mitzel Jr., a former special agent and intelligence officer with the U.S Department of State and a prolific author, tells the story of Lee Willis, a lowly clerk with the Internal Revenue Service. Willis had been stalking his ex-girlfriend for sixteen months. She thought she was safe, because her home address was kept secret, her telephone number was kept secret, and she made sure her friends and neighbors kept a lookout for the stalker.

Although 56,000 IRS employees have access to taxpayer files, Willis was not one of them. He did, however, persuade a coworker to illegally run a search for him. The ex-girlfriend was filing her tax returns under her true address! Willis raced to her apartment building. The lobby was locked, but he pressed all the buzzers and one of the neighbors let him in. At the last moment, the girl discovered he was in the building, called the police, and they arrested him. When they then searched Willis's car, they found a stun gun, rope, latex gloves, duct tape, and a knife.

Does that answer your question? Let's say each of the 56,000 IRS employees with access to the records has five close friends, and each of these friends has five close friends of his own. Are you willing to bet your life that not one of these 1.4 million persons would ever commit an illegal act, or coerce another into doing so?

Is it OK to put my true home address on the bags I check when making a trip by air?

Am I not getting through here? "Do not, as long as you live, ever again allow your real name to be coupled with your home address." This includes the address on baggage tags. Baggage handlers are just as tempted by money as anyone else, and some burglars pay well for the name and address of someone who has just left on a trip.

By the way, I never check luggage. If I need to carry more than will fit in my carry-on, I ship it ahead via FedEx.

How can I avoid giving out my daughter's Social Security number, as well as our street address, when she starts school next year?

Privacy in a public-school system is nonexistent—absolutely unachievable. To maintain privacy, you have two options:

1. a private school

2. home schooling.

In our own case, we raised our three children in Spain, at a time when—thanks to General Franco—drugs were simply not available and sex among teenagers was unknown. We put the kids in a private school (German, with professors from Berlin), and, when classes let out, my wife spent the next hour with them teaching them English. Although we took each child out of school at age fifteen, each was better educated than the majority of today's high school graduates, and could speak, read, and write in three languages.

Friendly tip: Raise your children to be self-employed when they leave home, so that their names will never, ever, go into the National Directory for New Hires. And just think of all the money you'll save by not sending them to college! (Like Bill Gates, I am a university dropout. I don't know about Gates, but I myself have never regretted dropping out during my senior year, back in the 1940s. Not for a day, an hour, or a minute.)

6

REPAIRMEN, HOME DELIVERIES, HOUSE CALLS, FEDEX, UPS

Shy and unready men are great betrayers of secrets; for there are few wants more urgent for the moment than the want of something to say.

—SIR HENRY TAYLOR (1800–1886),
AUTHOR OF *THE STATESMAN*

George Joseph Phillips, who lives in the 600 block of South "D" Street in Tacoma, Washington, is a photographer. His nightmare began when he called Washington Energy Services Co. to get a new furnace and water heater installed. When work began, an employee spotted some darkroom chemicals and, apparently unfamiliar with darkroom supplies, told his boss he saw chemicals in the home that he felt might be used to manufacture drugs. A company official then notified the police. Please pay more than the usual attention to what followed, according to an article in the *Seattle Post-Intelligencer* titled "Utility's House Call Became a Nightmare":

". . . Phillips's claims that after the company reported its suspicions to the police, a member of the Police Department asked the company to gather information from Phillips's home so police could obtain a search warrant."

The article goes on to report that the employees—yes, the ones Phillips was paying to install the furnace and water heater—then tried to take "pictures of the home's interior, searched through Phillips's personal effects, and opened dozens of boxes of light-sensitive paper." Further, he suspects *they also searched his computer files*, because his computer was broken and beyond repair after the search. Whether or not this was an illegal and unconstitutional search—and I think it was—let's benefit from this, shall we? The next time a worker enters *your* home, think beforehand about what could possibly give him a false impression. Then, when you let him in, stick with him.

OBTAINING CONSENT TO ENTER
BY DECEPTION

The following is based on information from the January 1994 *FBI Law Enforcement Bulletin,* now in the public domain. This applies to any home that federal agents would like to search but for lack of evidence are unable to obtain a warrant. Here is how it works:

A van that appears to be from a well-known courier service pulls into your driveway and the driver, with a package in hand, rings your bell. He asks for a certain person, and when you say no such person lives at this address, he asks to use your telephone "to call the company." If you allow him to do it, and if—while in your home—he observes anything that *might* be illegal, he may return within a few hours. This time he'll be with police officers who have a warrant to search your home, based on what the "deliveryman" observed earlier.

You and I are law-abiding persons, with nothing to hide.

Nevertheless, why invite strangers into your home? Just say no, and give the location of the nearest pay phone. Or, if you need an excuse, here are several:

- "My husband," says the wife, "told me never to allow strangers into the house when he's not here."
- "The phone's not working right now."
- "Our only phone line is tied into the Internet."

Sometimes, of course, no warrant is needed, as the following section explains.

FEDEX, UPS, DHL, AIRBORNE EXPRESS

The only sure way to avoid having someone send you an envelope or a package by courier is to never, ever, let anyone other than your closest friends know where you really live. The result is that, should a uniformed courier show up on your doorstep—or even a clown with balloons!—you automatically *know* that he or she doesn't belong there.

In fact, if you see someone coming up the walk—or observe them through the peephole I hope you have in your door—and do not know them, why open at all? When I was younger, cars were stolen, not hijacked, but improvements in car alarms have brought about a change. The same is starting to be true with house burglaries, now that locks and burglar alarms have improved. Thugs may just ring your doorbell. When you open, they slam their way in. Housejacking started in New York some years ago, and it may soon be coming to your hometown.

Now then, just in case you consider some of my advice to be extreme—and I admit that many do—I am willing to discuss some options. I don't recommend them, but better half an ounce of prevention than none at all.

HOME DELIVERY

Remember the cardinal rule? "Do not, as long as you live, ever again allow your real name to be coupled with your home address." If, then, you are going to have a delivery made to where you really live, it must not be in your name. All courier companies keep a national database of names and addresses, and countless thousands of their employees can run a search of your name. PIs know this, and many have contacts inside these companies.

If, in fact, you have *ever* received a letter or a package at your present address and under your real name, the only way to protect your privacy is to move. Once this move has been made, and if you are determined to have delivery made at your home, then it must be in another name. When you sign for the courier, you sign the other name.

You may get by with no problems doing this, as long as you do not order expensive items from out of state. If you do, however, keep in mind that in states with a sales tax, it is not uncommon for irate neighbors to call the tax department and report that the people next door are buying such-and-such to avoid the state's sales tax. (You do know, do you not, that you are obligated to "voluntarily" pay the local sales tax on merchandise purchased from out of state?)

The logical solution to anonymity with courier services would be to have your parcels come into one of their nearby offices and just pick them up there. Unfortunately, these companies do not employ logic. Whereas they never ask for ID at a private home, they absolutely demand it if you stop by one of their offices to pick anything up. I have argued this point in vain with the various home offices, pointing out that if I send a package in a certain name, I will sign a waiver to the effect that they may deliver to any person asking for it in that name. After all, this is similar to item number eight on all FedEx labels which reads RELEASE SIG-NATURE. *Sign to authorize delivery without obtaining signature.* In fact, if you really wish to remain incognito, have the sender sign on the line for this release and, when you see the FedEx truck arrive, do not answer the door.

But do not pick up at their office. I sent an e-mail to the FedEx main office, pleading for permission to send a letter to one of my clients who would not present ID when he picked it up at an office in Memphis. I received this reply, short but not sweet:

> *Thank you for your inquiry. FedEx requires a valid consignee name and phone number for shipments that are held for pick-up. More hold for pick-up information can be found on our website at:*
> *http://fedex.com/us/services/conditions/domestic/hold.html*
> *Thank you for your interest in FedEx.*
> *Susan Carr*
> *FedEx Webmaster*

MAIL DROP PICKUP

Although USPS regulations require that you show picture ID in order to receive mail sent to you as "General Delivery," the commercial mail-receiving agencies are apparently not bound by these regulations. So then, even though you have not rented a box at the CMRA, you can receive a shipment there in a business name, and no ID is necessary. Here's an example of how it works:

Assume I live in Plano, Texas. I wish to have a friend from New York City send me a small box that will not be identified with me in any way. Not by my name, and not by my address. I look up Mail Boxes Etc. in the Yellow Pages, choose one of the six offices listed, and have my wife make the call. The conversation goes like this:

"Hello, this is Mary Johnson with Triple R Services in New York. I wish to send a small box to your address, for pickup by one of our salesmen traveling through. Will that be satisfactory?"

"No problem—in whose name will it be?"

"We'll just send it to your address in the name of Triple R Services. Anyone that asks for a package in that name can pick it up."

"There is a small pickup fee, or course . . ."

"No problem."

I then call my friend, who ships the package. The following week I stop by, pay the fee, and pick up the box. (I have my wife make these calls, so that when I ask for the box, the manager does not recognize my rather odd accent and connect it with the "New York" caller.) Or I can send anyone else around on my behalf, anyone at all.

ROBBERS MAY IMPERSONATE THE POLICE

If no one knows where you live, it is extremely unlikely that police will ever show up at your door. If, therefore, you see what appear to be policemen coming up your walk, do not open the door. Call the police department, or even 911 on your cell phone, to check them out.

Several years ago, two men who identified themselves as police officers entered a home in a Los Angeles suburb with their guns drawn and tied up the couple who lived there. Both men wore dark clothing and caps with the word POLICE on the brow. They then stole $1,000 in cash and a laptop computer.

"Unfortunately, this happens too often," said LAPD spokesman Lieutenant Anthony Alba, "but generally on the east side or the south side of town, where recent immigrants might not be familiar with our law-enforcement officials. This one's a bit different." He referred to the fact that the victims were from a relatively quiet street in a predominantly middle-class neighborhood.

Later, two Los Angeles men suspected of committing more than thirty home-invasion robberies were arrested on suspicion of several theft, assault, and drug crimes. At a widely publicized press conference, police displayed more than one hundred items confiscated from the suspects' home, including night-vision goggles, official Los Angeles police badges, handcuffs, five handguns, a sawed-off shotgun, an assault rifle, and hundreds of rounds of ammunition.

In summary, a ghost address will give you not only protection but peace of mind as well. No longer will you have to wonder who is coming to your door. If it is not someone you recognize, then— since no one else has this address—they have no business there. The postman? Ignore him! Woman dressed in a FedEx uniform? Ignore her! Two or three guys in leather jackets? Don't even *think* of answering your door! (See how easy it is, once you eliminate all traces of your home address?)

PIZZA DELIVERIES

You may feel confident in calling in an order for pizza, because you give them a different name. However, it's safer never to have pizza delivered to your home under any name, and here's why.

Suppose all a PI has to work with is your unlisted number (567-1234), and he's after your name and especially your home address (677 Camino Privado). From the telephone prefix, he will know what city you live in. His next step will be to call every major pizza delivery company in town, because he knows that in most areas these companies log the numbers of their customers for quicker future orders. Here's what happens.

PI: I need a delivery.

Pizza Place: What's your phone number?

PI: 567-1234.

Pizza Place: Are you still at 677 Camino Privado?

PI: Yeah, same address. Oh, hang on a sec . . . wait . . . something's come up . . . Guess I'll have to cancel for now. Sorry!

Didn't take the man very long to get your home address, did it? And with the address, it won't take long to get your name. As I said earlier, the obvious solution is "to never receive anything at your home, no mail, no packages, no courier deliveries . . ." *That means no pizza, either.*

QUESTIONS & ANSWERS

Can a bounty hunter legally break into my home?

If you ever post bail via a bondsman, and fail to show up in court, then the answer is YES, INDEED. There have been a number of articles and programs about this fact. As reported on the CBS program *60 Minutes*, a bounty hunter—unlike the police—can search whatever he likes without a warrant. He can break down doors, read mail, power up computers, copy keys, whatever. The justification for all this is that anyone arranging bail through a bondsman signs a contract, and the bounty hunter is merely fulfilling the fine print in said contract. So if any of you readers ever forfeit bail, you'd better make sure your home address is *really* private.

A more likely danger is that, knowingly or unknowingly, you invite into your home someone who has forfeited bail. This might be a relative, a close friend, maybe even your brother, or grown son or daughter. You might wish to give this some thought, the next time a certain someone "stops by." In some cases, there is a danger even in *knowing* the persons the bounty hunters are after. One person interviewed on the *60 Minutes* program told of a couple being held and grilled for eleven hours by bounty hunters intent on getting enough information to track down someone this couple knew.

If someone pounds on your door and yells "Special agent!,"
you are about to meet one or more bounty hunters (who much
prefer to call themselves "bail recovery agents") in person. Do not
be fooled by the fact that they may wear uniforms, carry badges,
and at first glance appear to be with the FBI or the ATF. Or, they
may get you to open the door by dressing as employees of UPS,
FedEx, or the U.S. Postal Service. In one case, the hunters determined that one particular tough quarry—who was wise to all
normal ruses—had a young daughter whose birthday was coming
up. They waited until that day, then sent in a clown with balloons. He passed muster with the closed-circuit video, the door
was opened, and you can guess the rest.

**We are about to move to another state. Is it safe to use a
mover such as Allied, Bekins, or Mayflower?**

Not if you value your privacy. Most—if not all—interstate
moving services keep computer records, and PIs know and use
this. Keep in mind that even though you give the movers a different name, the computers can be searched by address as well. If,
therefore, an investigator tracks down your present address and
discovers you have moved, he will have an accomplice check the
records to see what name you used, and the destination street
address.

When we move, I pay a driver to rent the largest size Ryder
truck in *his* name. I then look under "Movers" in the Yellow
Pages. There is usually a subsection called "Student Movers," self-
employed husky young men who load and unload trucks for an
hourly wage. They load the truck, the driver drives it, and, at the
destination, another set of student movers unloads it. My driver
then either drops off the truck in a nearby city or drives it back
to the city of origin. Ryder puts everything into their computers,
but what do they have? Certainly not my name, and neither the
previous street address nor the new one. Incidentally, you will
often save a bundle of money with this method.

What about the cleaning lady or the carpet cleaner?

At the very least, use someone that your friends have used for years and will recommend without reservations. However, if you have secrets to protect, this precaution may not be enough. PIs have been known to offer serious money to obtain trash from a home office before it has been shredded.

My next suggestion maybe worth far more to you than the price you paid for this book. In the first edition of this book, I suggested you contact an active member of the Seventh-Day Adventists, Jehovah's Witnesses, or the Church of Jesus Christ of Latter-Day Saints (Mormons). Unlike with mainstream religions, you will seldom if ever find a longtime member of these three religions in jail unless—as in some countries—they are there for their faith. These people believe their Creator is watching them, and most would rather die than steal.

Now that the feedback from this suggestion has come in, I will limit my recommendation to Jehovah's Witnesses, who received a uniformly good report. I hasten to add, however, that there were no *bad* reports about the other two religions. Rather, there weren't any reports at all. I assume, therefore, that the other two groups do not have many members interested in cleaning. The Witnesses, on the other hand, do up to eighty percent of the nightly janitorial work in office buildings in major cities, and an even higher percentage in clinics. In almost any town, there are Witnesses with janitorial and carpet-cleaning businesses, as well as individuals who do much of the cleaning in upscale homes where security is paramount. They usually clean for a flat rate, work briskly yet carefully, and earn from $20 to $40 an hour. They seldom object to working odd hours such as late at night, very early in the morning, or on holidays (since they do not celebrate them).

Although they call their church buildings "Kingdom Halls," we look them up in the Yellow Pages under "Churches." Over the years, we have learned that the best time to call a Kingdom Hall is between 6:45 and 7:10 P.M. on a Tuesday, Wednesday, or Thursday. This is just before they have one of their meetings. Ask to speak to one of the "elders." If they are busy, leave your number and have them call back. When an elder comes on the line, do not use a title such as pastor or reverend—they do not use titles. Just explain what you need.

There is no need to be embarrassed about calling. Non-Witness persons often call Kingdom Halls to ask who is looking for work. (Besides janitorial, they are in demand in businesses where large sums of money are being handled.) If you are unusually concerned about privacy, say that you prefer a worker who is a "pioneer." This is the term Witnesses use for those who put most of their time in the Bible-teaching work. They cannot be pioneers unless they have an excellent reputation both within and without their congregation. And not to worry—they won't preach to you while on the job!

What about letting a baby-sitter into our home?

If the baby-sitter is Grandma, there should be no problem. Other than that, tune your radio into the *Dr. Laura Schlessinger Show*. Better yet, call Dr. Laura. Ask her what she thinks about abandoning your little trolls to a sitter. (Best to be sitting down for the answer.)

Even if you survive the phone call and are determined to call in a sitter, do you still harbor vague fears? Then spend about $60 for a voice-activated tape recorder with multiple pickup microphones. You may hear phone calls, boyfriends coming to visit, or sounds of child abuse. A better solution is to install a nanny-cam and see what goes on in living color. Perhaps she is checking out your computer or going through your drawers!

Actually, however, if you suspect the sitter may need electronic surveillance, your fears are probably right. Better to call in Grandma, or stay home yourself.

7

UNTRACEABLE TRASH, ANONYMOUS UTILITIES

Satisfaction Guaranteed or Double Your Garbage Back
—GARBAGE TRUCK, CAMBRIDGE, MASSACHUSETTS

This is a short but vital chapter, absolutely essential in order to achieve your goal. Let's start out with an opportunity for you to play detective. See if you can solve the mystery.

A bilingual private investigator in San Jose, California, takes a call from a law firm in San Diego. They wish to locate a certain Victor R——— in order to serve a subpoena in a civil lawsuit. They have only two pieces of information:

1. Victor, who was born in Ameca, Jalisco, is staying with friends from his hometown. They live "somewhere" near Lake Tahoe, on the California-Nevada border.

2. Victor has a younger brother named Fernando, who rents a one-bedroom unit in a sixty-four-unit apartment complex in San Jose. However, the PI is *not* to contact Fernando, because, if he does, Fernando will tip off his brother.

Worse, the lawyers want fast results, and yet they put a limit on what the PI may spend. If he needs any helpers, he will have to use slave labor. The intrepid PI takes the job, despite the following drawbacks:

- If Victor is staying with friends, there is no way to track him down via rental agreement, telephone, or utilities.

- There are more than ten thousand Latinos in the Lake Tahoe area, and nearly 80 percent of them come from the same place: Ameca, Jalisco (Mexico).

- A quick check shows that there is no telephone at Fernando's apartment.

Our resolute PI is on the job that very evening, prepared for action. What he wants is every bit of the trash that leaves Fernando's apartment for the next thirty days. He observes that there are two large Dumpsters near the entrance of the parking lot, and learns that they are dumped between three and four A.M. every day. There is no uniformity in the bags the residents are using. Some are paper, some are white plastic bags from the supermarkets, and some are large black trash bags. The PI knows of a Guatemalan family where three teenagers are desperate for work, any kind of work, even diving into Dumpsters.

Here is where you get to play detective.

How will his Guatemalan friends know which garbage belongs to Fernando?

[Take five, see if you can guess the answer. This is not rocket science.]

Okay, check your answer with what happens next. Later that evening, the PI goes from door to door, calling at each of the sixteen apartments that are on Fernando's floor. He wears a uniform with a name tag and presents each renter with a free supply of thirty trash bags, speaking Spanish or English, as the occasion warrants.

"This is part of an experiment by our company," he says with a disarming smile. "The idea is to see if these extra-strong bags will cause less spillage when our trucks unload at the processing plant. If you and your neighbors use these bags for the next thirty days, we may continue to furnish them at no charge."

A young, pregnant woman answers the door at Fernando's apartment. He gives her the pitch and hands her the bags.

"Muchas gracias," she says. *"Muy amable."*

"No hay de qué. Que tenga un buen día." Have a nice day.

Then the three Guatemalans get their assignment. They are to take turns drifting past the Dumpsters both morning and evening, checking to see if there is a bag from Fernando's apartment. For every bag they bring in, the PI pays them $20 cash. If he finds what he is looking for, there will be a $100 bonus.

In the next two weeks, they bring in eight bags, and, two days later, they bring in the bag that pays a $100 bonus—Fernando has a cell phone and he has tossed the statement in the trash after tearing it into sixteen pieces. Pieced together with tape, it shows six long-distance calls to the same number at Zephyr Cove on the Nevada side of Lake Tahoe. That is all it takes to track down Victor, at a cost of $280 to the kids and $96 for the bags.

Have you already guessed how the kids knew which bags to pick up?

Yes, it was just as you thought. At fifteen doors, the PI gave away dark green bags. At Fernando's door, he handed over dark blue bags.

That was the windup. Here comes the pitch.

To paraphrase Johnny Cochran:

> *If it can be read,*
> *Then you must shred.*

WHAT YOUR TRASH REVEALS ABOUT YOU

Trash is not the remains of food. That is garbage. Trash is everything else. Unfortunately, the two may be mixed, unless they
are coming from an office building. Trash is to a detective what
a gold nugget is to a prospector. Just imagine what investigators
would have learned about *you* and *your* family if they had
secretly gone through your trash for the last ninety days. We
shall assume they started with a blank sheet, having no idea as
to the occupants of your home. To put a picture together, they
would have watched for any of the items on the following list.
If there were any items that you had merely torn up (rather
than put through a shredder), they would have glued the pieces
back together.

- Bank statements with your name, address, account num-
  ber, and balance
- Telephone bills with your number, and the long-distance
  calls you made
- Utility and other bills, showing the name and address you
  use for those
- Credit card statements and receipts, invoices, automatic
  teller receipts
- Paycheck and/or money order stubs
- Empty bottles from prescription medicine, with your doc-
  tor's name
- Personal and business letters; all address labels
- Scraps of paper that may reveal a name or a phone number
- Matchbooks, inside covers checked for phone numbers
- Beer cans, wine and liquor bottles
- Anything to indicate drug use, including triangular scraps
  of paper

- Itemized grocery and pharmacy slips, for evidence of alcohol, illness, condoms, birth control pills, or anything to indicate homosexual activity
- Classified ads from newspapers, to see if anything is circled
- Magazines, travel brochures, or anything that would indicate interest in weapons or strange practices
- Any envelope with a foreign stamp to indicate a possible overseas connection

What else can you think of, in your particular case? Or that of your friends, relatives, or even your children?

Do you have a weekly arrangement for a woman to come in and clean? Does she have access to the trash?

If you work in an office, who handles the trash? Did you know that, in some cases, janitors are bribed to turn trash from a specific office over to private investigators or government agents?

Most likely, if you do everything else right, no one will be able to sift through your trash, because they cannot find you in the first place. But *if they do* (perhaps by following you home), then make sure all papers have been shredded and that there is nothing further to be revealed from your trash.

UTILITIES

By utilities I mean the companies that furnish electricity, garbage pickup, water and sewer connections, and natural or propane gas. (Telephones will be discussed in chapter 10.) Never give your true name—much less your Social Security number or date of birth!—to a utility company, nor to any other private company that will furnish a service at your actual residence.

Rather, if you own your home in the name of a limited liability company (see chapter 15), give each company the name of the LLC and insist that the name in the company database is in the name of the LLC only. In fact, do not give them your own name under any circumstances. Try a fictitious one, or use your wife's maiden name. Even then, this should just be her middle initial plus last name. Do not furnish her Social Security number or date of birth.

A quick and dirty method of setting up the utility accounts on short notice is to use a nominee (proxy), someone who will act on your behalf. (See chapter 13.) Usually, the utility company will demand a cash deposit in lieu of being able to check your credit by using your Social Security number. Fine, give them a money order or a bank check for the deposit. It will be returned to you after one year of timely payments. Make sure that the bills *never* come to your home address. Give them your "ghost" address (see chapter 5), explaining that (a) you do not have a mailbox at the street address, and (b) all bills are paid from your "business" (ghost) address.

What has been accomplished? Just this: If a private investigator—acting on behalf of a stalker or working with a law firm or insurance company—starts searching for you, one of the first places he will check (after cable TV) will be the utility companies. If your name is in any database, the PI will obtain the address. But as long as your name never shows up, the search will be in vain.

QUESTIONS & ANSWERS

How can I get rid of trash other than by shredding it?

If you have a fireplace or a wood-burning stove, perhaps you can burn it. Otherwise, toss your statements, bills, etc. into a box that is reserved for this purpose. Be sure to include all envelopes that indicate your name and ghost address. (Don't forget the junk-mail offers.) Then cut through the addresses and put one half of each address in one pile, the other half in a second pile. Bundle them up and toss the piles in separate public trash bins.

And then go out and buy a shredder!

Where can I buy a paper shredder and what kind should I buy?

Office supply stores, such as OfficeMax, Office Depot, and Staples, all carry paper shredders. Although the strip-shredders are the most economical, with infinite patience, the strips *could* be reassembled. For maximum security, I recommend a confetti-cut shredder. It will reduce your documents to thousands of $\frac{5}{32}$" by $1\frac{1}{4}$" particles.

We have a small business that has to do with top-secret information. How can we make sure that trash taken from our office building at night does not, under any circumstances whatsoever, fall into the hands of a private investigator from one of our competitors?

First on the list, of course, is to cross-shred everything. Then, give the job to janitors who are Jehovah's Witnesses (see chapter 6). Explain your circumstances to them and tell them never to leave the trash in a Dumpster or on the street. Instead, they are to take the trash with them and dispose of it in some other way. Also, stress the importance of calling you immediately if anyone approaches them and even *hints* at being interested in your trash.

Although they may charge you more than the lowest-bidder types, trust me on this one: It will be money well spent.

8

YOUR SOCIAL SECURITY NUMBER AND DATE OF BIRTH

*But there is nothing concealed that will not be disclosed,
and nothing hidden that will not be made known.*

—LUKE 12:2

In 1973, George Norman left Denver, Colorado, in a borrowed car. He was skipping out on an impending two-year prison sentence for embezzling some $500,000 from the now-defunct Rocky Mountain Bank. Over the years, he ran this "starter money" into $50 million by legal means, dabbling in oil in Houston and starting software companies in Oregon and Utah.

Although he knew that U.S. marshals were after him, rather than move to Mexico or Canada he stayed in the United States, relying on alternate names to protect him. Some of the names he used were George Larson, Max Morris, George Irving, Frick Jensen, Gunner Isoz, J. Blankman, and Dr. James Hill.

Had private parties been employing detectives to pursue him, the money would have run out before many years had passed.

However, with government agents, money does not run out. Twenty-three years passed before Norman, for whatever reason, felt compelled to give out a Social Security number. Rather than use his own, or invent one, he used the number of a person he knew was dead. This Social Security number came up on a government computer as that of Tom Dangelis, red-flagged as George Norman's wife Donna's deceased grandfather! The result was this headline in the Sunday, December 1, 1996, *Los Angeles Times*: "FUGITIVE MILLIONAIRE NABBED AFTER 23 YEARS ON THE LAM."

Yes, Norman needed catching, and they caught him. But the point is, privacy isn't only for criminals, it's also desirable for white-hat folks like you and me, and this story certainly illustrates the point about not using someone else's Social Security number. It also tells us, as I say in chapter 1, that when the chips go down for whatever reason, your first priority may be to gain time to sort things out. One way to find that time is to cross a border to the north or south. Even Denver's Deputy U.S. Marshal Bobby Lloyd wondered about this, as indicated in the closing paragraph of the *Los Angeles Times* article:

"A guy with this amount of money," said Lloyd, "why he didn't just leave the country, I don't know."

YOUR DATE OF BIRTH

No matter how common your name, you can be quickly identified in a database by coupling either your name *or* your birth date with your address. Keeping your true home address a secret has already been discussed. As for a birth date, I seldom give out any date whatsoever.

For instance, I recently stopped in at a shopping mall to have my eyes tested. The doctor's assistant handed me a long form to fill out, asking, among other things, my address, telephone number, Social Security number, and date of birth. I explained that I did not live in the area, did not give out my Social Security number, and my age was in the "early seventies." No objection was raised. During the exam, the doctor asked me what I did for a living.

"I'm a writer."

"Oh? What do you write?"

"Articles and books about keeping your private life *private*. Which is why I didn't give you a Social Security number nor a date of birth."

"Oh well," replied the doctor, "except for insurance cases, I don't need that stuff on the form anyway!" (But they don't tell you that when they hand you the form, right?)

My next stop was nearby, at one of those national chains that have optical shops in malls. I picked out the two frames I wanted and the young sales clerk started to fill in the form.

"Address?" she said.

"No local address, I live in Spain." After a puzzled look, she wrote down the address of the store itself.

"Telephone number?"

"Sorry, no telephone." She wrote down the number of the store.

"Date of birth?"

"Why on earth," I said, "would the purchase of two pairs of glasses require a date of birth?"

"The date of birth is how we identify our customers."

"I do not wish to be identified." Long pause. Then she left it blank. The next question on the form was for a Social Security number, but, at this point, the girl just shrugged and didn't even ask me.

Personally, I enjoy these challenges, but some of my clients do not. In fact, they hate confrontations of any kind. Often, if filling in a form yourself, you can just write "legal age." Another alternative is to give a fictitious month and day, and a year a bit before or after the real one. If you feel obligated to give some date of birth, choose one that is easy to remember, such as a national holiday. Why not make yourself a few years younger at the same time?

YOUR SOCIAL SECURITY NUMBER (SSN)

The Privacy Act of 1974 (P.L. 93-579) requires that any federal, state, or local government agency that requests your Social Security number must tell you four things:

1. Whether disclosure of your SSN is required or optional.

2. What statute or other authority requires this number.

3. How they will use your SSN, once they have it.

4. What will happen if you do not provide them with your SSN.

So then, if you are asked for your SSN by any federal, state, or local government agency (including any state university that accepts federal funds), look for the Privacy Act Statement. If it isn't there, ask to see it before you give your number. Since the subject of this book is privacy, not tax evasion, I see no problem in furnishing your SSN to the Internal Revenue Service.

YOUR DRIVER'S LICENSE

Public Law 104-208, passed in 1996, poses an unprecedented threat to the persons who use driver's licenses for ID purposes. Section 656 provided that after October 1, 2000, federal agencies may not accept for any identification-related purpose a driver's license issued by a state unless the license contains a Social Security number that can be read visually or by electronic means. Due to strong public objections, Congress has been delayed in putting this into force, but by the time this book is published, it may have been implemented.

Actually, apart from the state agency that issues driver's licenses, there's not much of a problem when you're dealing with government agencies. It's the *private* organizations that can give you industrial-strength headaches. The low-level clerk behind the counter expects you to fill out that form *completely*. After all, "everyone else does," and it's "the company policy." So let's consider some of these private agencies or organizations:

YOUR EMPLOYER

If you work for wages, the IRS requires the employer to get your Social Security number. Sometimes they will ask for it before you're hired, so they can check your credit and criminal (if any) record. Tell them you'll give your Social Security number if and when actually hired for the job. If this is not acceptable, ask yourself, "How badly do I want this job?"

If you do take the job, know that your name, address, and Social Security number must by law go into the database for the National Directory of New Hires within twenty calendar days. This applies to virtually every person who is hired in the United States. The only wiggle room here is with the address. Remember the rule? "Do not, as long as you live, ever again allow your real name to be coupled with your home address." Therefore, give your employer only your ghost address. (If you don't yet have one, perhaps you can use the address of a relative who lives in the same area.)

In some cases, you may be able to work as an independent contractor. This is easier than it used to be, because, in 1998, the IRS burden-of-proof rules were changed in the independent contractor's favor. An independent contractor is someone who works for another person or firm as a separate entity. The details are too complex to go into here, but if you think you might qualify, consult a CPA.

HOSPITALS AND DOCTORS

If you qualify for Medicare *and wish to use it*, you'll need to furnish your true Social Security number. Other than that, I know of no law that requires your Social Security number to be an ID number. Insurance companies can often be persuaded to use another number in lieu of the Social Security number. True, the insurance companies do send information to the Medical Information Bureau (MIB), but I've been told the MIB does not use Social Security numbers as identifiers, nor do they report Social Security numbers when making reports.

Remember, when a private investigator has an associate search for your records in the Medical Information Bureau, many identical names may come up. His first choice for picking you out will be your date of birth, and his second choice will be whatever address he may have for you (if any). The very last thing you want on your record is a consultation that indicates a nervous disorder, a psychiatric problem, or a sexually transmitted disease. For these, pay cash and use a false name. Better yet, pop over into Canada or Mexico. If you can afford it, skip Medicare altogether and just pay all bills in cash. No personal information needed for that.

BANKS

If you must have a U.S. bank account, open it in a business name or in that of another person. When cashing checks, do not use your driver's license for identification. Rather, use your passport, because:

- it does not show your Social Security number;
- it does not show any address for you, not even the state or country in which you live;
- unlike through the Department of Motor Vehicles (or whatever name it has in your state), you cannot easily be traced with your passport number.

Occasionally, after presenting my passport, I have been asked for my driver's license. I reply that I do not use my driver's license for

ID. In one small town, the bank teller confessed that she had never seen a passport before! I had to point out where the number was, so she could write it on the third-party check I was cashing.

If you do not yet have a passport, apply for one, even if you have no intention of traveling to foreign lands. From the time it arrives, this will be the ID to use at all times.

RENTING AN APARTMENT

Apartment managers present one of the greatest challenges a privacy-seeker will ever face. You, of course, wish to keep your rental contract private. The manager, however, has almost certainly had some bad experiences with renters in the past and he is determined not to repeat them. With the escalating amount of identity fraud and the increased security since 9–11, most landlords now require:

- Your driver's license (which may be photocopied) and a second piece of identification, such as a credit card.

- Your date of birth.

- The name, address, and telephone number of one or more references, preferably relatives.

- Your Social Security number, so he can check both your credit and a statewide database (i.e., blacklist) of undesirable tenants.

- The name of your employer, your monthly income, and perhaps a stub from one of your paychecks. Or, if you're self-employed, you may be asked for a copy of your most recent tax return.

- A completely filled out and signed contract, including a list of your most recent landlords, along with their telephone numbers. And yes, they will be called.

• The name of your bank, and perhaps the account number as well. Some will even demand to see a bank statement. (This is unusual but not illegal.)

In your present circumstances, you may find it impossible to get around these demands. If such is the case, my advice is to give in on most of the points but *not on the Social Security number.* (Once the Social Security number is used to check your credit, you can be targeted in a heartbeat.) Dress well, be polite, use your passport for ID, and offer to pay several months in advance. Above all, prepare beforehand to explain the reason—perhaps fear of a stalker—why you are simply unable to allow anyone to have your Social Security number. If you must furnish a copy of your tax return, black out your Social Security number, and then (to make sure it cannot still be read in front of a strong light) make a copy of that copy.

Warning: If you succeed in renting an apartment without revealing your Social Security number, never pay the rent with a personal check. Otherwise, a PI can trace it back to your bank and they *do* have your Social Security number. Instead, pay either in cash or with a money order purchased at a post office, a supermarket, or a convenience store.

If, at the present time, you see no way around acceding to all of the landlord's demands, do not despair. Get a short lease or rent month-by-month while you make your plans to move on to a more private location.

RENTING A HOUSE FROM ITS OWNER

If you choose to rent a house rather than an apartment, you may be able to solve the Social Security number problem, especially if you have money available from an emergency fund. Watch the classified ads and also check with real estate agencies. The objective is to deal directly with the owner of the property. Here's a recent example from a friend of ours, to whom I'll refer here as John Martin Tallman.

John moved to a new area where he was having a home custom-built. Due to myriad delays and problems, the builders were six months away from completion. He checked the classifieds and found this one:

> For lease: 3,000 sq. ft. home
> on golf course. $1,700/month
> plus $2,000 deposit. Credit
> check mandatory. Call Amy at
> 783-99xx.

The "credit check mandatory" did not scare John. As "Martin" Tallman, he called Amy for an appointment, showed up in a conservative suit and tie, introduced himself as an investor who was considering a move to the area, and asked to see the property. The house had been on the market for nearly a year. After six months, the asking price of $495,000 had been reduced to $449,000, but the home had still not sold. Amy's boss, who had built the home on speculation, had decided to lease it out until the market improved. Although the owner had hoped to lease it out for a minimum of one year, it was agreed that John could lease for just six months, with an option to extend the lease to one year.

"You mentioned a credit report in your ad," he said. "I prefer to keep my private affairs private, and for that reason I never give out my Social Security number. Since I always—"

"Sir, we need your Social Security number for a credit report."

"As I started to say, since I always pay cash, a file has never been opened for me in any credit agency."

"Nevertheless," said Amy, "we have to make a routine check. If nothing turns up—"

"Excuse me," said John with a smile, holding up his hand. "If you send in a request, they *will* open a file for me, and there goes my privacy. Now then, I totally understand that you do not plan to lease this home unless you are sure that the monthly payments will come in, right?"

"Of course, and that's why—"

"In my case, no monthly payments will be involved. I'll pay cash in advance."

"For all six months?"

"Yes, for all six months, and if I extend the lease at the end of that time, I will again pay for six months. I can give you the name of my attorney in San Francisco who will confirm that I am a law-abiding citizen. Here is my passport [showing it], and I will leave you a photocopy. We have no children, we throw no parties, my wife's only hobby in life is scrubbing and cleaning, we have no pets, and neither of us smoke. You can leave the utilities in the present name, and I'll leave a deposit with you to cover them. I can have a bank cashier's check for you within the hour. How shall I have it made out?"

"I'll have to talk to my boss."

"Fine, I'd like that. Is he here?"

"No, I'll have to call him. Could you come back at this same time tomorrow?"

The lease went through the next day. Note:

- No one was called for a reference
- No Social Security number was given
- The lease was in John's middle and last name only, and did not include the name of his wife
- He listed no previous addresses
- Not one of the utilities was put into his name
- He received no mail nor any delivery at that address
- He avoided giving his date of birth

Pay close attention to that last item. One problem with a passport is that it *does* list the date of birth, and the date of birth is sometimes used in databases in lieu of a Social Security number. John, however, was prepared in advance for that problem. He had previously photocopied his passport, eliminated the date of birth on the copy, and then copied it again. When he met with Amy the next day, he was ready.

"Here, again, is my passport. And," he said, producing his copy, "here is a copy for your files." The altered copy went into the files without a second glance.

At no time during the six months of the lease did John ever mention that he was having a home built in the area, and, when he moved out, he "neglected" to leave any forwarding address. (If you are thinking to yourself that very few persons can pay six month's rent in advance, please review the final question at the end of this chapter.)

TRAVEL TRAILERS AND MOBILE HOMES

No Social Security number is needed if you purchase a travel trailer or a mobile home for cash, license it in the name of an LLC, and do not put it on a firm foundation. For those of you who are determined to "own" your own home, I suggest buying a used mobile home in a park. You can sometimes pick up an older one in good condition for as little as ten or fifteen thousand dollars, which, hopefully, means you can pay cash.

You may even decide to make a little extra money this way, fixing up the mobile home and then selling it for a higher price.

REAL ESTATE PURCHASES AND SALES

A Social Security number is required for the IRS reporting forms, even if you do pay cash. Although I don't consider giving your Social Security number under this condition high risk— the IRS has it anyway, from your tax returns—you are not without options. One is to never actually *buy* real estate. Rent, lease, or take options. Or you can purchase and sell in the name of company or a trust, using its tax identification number (TIN) if you've obtained one.

FALSE SOCIAL SECURITY NUMBERS

A federal court of appeals has ruled that using a false Social Security number to obtain a driver's license is illegal. Other than that, there appears to be no legal penalty for giving a wrong number as long as there is no intent to:

1. deceive a government agency;

2. commit fraud; or

3. obtain a specific benefit.

If, then, you are someday asked for your Social Security number in an innocuous circumstance where you know this number will *not be checked*, you may be tempted to transpose two digits in the last four. (Never transpose any digits in the first three, because these are state ID numbers.) "If they ever ask," you might tell yourself, "I'll just say it was an accident."

However, I do not recommend this. You have no way of knowing whom the real number belongs to. What if it identifies a drug dealer, a child pornographer, or someone who died in 1975?

What I do recommend is that you either give your true number when absolutely required, or else no number at all. Nevertheless, knowing that you may someday be tempted to give a false number, here are three ways to come up with a Social Security number which, although false, will *not* identify you with anyone else.

1. Invent a number that lists the state of your choice in the first field, followed by 00 in the second field, as there are no legitimate Social Security numbers with all zeroes in any field.

2. Start the number with 987-65-, and then pick a number for the last four digits between 4320 and 4329. These are the numbers allowed for use in advertisements.

3. Fifty years ago, new wallets with a celluloid window insert came with a sample Social Security card included, and this number was always 078-05-1120. You might, therefore, jot this number down and keep it in your wallet or purse for emergency use.

There is a Web site, *www.informus.com/ssnlkup.html*, where anyone used to be able to check to see if a Social Security number has ever been issued. (It has since been changed to "subscribers only.") When I checked the above numbers a few years ago, items one and two were invalid. When I ran the third number, this was the response:

SSN 078-05-1120 was VALIDLY ISSUED between 1934 and 1951 in NY.

So, then, if you give that number as your own but fear it might be checked, "remember" that you were in New York at the time. It would also be helpful to look at least sixty-four years old, as Social Security numbers were seldom issued to children in those years.

Very important: Never use any of the above numbers with a government agency. Even lowly clerks will recognize them.

TIP

Who knows when you will

1. lose your purse or wallet;

2. have it stolen; or

3. have the contents searched, following a traffic stop?

Therefore, do not carry your Social Security card with you, nor *any* document that lists your Social Security number. (Since you will never again use your driver's license for identification, keep it hidden in your car.) If you carry a health insurance card, or are under Medicare, I suggest you photocopy the card and block out the Social Security number. You can give your Social Security number to the health-care provider orally, if and when required.

OBTAINING CREDIT

In some cases, it may be extremely difficult to obtain credit without revealing your number, so you'll have to ask yourself a question: *"How desperately do I need this credit?"* The correct answer should be, "Not *that* desperately!" In the *Computer Privacy Handbook*, author André Bacard quotes his grandfather's opinion of credit:

"I'm 80 years old and free because I never owed a dime. Young people are addicted to credit. Mark my words, André. Credit will lead to a police state in America. I hope I die before then."

My Scottish father and my Norwegian mother ran their lives the same way, quoting Proverbs 22:7 to my sister and me: "The borrower is a servant to the man doing the lending." The advice was sound. I pass it on to you.

RUN YOUR LIFE ON A CASH BASIS

If you truly wish to become invisible, never apply for personal credit. (There is occasionally a business exception, but credit in this case should be extended only to your corporation or LLC.) We raised our children to pay cash or go without, we recommend the same to all our friends, and we stand by our own example even when discussing the International Dream of "Owning Your Own Home."

Incidentally, home ownership is overrated. It is usually cheaper to rent or lease your living quarters. Further, should disaster strike from whatever direction, as a renter you can move before the sun rises tomorrow morning. The homeowner, on the other hand, will dawdle and procrastinate, and, in some cases, this delay can be fatal.

Until my wife and I were in our fifties, we *rented*, period. When we finally did build our first home on Lanzarote Island, perched on a cliff 1,500 feet above the Atlantic, we followed the Spanish custom and paid cash for every brick and rock and block. *Un*like the Spanish way of thinking, however, we were mentally prepared to walk away and leave it if we had to. Since then we've built homes both there and in North America, always for cash, and only because we can afford this totally unnecessary luxury.

When the day comes that we can't afford to walk (or run) away and leave a house behind, we'll sell it, stash the cash, and go back to renting. In, as always, another name.

QUESTIONS & ANSWERS

Isn't giving out a false Social Security number a federal offense according to U.S. Code, Title 42, Section 408?

Before preparing this chapter, I read 42 U.S.C. 408 and also Case 94-5721 in the United States Court of Appeals for the Fourth Circuit: *United States of America v. Eunice Arnetta Harris Sparks*. I am not an attorney, so this is just a layman's opinion:

There does not seem to be any basis for a court case if there is no intent to deceive, and if no benefit is obtained. (In the above court case, the defendant purchased a car on credit, gave a false Social Security number, and then failed to make the payments.)

Can I get by without a passport and still maintain my privacy?

Yes, of course . . . if you never travel by air, never pay in a store by check, never cash a check at a bank, never receive a registered letter, and are never otherwise called upon to prove your age or identity. Since this may not be practical for you, let's discuss another aspect of drivers' licenses.

A recent news program on national television discussed the sale of pictures that goes with state drivers' licenses. The buyer is a company called Image Data. What had previously been kept secret was now made public (i.e., that the source of Image Data's financing came from the U.S. Secret Service). Image Data *says* the only use for these pictures will be for businesses that accept checks. They will scan your driver's license and check the picture on the screen to be sure it is really you. Two questions arise:

1. what use does the U.S. Secret Service have for these pictures?

2. why was Image Data attempting to hide the U.S. Secret Service connection?

I cannot answer these questions. What I can do, however, is continue to urge you not to use your driver's license for anything other than showing it to a policeman if you are stopped for a violation. (And do all within your power never to be stopped!)

Remember, for the past twenty-five years, most states have been selling the data from driver's licenses. This includes your height, weight, and "home address," none of which shows up on a passport. Also, as I have said before, if an investigator wishes to check you out, one of the first places he will check is the DMV in the state in which you live. I therefore say—once again—that one of the very best ways to maintain your privacy is to obtain a passport and use it alone for identification. (On the rare occasion when a second piece of ID is required, use something other than your driver's license.)

What if a Social Security number is required for a hunting or fishing license?

Many states do require a Social Security number for registering a boat or buying a hunting or fishing license. The boat, of course, can be registered in the name of an LLC. You may wish to hunt or fish in another state—one that does not require a Social Security number. The nonresident license will cost you more, but if saving money is your goal, you'll cut expenses when you shop for your meat and fish at the local supermarket.

Can't I just apply for a new Social Security number?

Many books have been published with advice about how to illegally obtain a new Social Security number. Some authors recommend you tell some wild story about how you were living in the jungles of New Guinea and just got back. More often, it is suggested you comb old newspapers for children who died young, and obtain—or fake—their birth certificate. These books are out of date because the Social Security Administration now requires anyone eighteen or older to show up in person with original or certified documents to prove age, identity, and United States citizenship, along with an airtight explanation as to why no card has ever been issued previously. There are just three exceptions. These are for:

1. Those relocated with new identities under the Federal Witness Security program.

2. Individuals who can prove they were victims of "identify theft" when criminals used their number repeatedly to get credit cards, make loans, and engage in other financial transactions.

3. Abused women who are hiding from husbands, ex-husbands, or former lovers. Until the latter part of 1999, only about 150 new numbers were granted each year. Since then, however, the Social Security Administration has been

granting new numbers much more freely. In addition to original documents establishing your age, identity and U.S. citizenship or lawful alien status, you will be asked for both your old and new names if you have changed your name. You must also present evidence showing you have custody of children for whom you are requesting new numbers; and evidence you may have documenting the harassment or abuse. The best evidence of abuse will come from third parties, such as police, medical facilities, or doctors. Other evidence may include court restraining orders, letters from shelters, family members, friends, counselors, or others who have knowledge of the domestic violence or abuse. (For additional information about new numbers for abused women, go to the agency's Web site, *http://www.ssa.gov/pubs/10093.html.*)

Can I avoid giving my Social Security number on the basis of Revelation, Chapter 13?

I assume you are referring to the belief, held sincerely by some, that a Social Security number is the "mark of the beast." It is true that, in the past, several persons have won court cases objecting on religious grounds to state requirements for a Social Security number as a condition to receiving a driver's license. In *Leahy v. District of Columbia*, the circuit court upheld John C. Leahy's religious objection to providing his Social Security number in order to get a driver's license.

Later, five plaintiffs sued the City of Los Angeles on religious objection grounds, objecting to the state's requirement that driver's license applicants must provide a Social Security number as a condition to getting a license. They won the case in the State Superior Court, but I have since heard the state appealed that decision.

An October 25, 1997, a headline in the *Los Angeles Times* said, "RELIGIOUS OBJECTIONS TO DMV UPHELD." The subtitle was, "Judge Says Five Men Do Not Need Social Security Numbers To Get

Licenses. They Contend That The Identification Is The Satanic
'Mark Of The Beast.'" The article, written by staff writer John
Dart, reads in part:

> In the first court decision to declare that a driver's license
> applicant can refuse to give the Department of Motor Vehicles
> a Social Security number for religious reasons, a Los Angeles
> Superior Court has ruled that the DMV must accommodate five
> men who contend that the numbers are the "mark of the beast"
> in the Bible's Book of Revelation. In handing down the decision,
> Superior Court Judge Diane Wayne said last week that the state
> agency could use another method of identification in light of the
> men's "sincerely held religious convictions . . . that anyone who
> uses his or her Social Security number is in danger of not receiv-
> ing eternal life."

If you really, truly believe that the use of a Social Security number violates your religious beliefs, then take your stand. If you go
to jail—and some have—you will be suffering for what you feel is
a righteous cause. But if you are thinking of challenging the
authorities and just using religion as an excuse, then I urge you to
back off. Join the rest of us who do furnish the number when
absolutely necessary . . . but never otherwise.

*You cited an example of a friend who paid his rent six
months in advance in order to avoid giving out his Social Security number. But what if we can barely scrape together a deposit
and* one *month in advance?*

If you are that broke, set the privacy issues aside for the
moment. Get right to work on setting up an emergency fund—
$5,000 minimum. (If you are making monthly payments on
nonessentials like furniture, TV, or a fancy car, *sell them.*) Until
you reach your goal, pay for nothing other than rent, gasoline,
minimal repairs on an old car, utilities, insurance, and groceries.
No cable TV, no movies, no newspapers, no soft drinks, no eating

out, no alcohol, no cigarettes, and no new clothes or shoes. Don't tell me it cannot be done. I know Mexicans with minimum-wage jobs who send money to their parents back in Mexico *every month*.

Personally, I prefer to keep my emergency fund in a combination of cash, well-hidden (as explained in chapter 20), and traveler's checks. However, if you feel more comfortable keeping it in the bank, do so. The main thing is to have this emergency fund in place. Then—when necessary—pay your rent for six months in advance. Paying rent in advance is the same as money in the bank.

9

YOUR ALTERNATE NAMES AND SIGNATURES

Why be difficult when, with a bit of effort, you can be impossible?

—ANONYMOUS

Anyone can sign your name. If your attorney, CPA, or anyone else warns you that you cannot legally sign another person's name, ask them to prove it. (They will be unable to do so.) The only caveat is that the person whose name you are about to sign must authorize this by telephone at the time of signature.

Example: You have the tax return for your Wyoming corporation, Oliver's Oddities, ready to mail on the due date. Problem: you forgot that your cousin Oliver, who is substituting for you as the sole director, will have to sign. Although Oliver is currently on an Arctic fishing trip, you reach him by telephone at the Frontier Lodge on Great Slave Lake.

"Oliver, we need to mail the tax return to the IRS today. OK if I sign your name as president?"

"Sure, why not?"

That's it. Go ahead and sign his name. All the IRS wants to see is *a* signature. My only suggestion here is that, when Oliver returns, have him sign an acknowledgment affirming for the private corporate records that permission was given via a telephone call the same day. Clip this to your copy of the return.

IF YOU *SAY* IT'S YOUR SIGNATURE, THEN IT'S YOUR SIGNATURE

Example: Your husband, John, is off hunting elk in the Rocky Mountains when an unforeseen emergency leaves you short of cash for Saturday night bingo. In the morning's mail comes his Social Security check. You cannot reach John, because he is camping out and doesn't have a cell phone. Question: Can you sign his name and deposit his check in your joint account?

Yes, because you know that, if any question comes up later, he will acknowledge your signature as his own. Naturally, you sign the check *before* you go to the bank. (*Note:* Many husbands and wives practice signing each other's signatures for just such purposes as this, and some are skilled enough to fool any banker in the land.)

Warning: If, instead of going hunting, John ran off with Flossy Floozie from the office, he will *not* want you to sign his name, in which case, repeat after me:

"*DO . . . NOT . . . SIGN!*"

YOU CAN USE ANY NUMBER OF DIFFERENT SIGNATURES, INCLUDING ILLEGIBLE ONES

In fact, among European businessmen, illegible is the order of the day. I used to work with a banker in Santa Cruz de Tenerife.

His name was Hector Adelfonso de la Torre Romero y Ortega. This was his signature:

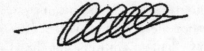

"But why," I'm often asked, "would anyone want an illegible signature?" Well, for signing letters to your friends, you do not want one, but why not have an alternative, illegible signature you can reproduce at will? Here are several reasons why such signatures are used so widely in Europe:

- If a copy of a secret letter comes to light, the identity of the signer will not be evident.
- For faxes, the signature is recognized only by those with the right to know.
- Bank accounts can be in the name of another person or in the name of a legal entity, and the one receiving such a check will have no clue as to the signer. (*Note:* There should be no problem, in any event, with the bank itself. Only the smallest of banks actually check signatures.)

AN ALTERNATE NAME

Why would you, a model citizen and taxpayer, ever temporarily need another name? The reasons given in many books include overwhelming debts, threatened vengeance by wrathful in-laws, a marriage gone bad, or getting on a Mafia hit list. But circumstances and situations can change in a heartbeat, and thousands of persons living a tranquil life one day have resorted to flight the next. The fact that you are right and the charges are wrong may be meaningless—just ask any lawyer if he can get you justice. The stock answer is, "How much justice can you *afford?*"

By the way, let's not call your second name an "alias," that's only for the criminal types. What you want is a perfectly respectable alternate name, an assumed name, a nom de plume, nom de guerre, also called a pseudonym. (These can be used almost anywhere, as long as there is no intent to defraud.) Have you ever thought about being in the movies, even as an "extra"? Then you'll want a *stage name*. Or perhaps you'd like to be a writer, like Samuel Clemens, aka Mark Twain? If so, your journey will begin with the first step, choosing a *pen name*. (Women often use their maiden names in business, and either men or women can adopt the British custom of using a hyphenated name. If Hillary Clinton did this, she would write her name Hillary *Rodham-Clinton*, and, in an alphabetical listing, such a name would be under "R.") However, a pen name can be any name you like.

For privacy, nothing beats a common name, because it is so hard to identify which one belongs to you. (Just ask any PI.) If your name is, for example, Meinhard Leuchtenmueller, you will want to use a much more common name where possible. Suppose you will be working out of an address in Minneapolis. Why not use something like M. Anderson for your mail-order business? (There are more than ten thousand M. Andersons in the United States, most of them in the upper Midwest.) Or, if you work out of Miami or Los Angeles, you might try M. Hernandez. Check the local telephone directories for the most common names in your area.

TITLES

A surprising number of people—even in America—have a desire for some sort of title that will make them feel important. If they wish, they can call themselves a doctor, a lawyer, a CPA, or a captain with Northwest Airlines. That is, in the United States. (Do not try this in Europe!) In the Land of the Free, it is not what you call yourself but what you practice. If you are a "CPA," do not advise anyone on taxes. If you pose as a lawyer, do not give any opinions on the law.

For many, the title of choice will be "doctor." Here are some guidelines for wanna-be doctors:

Do not give advice. Explain that you are not "that kind" of a doctor. Maybe you deal only with viruses from Chad. Also, you will certainly be truthful when—if called upon for some emergency—you say you are not in "practice" and do not therefore carry malpractice insurance. Frank Abagnale Jr., in his intriguing book *Catch Me If You Can*, says that when passing himself off as a doctor in the state of Georgia, he had a standard answer for anyone who asked what kind of doctor he was.

"I'm not practicing right now," he said, identifying himself as a pediatrician. "My practice is in California and I've taken a leave of absence for one year to audit some research projects at Emory University and to make some investments."

However, Abagnale did not always stick to his standard answer. On one occasion, an attractive brunette mentioned an "odd, tight feeling" in her chest. He did examine her privately. His diagnosis was that her brassiere was too small.

Do not do as he did, unless you are willing to risk both civil and criminal charges of assault.

It is permissible to act the part. Subscribe to a couple of medical magazines and carry one around. Wear a smock with a stethoscope in the pocket.

"You can even join the county medical society," says Jack Luger in his book *Counterfeit I.D. Made Easy*. He says you can simply explain that you are not licensed in the state because you're doing research rather than holding a practice, and that the most that can happen is they'll refuse to accept you.

MEDICAL RECORDS

From a long article in the *Los Angeles Times*, February 8, 1999, under the subtitle "Some Fear Seeking Care":

> It's 10 P.M. Do you know where your medical records are? . . . Your medical records can turn up in places you'd never imagine, read by people you've never met . . . It's hard to believe that in a country where video rental records are protected by law, medical records are not. . . .
>
> A survey commissioned by the California HealthCare Foundation . . . documents that one in six Americans engages in "privacy protected behaviors," such as paying out of pocket for care otherwise covered by insurance, lying to their doctor about their medical history or being afraid to get care. . . .
>
> LaTanya Sweeney, an assistant professor of public policy at Mellon University in Pittsburgh, demonstrated how easy it is to pierce the privacy in so-called anonymous medical records. Even when names have been stripped off records that contain date of birth, sex, race and diagnostics, she can readily re-identify the individual by cross-referencing with a $20 voter registration list . . .
>
> In one instance, she looked at data from the city of Cambridge, Mass., population 54,000, and was able to identify former Gov. William Weld because only five people in the city—and only one in his ZIP Code—had his date of birth.

The conclusions that some people may draw from articles like this are listed below, along with my comments in brackets:

- Do not give the doctor a complete medical history. (If you are going to a doctor for some normal medical reason, why—*assuming it does not apply to the case at hand*—would you list any visit to a psychiatrist for depression, or admit to any history of a venereal disease?)

- Change the birth date. Use a false Social Security number. (If you are using your medical insurance, or making a claim to Medicare, you must, of course, list the true date and Social Security number. If you pay cash, however, why not change the date of birth? Either refuse to give your Social Security number, or use only one that is not that of another person, as outlined in chapter 8.)

- Get off voter rolls and never return. (Whether or not to do this must be a personal decision.)

WEB SITES ADVERTISING FAKE ID

If you have an e-mail account, you are most likely getting offers to purchase either fake driver's licenses or computer programs that will generate fake ID. Or, if you search the Internet for "Fake ID," you will come up with an endless supply of offers. Because my clients kept asking me about these Web sites, I started sending in money orders to check them out. Sometimes I received a grossly inferior product. Other times I received nothing at all. Eventually I stopped wasting time and money this way.

Lee Lapin, author of *How to Get Anything on Anybody—The Newsletter*, came to the same conclusion. In one of his issues, he wrote, in capital letters, "AS OF THIS WRITING I KNOW OF NO, ZERO, SITES THAT SELL ANYTHING EVEN VAGUELY WORTH BUYING!"

QUESTIONS & ANSWERS

How can I change my name legally?

This is seldom recommended. After all, you may use one or more additional names and still retain your legal name. However, to answer the question: When you legally change your name, you *abandon* your present name and choose a new one of your liking. I suggest you choose a common name, one that will be shared with thousands of others. In the USA, 25 percent of men of retirement age have one of the following names: John, William, James, Charles, or George. As for a last name, why not pick a family name from the Mayflower? Here are some of the more common names, culled from a complete list kept by Christopher Jones, Master, A.D. 1620:

Alden	Fuller	Turner
Browne	Martin	Warren
Carter	Priest	White
Clarke	Rogers	Williams
Cooke	Thompson	

The usual rules apply, i.e., the new name may not be the same as that of a famous person, nor can there be intent to defraud. There are two methods to do this:

The use method: The *use* method requires no lawyer, no trip to the courthouse, and is not legally registered anywhere. You simply begin using your new name everywhere. Keep in mind, however, that you will not be able to open a bank account nor obtain a driver's license with the new name. However, if you pay cash, you may be able to get by with no problem. You will, of course, always use your true name (1) when stopped by the police and asked for your license, (2) for your auto insurance, (3) for your income tax return, and (4) when purchasing a plane ticket and later identifying yourself at the airport.

The court method: State statutes regarding legal name changes vary, so if you dislike the requirements in one state, check those in another. A lawyer is not necessary, so do not use one; they keep records in their files. Various books on name changes are available, and you may find one or more of these at your local library. A date will be set for a court appearance, and the judge will question you to make sure you are not changing your name for a deceitful purpose. If no such reason emerges, you can expect approval of your new name, and this name change will be valid in all fifty states and the District of Columbia. You will now be able to obtain a new passport and a new driver's license. With this method, of course, you have left a paper trail. There is a file in some file cabinet that contains the name you were born with.

Warning: Some name-changers have been known to bribe an employee to take their old file and accidentally "misfile" it inside another, thicker file—some old case that's long since been settled. Although that does solve the "paper trail" problem, do not do it. It is a criminal action. Some doing this have been caught. Further, it is not necessary. I have already outlined ways to use alternate names in a 100 percent legal way. Reread this chapter again.

What do you think about fake passports?

In 1992, I was offered a passport from the "Dominion of Melchizedek." I turned it down. (As you may remember, Melchizedek was the King of Salem, mentioned in Genesis. No country was ever named for him.) Less than a year later, I read about one of the promoters being arrested at Incline Village, on the Nevada side of Lake Tahoe. What surprised me wasn't that he was arrested—I expected that—but that before being caught he'd sold *thousands* of the fake Melchizedek passports at inflated prices. Another "country" currently being touted is Sealand.

Remember the murder of Gianni Versace? An article in the Billings, Montana, *Gazette* titled "Cunanan Shaved His Head, Grew a Beard," mentioned Miami Beach houseboat owner Torsten Franz Reineck. I quote from paragraph eight:

Reineck, 49, claims to be from an unrecognized nation called the *Principality of Sealand*, according to law enforcement authorities. The *Miami Herald* reported yesterday that Reineck claims to be a diplomat from Sealand, which issues its own passports. He drives a car bearing diplomatic plates from the make-believe principality, the paper said."

I never recommend false passports, not even from former nations such as British Honduras (now Belize). Nor fake license plates. All this does is draw attention to you, which you do not need.

How do private investigators track down celebrities to serve subpoenas?

First, they track down the name they were born with. Next, they discover the true date of birth. Once they have that combination, they investigate property purchases, marriages, family members, churches, charities, clubs, lawsuits, pets, memberships, schools, and vehicles.

The PIs who have a 100 percent success rate in doing this are the ones that have unlimited backing. Offer one of these specialists enough money, and they will track down any celebrity, anywhere on earth. They could also track *you* down, as I say in the beginning of this book, but unless you've made some mortal enemies who have the necessary funds and are willing to spend them, don't lose any sleep over the prospect.

What if someone like Sears demands my name before they will sell me a large item?

First, allow me to describe my own experience with Sears. A few years ago, my wife and I went to a Sears store to buy an upright vacuum. The first hint of incompetence came when I asked the salesperson if I could speak to someone who thoroughly understood the differences between the models. Puffing out a more than ample chest, she assured me that *she* was that person.

"OK, fine. How many motors does this Whispertone upright have?"

"Hey, *Anna!*" she yelled at a woman three aisles over. "How many motors in this red one?" Anna told her there were two, as I suspected. So much for this clerk's expertise. But "this red one" looked good, so I said I'd take it, and would she kindly take the cash and ring it up as we were in a hurry? Here is the conversation that followed:

"Name, address, and telephone number?" she said, chubby fingers poised over the computer keyboard at the cash register.

"We live in the Canary Islands and have no local address. Besides, this is cash, remember?"

"Doesn't matter, the computer won't accept the sale without a name, address, and telephone number."

"You mean to tell me you refuse to sell me a vacuum cleaner unless I identify myself?"

"That's right, I can't sell it without putting a name, address, and telephone number into the computer."

"Call your supervisor."

The supervisor appeared out of nowhere, got the picture at a glance, and whispered to the clerk, "Type in 'Sears' and pick any name whatever." So she typed in "Sears," chose the name "Donald Searson," and, as far as Sears is concerned, Donald bought a vacuum that day. I went back to the shipping department, handed in the slip, and three minutes later the vacuum came out on a hand truck.

"Donald Searson?" said the young man, looking around.

"Here!" I said. And that was how we got our vacuum cleaner.

Now, to answer your question: Don't make waves as I did. (For me, making a fuss is just a hobby, but my wife is still embarrassed when I say, "Call your supervisor.") Just memorize a fake name, address, and telephone number that you can rattle off with ease. Or go through an old file of business cards (you *do* save them, don't you?), pick a name and address you like, and carry the card. When asked for your name, address, and phone number, just have the clerk copy the information on the card.

10

TELEPHONES AND ANSWERING MACHINES

Question: *What do the police call an illegal wiretap?*
Answer: *A "confidential Informant."*

In 1977, California millionaire Gary Allen Bandy purchased land near the rural community of Gardiner on Washington State's Olympic Peninsula. He then proceeded to build a castle and other medieval buildings, bringing in artists to carve intricate Norwegian trolls on wooden posts. He was subsequently featured in the *National Enquirer* as an eccentric millionaire surrounded by his medieval buildings and trolls.

In 1991, a son was born to Gary and his wife, Eva. Later, they separated, and in 1995, divorce proceedings were begun. Eva hired attorney Natalie De Maar. Gary hired attorney Steven Fields. Bitter charges flew back and forth as Gary and Eva battled for custody of son Geoff, now four.

Eva Bandy rented a home in the upscale community of Gig Harbor, at the northern end of the Tacoma Narrows Bridge. The owner lived just across the street. His name was James Wilburn, and he was a private investigator. What followed next was the subject of an article in the *Peninsula Daily News*:

> Bandy's attorney, Steven Fields, was leaving a voice-mail message for Eva Bandy's attorney, Natalie De Maar. He was using the speakerphone. Sitting in his office were Bandy and another attorney. Fields thought he had disconnected the speakerphone and proceeded to have a conversation with Bandy.

What Fields failed to realize was that the speakerphone had not been disconnected. Therefore, when Bandy admitted that he had hired an investigator to put a wiretap on his wife's phone, his words were being recorded on attorney Natalie De Maar's answering-machine tape. For some reason never made clear, the tape eventually wound up in the hands of the FBI, who then raided Bandy's home at Gardiner Beach and his fifty-foot yacht at a nearby marina. A week later, Bandy was arrested while on a trip through Idaho.

What have we learned so far?

1. Some PIs will bug cars and residences if the pay is right.

2. Some lawyers cannot be trusted with confidential information.

3. When it comes to speakerphones and answering machines (to paraphrase Murphy's law), any mistake that can be made will be made, and at the worse possible moment.

We can learn more. Because he ordered an illegal wiretap, Gary Allen Bandy was sentenced to two months in prison and five years of probation. He was also fined $21,138. He will be subject to drug and alcohol testing, and, as a convicted felon, will be prohibited from possessing any firearms.

Attorney Steven Fields did not go to jail. There are no laws against stupidity.

The private investigator did not go to jail. The article did not say if he turned state's evidence, so I can only state a general truth: No matter how much you trust an attorney, a doctor, a CPA, or a private investigator, when a prosecutor starts talking jail time, these and other professionals will give you up in a heartbeat. (The G. Gordon Liddy types are a disappearing species.)

TELEPHONE SECURITY

"Telephone security" is an oxymoron, because a telephone conversation is never secure. It goes over land lines, may be beamed up and down from satellites, or travel via digital or analog radio waves, and it can be intercepted. There are other ways to communicate, and thousands of privacy seekers in Europe and North America have come to the same conclusion. So here is my very best advice to you, right from the start: *Get rid of your land-line telephones*. (By "land-line" I mean a telephone that is connected to your home by wires, as opposed to a cell phone which—since it uses radio waves—is not physically tied into a specific address.)

In the following chapters, cell phones, pagers, and two-way radios will be discussed. Nevertheless, I know that most of you will opt for one or more land-line telephones in your home, especially if you require a connection to the Internet. Although the information that follows is written primarily for when you move, rest assured that it is also possible—as will be shown—to make the necessary change at your current address.

UNLISTED NUMBERS

An unlisted number is no longer the protection it used to be. Many unlisted telephone numbers now appear on the Internet as well as on the ubiquitous CD-ROM directories, and these allow for reverse searches.

Example: Your wife gets the telephone in her maiden name, Harriet Helpless. It is unlisted and has call-blocking. Nevertheless, from time to time she calls toll-free numbers. *All* toll-free numbers have Automatic Number Identification (ANI), and these numbers are captured. Eventually this number will be in various databases available to private investigators. It may even show up on databases available to the general public.

To check on the latter, go to *www.freeality.com* and click on FIND PEOPLE. Then enter your name in each of the search engines listed for the White Pages. Similar information is also available at *www.switchboard.com* or *www.databaseamerica.com*.

The conclusion, then, about unlisted numbers, is that they are not secure. Always remember that if you give out a telephone number that is on a land line, a reverse search may reveal whatever name you used to obtain the service, plus the street address. Therefore, never give out such a number to those not entitled to have it.

HOW TO LIST YOUR NAME

Given that—despite having an unlisted telephone—the name you give the telephone company may show up on a national database, do your best to disguise it. Try one of the following:

- Wife's middle name and maiden name
- Your middle name or initial, and last name
- The name of a friend or relative (find someone with a very common name) who is willing to have the phone put in their middle/last or middle/maiden names

Another system that many have used successfully is to explain that you are a writer and that your telephone must be listed in your well-known *pen* name. (In this case, you may choose to have the name listed.) The usual procedure is that you will be instructed to go to one of the company's offices and prove your true identity, so they have that for their files. They will then allow you to list whatever name you've chosen. The trick here is to choose the most common name you can think of, with no middle initial, so that the name will be lost in a sea of similar names.

I am partial to first names like John, Robert, Mary, and Elizabeth, with surnames such as Johnson, Cohen, McDonald, Anderson, Rodriguez, and Brown. If moving to a new area, I'd first spend an hour or two with the local telephone directory—checking for the most common names in that area. Many will be identical, which is, of course, what you want.

HOW NOT TO ANSWER THE TELEPHONE

Let's say your names are Lawrence and Jennifer Barrington, but your telephone is in the name of Jennifer's middle name plus her maiden name, i.e., Suzanne Martin. Until the present moment, you or members of your family may have been answering the telephone with phrases such as:

"Larry Barrington here."

"Barrington residence."

"Hi, this is Jenny!"

However, what if the telephone company is calling? Remember, the name *they* have for this residence is Suzanne Martin. Or it could be a private detective on the line, or a process server with a subpoena in his pocket. Therefore, a simple "Hello" or "Good morning" will suffice. Let the *caller* be the one to mention a name, and, when necessary, answer with a question. For example:

Caller A: Good morning! How are you today, sir?

You: What are you selling? (When "How are you?" rather than your name follows "Hello," you know it's a salesperson.)

Caller B: Ms. Suzanne Martin?

You: What is this in reference to, please?

Caller B: This is Cora with the Crystal County Sheriff's Department.

Not to panic. Don't speak; *wait for more information.*

Caller B: We're sponsoring the Crystal County Crusade Against Crime, and for a small donation you can—

You: Suzanne won't be back from Italy for at least two months, but thank you for calling, good-bye.

Practice beforehand, and, in time, you'll stop getting sweaty hands and an accelerated heartbeat.

ANSWERING MACHINE MESSAGES

We've all heard instructions like "Please leave a message for Buddy, Betty, or Little Boseefus." Not cool. A simple "Please leave your name, number, and message at the sound of the beep" will do fine.

Some of our antisocial friends do not want messages left by anyone other than friends who know them. If we call Buddy and Betty, this is the message we get:

"Hello, we never answer this telephone in person. Please leave your first, middle, and last name, Social Security number, date of birth, street address, and telephone number. Sorry, but if you fail to leave complete information, your call will not be returned— *beeeeep!*"

If we call Nick and Amy, we get this message:

"Congratulations, you've just reached the Niccolo Machiavelli Misinformation Centre. Since we never answer in person, be sure to leave your name and number. After we've doctored the tape, your message will implicate you in an al-Qaida plot to poison

L.A.'s Stone Canyon Water Reservoir; the tape will then go to the FBI—*beeeeep!*"

Friends of these two couples know they can go ahead and leave a message anyway.

CHANGING YOUR LISTING

If you are not yet willing or able to move to a new location, you may still contact the telephone company to say you are moving away. (If asked, tell them you are moving to Mexico City or to London. Set a date for the service to be discontinued.)

A few days or weeks later, order a new telephone, which will, of course, have a different number. If you are using a nominee— an alternative person—have him or her make the call. This person will *not* admit to having had service before, nor will a Social Security number be given.

Since no credit history is available, the telephone company will ask for a cash deposit to ensure payment. Stop by their offices or mail in a money order for the requested amount—usually a few hundred dollars. Assuming you pay your bills on time, expect your deposit to be returned to you at the end of one year.

A GREAT IDEA THAT STILL NEEDS WORK

In the first edition of this book, I listed the names and addresses of two companies that sold call-filtering units manufactured in Taiwan. You could set these little boxes to any easy-to-remember four-digit code, such as 1492, 1776, 1812, 1914, etc. If someone tried to call you, the unit would intercept the call and reply in a recorded voice:

"Hello, this is a security feature. Please enter the code."

When your friends enter the correct numbers, the voice would say, "Thank you, now ringing," and the unit itself would ring, to announce the call. If a caller entered a wrong number, however, or no number at all, you would be unaware of it. Instead, the recorded voice would say "Security violation" and hang up.

Problem 1: Your telephones do not ring. The only ring comes from the unit itself, and it is not very loud. Therefore, if you are not in the same room as the unit, you may miss your call.

Problem 2: Some of my readers tried another model, but the unit cut down on both the quality and the sound of the caller's voice, so they, too, gave up on using it.

Problem 3: It appears that the various outlets in the United States that sold these units have since discontinued them, so you probably can't buy one even if you try.

Attention, entrepreneurs: Find someone to build these units up to standard. If it works flawlessly and lets the telephones themselves do the ringing, I'll recommend it in the next edition of this book.

CALL INTERCEPT

This is an automated service that is currently available in thirteen states. It works in conjunction with Caller ID and adds about five dollars a month to your bill. If someone who has Caller ID–blocking tries to call you, they will get a recorded message asking them to identify themselves. At this point, telemarketers usually hang up. If, however, the caller states his or her name, then your phone rings. You can listen to the name that was given, and, at that point, accept or reject the call.

A few of our friends have it, but others (including me) think it's more trouble than it's worth. For further information, and to find out if this service is available in your state, go to *www.verizon.com*, click on PRODUCTS AND SERVICES, then on CALLING FEATURES, and finally ON IDENTIFY YOUR CALLERS.

CORDLESS PHONES

A few years ago, ABC television show *Good Morning America* ran a feature about the extreme dangers inherent in the use of cheap cordless phones. Charles Gibson quoted authorities that say 65 percent of all Americans have a cordless phone in the house, and "90 percent of all conversations can be listened to." And many are!

One unhappy cordless owner, interviewed in shadow, said he was suing the manufacturer because the instruction booklet said his cordless phone was "secure." He was also suing the dealer because the salesman confirmed that conversations would be secure. Believing what he heard and read, he then used this phone to talk about intimate details of his life with his lawyer, his doctor, and others. When a friend finally told him that neighbors were scanning every conversation—and laughing!—he was so embarrassed that he sold his home and moved away.

If you still want cordless, purchase an upscale digital (not analog) spread-spectrum model that transmits in the range of 2.4 GHz or 5.8 GHz. Can these digital cordless phones be scanned? When I queried international scanner expert Keith Carcasole, he had this to say:

> The real question is, who wants to listen? The average scanning enthusiast won't be able to listen in on your spread-spectrum cordless phone conversations; however, this doesn't mean that your conversations are private. Digital security codes only operate between the base and the handset, and if, perchance, your telephone line is tapped, digital security in your cordless phone will be of no help. The signals from your cordless phone leave your home on the same lines as your regular, corded phones. If you are suspected of wrongdoing, NSA and other authorities could monitor your phone conversations. A private detective can pick up conversations you have with others in your

home by using a special laser device that detects windowpane vibrations caused by your voice.

THE TELEPHONE AT THE OTHER END

When you make a sensitive call, do you make sure the person at the other end is on a secure line? Earlier this year, I made a sensitive telephone call to a certain person who lives in a large trailer court on one of the islands in Puget Sound, Washington. As the conversation grew more serious, she said, "Just a minute, Jack, I'm going to switch to a more secure telephone on a second line." (*Oh-oh!*) When she came back on the line, I learned she had been on a cheap cordless phone that was several years old. And listen to this: She then told me she *knew* her calls were being monitored. She said there were some "militia types" in the trailer court, and that some of the neighbors had made comments about conversations she'd had on the portable phone! Obviously I should have asked her *at the very beginning*, "Are you on a portable telephone?"

A more serious problem arises when you call someone whose telephone—unknown to them—is tapped. In that case, no matter what preventive measures have been taken, your home number will be revealed. If, therefore, you are wary that the person you are calling may be under surveillance, go to the extra trouble to use a prepaid card.

PREPAID TELEPHONE CARDS

There have been a number of scam operations, selling prepaid cards that do not work, so make sure you purchase your prepaid cards only from a legitimate source. I buy mine at Costco—670 minutes for $19.95, cheaper than any of the long-distance carriers.

If there is no Costco in your area, just call a friend, who is a Costco member, anywhere in the country and have him buy you a card. He doesn't need to mail it to you; he can just call you and read off the access number and the PIN number. The cards are good for two years after you make your first call.

At one time, these were a great way to protect your privacy. Whether they still are or not depends on where you live and which area you call. A police detective friend uses the cards from Costco whenever he has to make a sensitive call from home. However, at least once a month he calls a friend who has Caller ID and lives in the same city.

"Bob here, what shows on your screen?"

"Unknown caller."

Thus assured, he continues to use his card for another month. In my own case, if I call anyone nearby, the same message shows up. When I call a friend in Ohio, however, the ID that comes up on his screen is "SBC Worthington," a local exchange in that area. This, of course, is still okay for privacy. Just remember that, when you first purchase a card, it's a good idea to check it out by calling a friend who has Caller ID.

Even if the Caller ID does show your number, however, it will still be useful when you are traveling, to avoid the ghastly fees many hotels and motels charge for calls from the room. If you consider yourself mildly paranoid, don't carry the card itself, because if the card is found, all numbers you called from that card can be obtained from the issuing company. Instead, copy the correct access number but alter the last two digits of the PIN number. (Use the same system for all future cards—always adding or subtracting the same easy-to-remember two-digit number.) You may wish to use separate cards for unrelated sensitive calls, so that if the calls on one card become known, there will be no crossover to the second party. Or, if you are *seriously* paranoid, make just one single call using a new card, and then destroy it!

PREPAID PHONE-CARD TRICK

Take care never to fall for an old phone-card trick used by PIs from coast to coast. If the private investigator has your mailing address but does not know where you actually live, he or she may mail you a "free phone card." And yes, it will indeed have free minutes—lots of free minutes.

Or the card may even come from your spouse. For example, if a wife goes to a private investigator to have her husband checked out on a business trip, the PI will give her a prepaid card and tell her to give it to her husband. If he uses that card on his trip, the PI will be able to come up with every number he called while away, and with those numbers he'll come up with names and addresses.

How does this work? Simplicity itself. A number of companies issue cards along with a Web address where—if you enter the PIN number—a list of all calls made with that card will show up. With these numbers, it's a simple matter for the investigator to come up with every name and address that the husband called. It's just one more step for the PI to then furnish the wife with a name and address for every number her husband called.

Telltale clue: All prepaid cards come with a PIN number that is covered, and the covering must first be scratched off. Before passing the cards on to the target, the PI very carefully removes this covering.

"But don't your targets get suspicious," I said to a friend in the business, "when the PIN number's right out there in plain sight?"

"Never happens. They just assume it came that way!"

So, readers, the next time someone gives you a prepaid phone card, check to make sure the PIN is still covered. If not, and if the card came from your spouse, your marriage may be in trouble.

CALLS TO 911

When you call 911, your true address shows up on the operator's monitor, along with whatever name your telephone is in. If it is listed in another name, will you be able to give a reason for this when the police arrive? (Even if the call was for an ambulance, the police usually arrive first.) To illustrate both the problem and the solution, consider the recent experience we had in a western state.

I was sitting at my computer, working on one of the chapters, when I happened to glance out the window. Here came Walter, one of my neighbors at that time, dragging his big black dog on a leash, racing up to my door. He started pounding on it before I could get there to open.

"A horse just fell on Julie," he exclaimed, pointing to the east pasture, "and she broke her leg! *Call 911!*"

At this particular home, I unfortunately did have a land line, used only to receive incoming faxes from a forwarded 800 number, but, of course, I can call out in an emergency, and Walter knew it. Thoughts raced through my aging brain:

If I call 911 on the land line, my call blocking will not work. The name the telephone is in (not mine) will show up, and my address as well (the home is not in my name, either). They will ask my name and where I live, compare it with the readout on the computer screen, and the conversation will be recorded and filed. While I stood at the door, hesitating, not more than two seconds, Walt spread his hands out and shouted, "JACK, CALL 911!"

I grabbed my cell phone out of its charging unit and called 911.

"This is 911," said a female voice, adding the name of the county.

"I'm calling from a cell phone and—"

"Yes. I know. What is the emergency?"

"A lady just had an accident with her horse and broke her leg."

"Where is the location?" (I described the general location of the pasture.)

"How old is this lady?"

"I don't know, maybe fifty or sixty."

"Where are you now?" (I named the road and said I would wait there to direct the emergency vehicle.)

"What is your name and where do you live?"

"One moment please, something has just—" and at this point I punched the power off on my cell phone.

I went to the street and was there to direct the emergency vehicle in on the proper lane. A neighbor was already on the scene with a blanket, so I evaporated before any of the crew could ask me if I was the one who called.

Some say that the 911 system may not be able to bring a cell phone name and number onto the screen, but I suspect that, since the events of the other 9-11, it often can. In this particular case, however, even if the number had come up, the screen would have shown only a fictitious name plus a mailing address in a far-away state.

In chapter 5, I discussed the case of a Miami police detective's wife who called 911 and thus revealed their true address. They then had to sell their home and move. But did she have any options? I think she did, and you would do well to review these alternatives with other members of your family.

1. If they had a cell phone (and they should have!), she could have used that to make the call to 911.

2. Had prior arrangements been set up, she could have called a friend who would, in turn, call 911 from *her* home, directing the ambulance to such-and-such an address where the detective's wife was *visiting*.

3. When checking in at the hospital, she could have given their ghost address, adding that she was just house-sitting for a friend when the emergency came up.

WATCH OUT FOR THIS SNEAKY TRICK

Suppose a private investigator wants to hear you talking to your lawyer (or mistress, or whomever). He may place a conference call, recording every word. Here is how it works. The first call would go to you, and, when you answer, the PI punches HOLD and then speed-dials your lawyer. You start saying "Hello? Hello?" Then your lawyer comes on the line. He recognizes your voice. Each of you might then *assume* the other person placed the call, and start to chat!

Remedy: When a call comes in from a sensitive party, and there is some confusion about who called whom, *ask.* If neither called the other, you have just had a heads up that someone is after one or both of you.

QUESTIONS & ANSWERS

Is it okay to recharge my Costco card with a credit card?

No! Listen to one reader's experience: "When I went to recharge one of my cards (big mistake!), I learned that the company keeps records on every call made through the calling card. Some of these calls were made two and three years ago. They also keep records of which credit cards you use to recharge the cards in the past."

Is there any quick-and-easy way to get a residential telephone in a totally different name?

I haven't tried this, but one of my readers, Alan G———, uses Reconex. (For details, go to *www.reconex.com*.) This is normally good only for *local* calls. Alan says, however, "Prepaid phone cards work well with this service [for long distance] and, after three months, MCI calls you up and offers a complete local, long distance, and international calling service for $49 per month. They register the phone in the name used at Reconex."

In the case of a life-or-death situation where neither privacy nor legality matter, what is the fastest way to get help?

Call either the fire department or 911 and report a fire in progress! Captain Robert L. Snow, in his book *Protecting Your Life, Home and Property*, says that if you live in a high-crime area and call 911 on a hot summer weekend and/or a busy day, there may be a delay in getting a policeman to your home. He says there have been cases where police dispatchers have listened as a caller was murdered before the police arrived.

Under these circumstances, some persons have called the fire department and reported a fire. "This should be done only in desperate situations," says Snow, "since there will likely be some legal consequences later, because of calling in a false fire alarm. . . . But if you have absolutely no doubt there is an intruder who knows you're in the home and is trying to get in anyway, there's a very good chance you will be raped, beaten, and/or murdered. At a time like this, you can't really worry about legal niceties. There's not much point in being completely law-abiding if you're dead."

How safe are public telephones?

Even before the events of 9-11, some public telephones, especially at the larger airports and bus terminals, were tapped. Now, many more of them are. Nevertheless, there shouldn't be any problem using one in your own neighborhood, assuming it's not in an area known for prostitution or drug dealing. Pay with coins or use a prepaid calling card. But be careful *whom* you call—the telephone *at the other end* may be tapped.

Sometimes I hear clicking noises on my telephone. I brought in a detective to check for bugs, and he said there weren't any, but what if he was wrong? How can I be sure my telephone isn't tapped?

If the government is after you, they will do the tap at a central office, and no detective will ever track that one down. In fact, a little test might be to have detective A install the best tap he knows, and then see if detective B can find it. (Let me know if you do that; I've got $20 that says detective B will miss it.) Here is the best advice you'll ever get about telephone security: Have a little label stuck on every telephone, which says, THIS LINE IS TAPPED.

Can you recommend a hacker-proof answering machine?

There is no such thing. If I were an electronics engineer, that would be my first project, to invent a secure answering machine. One PI I know, with six agents, says this is Numero Uno on his wish list—a number where his agents could call in to leave and pick up messages in absolute secrecy.

The truth—sad to say—is that a number of companies sell answering-machine code-breakers that can break into a machine in about ninety seconds. Also, government agents have some interesting equipment, as outlined in *Manhunter*, a book by U.S. Marshal John Pascucci. He was in England, trying to get Scotland Yard to put a tap on a certain producer's phone. They refused.

"After we struck out on the phone tap," says Pascucci, "I called the producer's house to see if he had an answering machine. He did. So I had my computer guys make me a list of all possible three-digit access codes. Finally we hit the right number and started monitoring his messages."

How can I turn off the "redial" feature on my telephone?

You mean, so no one can check your telephone in your absence, to see whom you last called? Although this feature cannot be turned off, it can be easily defeated. When you finish your call, hang up. Then pick up the receiver, listen for the dial tone, and punch in a single digit. Then hang up. If anyone checks the "last number called," all they will find is that single digit.

Can international telephone calls be monitored without a warrant?

Of course, if they are beamed by microwave transmission. The National Security Agency (NSA) does this all the time. No warrant is needed to monitor microwave transmissions.

If I have Caller ID, will it always show the true number of an incoming call?

Not if the call is from a government agency. Even back in 1999, Mickey Hawkins, head of the FBI office in Tulsa, Oklahoma, in an interview for an article in the *Los Angeles Times*, said: "We use a device that gives a different number."

Since then, at least a few of the high-tech PIs learned this trick as well.

What is a "trap line?"

A "trap line" is a toll-free number used by private investigators to identify the location you are calling from. As soon as the target makes a call, the company providing this service contacts the PI to report the number and location of the incoming call. Remember, since the trap-line number starts with a toll-free area code (800, 888, 877, 866, or 855), you cannot block the transmission of information.

If you are the target, and the PI has only your ghost address, he may send you a convincing postcard or letter, asking you to either call him or send a fax. If you call or fax from home, he's got you.

Or perhaps he does not have an address for you but he does have a telephone number for a friend or relative. He will call them while they are away at work, hoping for an answering machine. If there is one, he will leave a message—have so-and-so call me before tomorrow midnight! "Urgent, there is a deadline, can't wait!"

On the other hand, in the case of a dispute between husband and wife, the wife may go to a PI to find out if hubby really is "working late," or "on a business trip." In this case, the PI knows his address and home telephone number, but he wants to know where the husband is at the times he is absent. Assume the husband carries a pager with voice mail. The wife gives this number to the PI and suggests he leave an urgent message. During the next suspicious absence, the PI calls the pager number and leaves an "extremely urgent" request to call him at the number he then leaves. Perhaps the husband was supposed to be on a trip to Sacramento, but the call comes in from the Kit-Kat Ranch in Nevada's Storey County . . .

CELL PHONES
AND PAGERS

The young man knows the rules, but the old man knows the exceptions.

—ANONYMOUS

For some years I've used one of the mainstream cell-phone providers. I gave them a bank cashier's check for a $1,000 security deposit (in lieu of a Social Security number) and my middle and last name, and they handed me a new phone on the spot. A year later, my deposit was returned to me.

This cell phone cannot be traced to my home address, since the bills go to a remote address and are paid from there. It is never turned on except when I do so to call out. Therefore it is almost impossible to locate the phone, should anyone try to do so. (When a cell phone is left on, it sends out a continuous signal identifying the nearest cell tower.) The service includes voice mail, which I check twice a day.

One of the better ways to obtain your cell phone is to find a nominee—someone who is willing to furnish his Social Security number. Pay him $100 (or whatever it takes) to get a telephone in his name. Furnish your ghost address for the monthly bills. (Make sure that mail can be received there in his name, along with whatever other names you are using at that location.)

Prepaid cell phones. Although the per-minute cost is high, if you carry a cell phone only for the occasional emergency, a prepaid cell phone may be your best choice. You choose how many minutes you want and how much money you want to spend. Advantages:

- No deposit
- No contract
- No credit check
- No minimum monthly fee
- No identification required
- *No request for a Social Security number*

Some are even disposable. You'll find them at stores such as Wal-Mart, RadioShack, and JC Penney, as well as at many places on the Internet. I suggest you first go to Amazon.com, click on ELECTRONICS, search for "prepaid cell," and study the reader comments for each phone on the list.

Note: In Switzerland, picture identification is now required before one may purchase a prepaid phone. Will this ridiculous requirement someday come to the Land of the Free? Only time will tell.

SCANNING A CELL PHONE

In an article discussing so-called privacy protection for the next-generation digital cellular telephones, the *Los Angeles Times* had this to say:

"Bruce Schneier, a well-known expert on code breaking, and other researchers have found a way to easily monitor any numbers dialed on a digital telephone, such as credit card numbers or passwords. In addition, they say, voice conversations can easily be deciphered. The findings could be a setback for the telecommunications industry, which has touted the security features of the new digital cellular and PCS systems."

Many cell phone users dismiss Schneier's warning, however, with the comment, "U.S. law *prohibits* the sale or import of scanners that cover the cell-phone frequencies." True enough, but there is no such law in Canada. The result is that PIs and others are constantly bringing these unblocked scanners across the border, and thus the danger remains. And, by the way, if you yourself are thinking of obtaining an unblocked scanner, please note:

Many scanners sold in Canada *are* blocked, because they were manufactured in the United States. I recently spoke with the manager of a RadioShack store in Surrey, British Columbia. He said the scanners in his store all came in from RadioShack in the States and were, therefore, blocked, even though Canadian law does not prohibit him from carrying unblocked Unidens if he wishes to do so. One store that does sell unblocked scanners is Durham Radio Sales and Service Inc., 350 Wentworth Street East Unit #7, Oshawa, Ontario, Canada (*www.durhamradio.com*). When preparing this chapter, I called owner, Keith Carcasole, to ask if he would ship unblocked scanners to U.S. addresses, but he said absolutely not, citing U.S. law.

This does not mean that the bad guys are out there night and day, searching for your cell-phone conversations. It does mean, however, that you should think twice before having any sensitive conversations, and, in any event, you should never identify yourself by your full name.

TRACING AND IDENTIFYING A CELL PHONE

Even years ago, cell phones could be traced to your general location (as O. J. Simpson found out when he was in the white Bronco), but the number of the cell phone would remain unknown. By the time you read this, not only will your location be identified, but—if you make a 911 call—your cell-phone number will show up on the screen as well. (Although the FCC deadline for providing the number to 911 centers is December 1, 2005, many already have this service in place.)

Nevertheless, I still prefer a cellular phone to a land line, for the very real reason that it is not tied to a physical street address. Remember, too, that as long as your cell phone is not turned on, you remain invisible. Read with care this following section:

USE A PAGER WITH YOUR CELL PHONE

Although clerks in electronics stores may tell you, "People don't use pagers anymore," pay no attention to them. I am a great fan of those small, cheap pagers that cost less than ten dollars a month. A big plus is that—unlike cell phones—*they cannot be tracked*. A cell phone, which both receives and transmits, is tied to a single tower. As you move down the highway with the cell phone on (even though not in use), it transfers your number from tower to tower. With pagers, although they, too, use towers, there is a vital difference: Each tower broadcasts *all* the messages, and there is no clue as to which tower is used when your pager rings. For example, suppose a friend is trying to locate you at a huge airport. A message goes out on all the loudspeakers: "Miss Loretta Lindstrom, please meet your party at gate 10 on the B concourse." Unless you decide to show up (only to discover a stalker, a PI, or the police), no one can possibly know you were even in the airport, much less in which part. The small, cheap pagers offer you this same protection.

The best way to use your pager is in conjunction with a cell phone *that is not turned on*. If you receive a message that appears urgent, either turn your cell phone on just long enough to reply, or go to a pay phone. Here is a simple code used by one of my readers. He carries a pager clipped to his belt and keeps his cell phone in his car. The pager is always on (since it cannot be traced), whereas his cell phone is always off unless in use.

The first digit is always 1, 2, or 3:

1. Call me in the next day or two.

2. Call back as soon as convenient.

3. Emergency!

The second digit is between 1 and 8:

1. Call wife at home.

2. Call wife on cell phone.

3. Call wife at work.

4. Call secretary.

5. Call parents.

6. Call friends Larry and Carol.

7. Package received at ghost address.

8. Check the pager's voice mail.

The last option requires two calls to the pager, of course. The first call is to leave a recorded message. The second call is to advise that the message is there to be retrieved. Look how simple it is to translate these two-digit codes:

22. Call wife on cell phone as soon as convenient.

15. Call parents, perhaps this evening.

18. Someone who has your page number has left an urgent voice-mail message. (Procedure: Dial the pager number, press 0, and then press the four-digit password number.)

How often have you been asked for your telephone number and have been reluctant to give it out? (One such example is when you're arranging a blind date!) From now on, *give out your pager number*. Take the time to record a greeting in your own words, such as: "This is Hillary. Please leave a message." (You will, of course, check for messages from time to time.)

AN UNUSUAL TOLL-FREE NUMBER

If you'd like to give out "your" toll-free telephone number with no fear that (1) it can be traced back to you, or (2) that you will ever have to actually answer it, use 1-800-720-9109.

This little tip comes from a supersecret conference for private investigators. *The line is always busy!*

QUESTIONS & ANSWERS

When I leave my car at the dealer's for servicing, shouldn't I give them my cell phone number and then leave it on, so I'll know when my car is ready?

If you carry a small pager, just give them that number and tell them to enter some simple number several times (such as 1111 or 7777) after the beep. This works equally well when you're waiting to pick up eyeglasses at the mall, at the golf course when your tee time is ready, or when your wife is ready to be picked up after the baby shower.

Are there any dangers with cell phones that have extra features?

If you refer to instant messaging, "always on," and "wake on ring," then yes, indeed. The carrier will be able to locate you even when your phone is powered off. Your only protection with such a phone is to remove the battery when you do not want to be tracked.

Why don't you recommend two-way pagers, such as the RIM Blackberry?

First and foremost, as long as the pager is on, you can be tracked. Second, you must pay heavy monthly fees for this service, sometimes as much as a cell phone. Third, coverage is lacking in many of the smaller cities in the "fly-over" states.

Do you still recommend satellite telephones, if money is no object?

You'll see these advertised in *Power & Motoryacht* and other yachting magazines. They were developed for oceangoing ships, but some airlines use them now for passengers, and you and I can use them anywhere, even in an isolated mountain valley or while crossing the Sahara. At one time, it appeared that communications via satellite were reasonably safe. However, as we later learned, Osama bin Laden—who used one in Afghanistan—had his calls monitored on a regular basis. So no, I no longer recommend them unless you have an oceangoing yacht or plan a trek to the South Pole.

Can my cellular phone's location be pinpointed when I'm in a moving car?

Even when you are *not* moving, it takes several minutes to plot your cellular phone's location. When you are moving, it will take double that time. In other words, if your call is made from the ten-mile marker, you may be at milepost seventeen before the ten-mile location comes up on the screen.

Prepaid cellular phones are 100 percent safe, right?

Safety is relative, and nothing is 100 percent safe. Suppose, after you've used your cell a few times, it ends up in the hands of a government agent who is trying to find your home address so he can order a warrant for a surreptitious "sneak and peek" search. He will pull a record of the calls from that phone. *Did you even once call home?*

What number should be used for medical contact informa-tion and/or work phone trees, where numbers are needed in a crisis?

A pager is ideal, assuming it is always on.

What do you mean by "sneak and peek?"

Since 1997, law enforcement officers have been obtaining sneak-and-peek warrants, which are issued "when there is a legit-imate need for the government to covertly uncover information that could not be obtained through other, more traditional means of investigation." They are just as the name implies. Offi-cers will enter surreptitiously and search for evidence that could later be the basis for a normal search warrant. The victim will almost never know an entry has been made. The number of these warrants issued has skyrocketed since the passing of the Patriot Act.

12

HANDHELD TWO-WAY RADIOS

Panic comes suddenly like thunder from a blue sky. No shrewdness can foresee it and no talent avert it.

—MATTHEW SMITH

On Sunday afternoon, September 24, 2000, eleven-year-old Mikayala Whitley was playing with her small yellow Family Radio Service (FRS) radio in the yard outside her home in Marysville, a small town in northern Washington State. When she suddenly heard a man's voice calling for help, she ran into the house to tell her parents. The caller was Michael Wyant, who had suffered a serious fall while hiking alone along a mountain trail, and was desperately seeking help. His radio, except for the color, was identical to Mikayala's. Although these small "walkie-talkies" normally have a maximum range of two miles, Wyant was calling from the Cascade Mountains, dimly visible from the Whitleys' front porch, *one hundred miles to the east.*

Mikayala's parents called the Chelan County Sheriff's Department. A rescue party set out for the mountains with the Whitleys acting as a communications relay between the hiker and rescuers. Within hours, the forty-nine-year-old hiker was picked up by a helicopter and taken to the Central Washington Hospital in Wenatchee.

What do you think Michael Wyant thought his little radio was worth?

ADD RADIOS TO YOUR ARSENAL

Unless otherwise identified, when I talk about radios in this section, I refer to transceivers, aka handheld two-way radios, aka walkie-talkies—a term dating back to World War II. In addition to the normal complement of AM/FM radios in our home, we have a baker's dozen of other units equipped to pluck RF (radio frequency) beams from the air:

1. An old Uniden Bearcat scanner that picks up frequencies that are blocked in the newer ones.

2. Two Standard VHF marine transceivers, for use on the water.

3. A TruTalk TK-514 weather receiver/FRS radio (for emergency alerts).

4. A Grundig Satellit 900 AM/FM/SW radio (continuous frequency coverage between 100 KHz and 30 MHz plus FM) with an exterior antenna.

5. Three cellular telephones and three pagers that work as pairs. One set is in my pickup, another in my wife's Mazda, and the third in a secret or "panic" room.

6. Two GMRS (General Mobile Radio Service) Motorola TalkAbouts, set to operate on the same frequencies.

You'll quickly note two obvious omissions in the above list. No ham radio. No satellite telephone. Nevertheless, assume for the moment a statewide emergency—an 8.4 earthquake, a terrorist attack, or whatever. I'm at home, working, and my wife is out shopping somewhere. Our telephone lines go dead. The cell phone towers—if any remain—are so jammed with calls that they become useless. The TVs are dead and I get nothing but static from the little AM/FM radio in the kitchen.

Is *anything* still working?

Well, the scanner may pick something up, and the marine radios should pick up any transmissions from the nearby ships in the harbor. Also, there'll be news on the battery-powered Grundig's shortwave bands. Before all else, however, I call my wife on her GMRS radio. And when I hear her voice and she tells me where she is . . . what do you suppose I'll think our little radios are worth?

MULTIPLE USES

Family outings You'll find radios will often be better than cell phones for coordinating a group of friends and family, because, with multiple radios, your whole group can listen in. (Also, how many families can afford to furnish a separate cell phone for each of the children?) Remember, with radios there are no charges for airtime and no need to dial up and wait for a connection every time.

Caravans Another obvious use is when you are traveling with two or more vehicles and want to keep everyone informed. You can stay in touch within a half mile or so while using radios inside the vehicles, and unlike using cell phones, *you can almost never be traced or monitored from a distant location.*

Shopping A common use for these radios is to keep in touch while shopping separately at the mall. Also, if an elderly relative or a handicapped person must wait in the car, why not share your experiences with them as you shop? One woman leaves a radio on in the car when she leaves the dog in there for any length of time, and calls every so often so he won't get lonely!

Single parents A set of radios may be the ideal way for a single parent to stay in touch with his or her kids at home. One of my readers, Dorothy B———, is a big fan of two-way radios. She writes, ". . . I even loan them out to neighbor kids. Radios are much cheaper in the long run than cell phones . . . and once a prepaid cell phone is broken, that's all she wrote. (And kids do break radios and phones. . . . that's why I keep so many.)"

Events They come in very handy when with a group at a ski resort or at an amusement park, and can be used to keep things under control at a big event. If the event is a wedding, the airwaves will crackle: *Where are the flowers? Call the caterers! Anyone heard from the groom?*

FRS VERSUS GMRS RADIOS

Both types of radios are readily available both on the Internet and in major chain stores such as Costco, Target, Office Club, OfficeMax, and Wal-Mart. The cheapest ones are the FRS radios, with prices as low as $35 a pair, online.

FRS stands for "Family Radio Service." FRS radios use up to fourteen channels in the UHF band (462–467 MHz). Although no license is required, there are two drawbacks to these radios. First, they broadcast at just half a watt, so the range is often less than a mile outdoors, and much less when inside a building. Second, there are so many of them, and so few channels, that you may have a hard time finding a channel you can use yourself

The General Mobile Radio Service is another personal radio band in the ultrahigh frequency spectrum, located with some other radio services in the range from 460–470 MHz. GMRS radios cost more but are superior in that they have up to twenty-three channels and are more powerful. At the allowed maximum of two watts, they can transmit up to five miles under ideal conditions. (There is an overlap in the GMRS/FRS frequency range so GMRS radios can communicate with FRS radios.)

DO EITHER OF THESE RADIOS REQUIRE A LICENSE?

FRS radios do not require a license. According to the law, however (of which more will be said in a moment), GMRS radios do. The FCC requires you to fill out several forms, pay $75 for a five-year license, and identify yourself by your callsign every time you make a call.

When I bought our current GMRS radios ($99 at Costco for a pair of Motorola TX6400WX TalkAbouts)—law-abiding fellow that I usually am—I decided to go ahead and get a license. To avoid giving personal information, I planned to register them as a foreign business, i.e., one of my LLCs with an address in Spain. An hour later, after fruitless efforts trying to do this online, I called it quits. (In any event, I had no plans to identify myself every time I made a call.) I later picked up the following on the Internet:

"Our staff spent several frustrating hours reading through the FCC Web site, trying to download the proper forms, and calling their telephone help line to try to figure out the maze of paperwork required to obtain the necessary license. To quote one staff member, 'it was as bad as doing my taxes!' "

So then, should *you* bother with a license? In the first chapter of this book, I said that I would warn you ahead of time if any of my suggestions might be illegal. Consider yourself warned . . . and read on. I just made a tour of four stores selling both kinds of these two-way radios, and asked the same question at each: Do I need a license to operate a GMRS radio?

Office Depot: I don't know, but I don't think so.

Wal-Mart: Doesn't it say on the package? [Not on the *outside.*]

RadioShack: I don't think anybody bothers with that.

OfficeMax: No, *no radio in this store* needs a license.

I then checked with some of my readers and also ran a search on the Internet. The following three comments are typical of many:

1. "Both FRS and GMRS radios are usually right next to each other on the store shelf or in a catalog, and not many sellers tell their customers about the difference. In some cases, manufacturers pack that information *inside* the package, giving a surprise to the buyers when they get home and open the box. At that point, they will usually just shrug their shoulders and then forget about it."

2. "My experience with two-way radios is extensive. . . . In several years of constant use, I've never had a problem . . . My impression is that the FCC does no surveillance, and only does enforcement if there is a complaint, but most likely not even then."

3. "I've used these little radios for a long time. . . . It is unlikely that anyone would get caught without a license unless they are high-profile and do something stupid. If they use the radio to talk to people they know . . . then it is unlikely that anyone will know they are using it illegally. . . . As an example of how difficult it is to catch [the violators], there are taxi companies in NYC that use amateur radio and do not have licenses (nor could they use those bands for commercial purposes anyway), and the enforcement office at the FCC is powerless to stop them."

CONCLUSION

To be 100 percent legal, either use FRS radios or get a license (if you can figure out how to do it) for the superior GMRS radios. If you choose to use them without a license, you are on your own. My personal opinion, however, is that if you use them sparingly for personal use only, chances are slim that you will ever be called to account.

By the way, never count on a miracle like that between Michael Wyant and Mikayla Whitley, who communicated with off-the-shelf TalkAbouts although they were a hundred miles apart. Writer Rick Dreher, an authority on backcountry communications devices, attributed it to "absolute dumb luck." Another authority suggested it might be due to "bounce," a term that refers to the signal hitting a surface, such as water or snow, and being sent a greater distance than what was expected.

Mikayla, however, when accepting a "Little Hero Award" from REACT—a nonprofit volunteer emergency communications organization—had another explanation:

"I think God really helped a lot."

QUESTIONS & ANSWERS

How do GMRS radios compare to CB radios?

Since CB radios are on different frequencies (around 26–27 MHz), the radio waves propagate differently—someone might be listening to your conversation in another state. Worse, the things you hear on a CB radio are frequently bizarre, weird, silly, nonsensical, and obscene. Personally, I wouldn't have one. However, to be fair, I'll quote a friend who swears by them: "Nothing has or will in the foreseeable future replace CB radio for traffic reports. Truckers across North America depend on their radios every day for up-to-the-second traffic reports and alternate routes. If you need good traffic reports and require decent local information, CB—despite all its shortcomings—is still viable."

Is there any way to extend the range of a GMRS radio?

Yes, if you are willing to pay the price (and obtain a license) for a GMRS repeater. The repeater will easily extend your range to as much as fifty miles. The details are beyond the scope of this chapter, but you'll find abundant information on the Internet.

Are children using radios at risk from predators?

True, a few child molesters have been known to drive around neighborhoods while monitoring the FRS and GMRS radio frequencies. However, the likelihood of your child coming in contact with a child molester is remote. Simply teach your children how to be careful on the radio. Warn them never to talk to strangers, never to call out randomly in hopes to find someone to talk to, and never to give out information that could lead to harm. This includes names, street and e-mail addresses, telephone numbers, the name of the school, times when the parents are not home, and where the spare key is hidden. Make sure the children understand that they have no exclusive rights to any channel, and that they are probably being heard up to two miles away.

Can we use our radios when we travel overseas?

No, because other countries use similar frequencies for emergencies and other noncivilian uses. If they catch you broadcasting on an illegal frequency, the penalties can be severe. (Exception: Although GMRS radios have never been type-accepted for use in Canada, FRS radios *are* allowed.)

Where can I learn more about shortwave radios?

For general information, try The Shortwave Store. Their home page is *http://usa.shortwavestore.com*. In the right column, around halfway down the page, you will find an ARTICLES section. Click on the link titled INTRODUCTION TO SHORTWAVE SERIES to access a series of articles by shortwave expert Ken Alexander. Another

article in this section outlines how to choose a shortwave radio. If
you still have questions, e-mail Keith Carcasole at *questions@usa.
shortwavestore.com*. If Keith doesn't know the answer, he'll find
out for you.

If money is no object, which handheld two-way radios are the most secure?

Computer guru Michael Spaulding recommends the XST
3500 from Motorola if you're seeking the best security features.

"However," he adds, "the iCom F30 and F40 both have digital
scrambling capabilities and I would recommend them as well."
For details and prices, go to *www.discounttwo-wayradio.com/
brochures/f30f40.pdf*.

Is there any danger in using a wireless video camera?

If you have one of these so-called "nanny cams" in your home
(such as the popular Xcam2), be aware that these cameras can
transmit an unscrambled analog radio signal for a distance of several blocks. These signals can be picked up by the receivers that
are sold with the cameras. In theory, the signal should be scram-
bled, but, to keep the price down, none are.

13

HOW TO FIND AND
USE NOMINEES

"Of that which nothing is known, nothing can be said."
—LUDWIG WITTGENSTEIN,
TRACTATUS LOGICO-PHILOSOPHICUS

As you know, an attorney filing a lawsuit may name anyone he pleases. If he is suing a corporation, he may also name the directors, the officers, and even the part-time secretary who writes the checks.

No matter how innocent you are, if you are *named*, you have to defend yourself, and that costs time, money, and extreme aggravation.

So then, if you wish to remain invisible, your name must not surface anywhere. Is that difficult? Yes! But is it impossible? No, but you cannot do this without the help of a proxy, or *nominee*. (Although the word *nominee* usually refers to a person nominated for a political office, in this book I use it in its secondary meaning: someone who takes your place as the apparent owner or manager of a company you own, or who opens a bank account for you, or obtains your cellular telephone, or signs up for your utilities.)

Who might be an ideal candidate? You may already have someone in mind, but, if not, here are a few suggestions:

- A homeless person who has not filed a tax return since Truman beat Dewey
- That illegal Guatemalan whom a friend uses to take care of
  the kids
- The town drunk, who sobers up just long enough to sign
  some "papers" in return for a case of Thunderbird
- A relative or close friend who will do this as a favor
- Someone who owes you money, is not in a position to pay
  you back, and would act as nominee in exchange for clear-
  ing the loan

On the other hand, here is whom *not* to use:

- Do not use a lover or a mistress—when the affair goes sour,
  he or she will see you drawn and quartered!
- Do not use an unwilling candidate. Example: "Look, Bill,
  either I name you as a member and you give me a notarized power of attorney, or I'll tell your parents about the
  time the police nailed you in that porno palace." This is
  blackmail.

Whatever the case, you should choose someone who has no assets,
otherwise known as "judgment-proof." Then, when a lawyer discovers there are no assets to recover, no lawsuit will be filed.

Age: From time to time, I do use a young person, especially if
from Spain or Mexico. However, all else being equal, older is better, and *really* old is best. There are several problems involved in
using young persons.

For one thing, although broke now, they may get their ducks
in a row and start making money. Or they might inherit money
when their parents or grandparents die. Or they might be injured
in an accident and receive tens of thousands of dollars in com-
pensation. At that point, they would *not* be judgment-proof.

PROTECT YOURSELF WITH A WRITTEN AGREEMENT

The sample form below, although not drawn up by an attorney—again, I'm not a lawyer, and this book doesn't provide legal advice—is nevertheless clear and understandable. The various clauses are merely an example. They can be changed to suit your purposes. I do strongly suggest you have your nominee sign it before a notary public. Keep the original in a safe place.

LIMITED POWER OF ATTORNEY

BE IT KNOWN that I, [name of nominee], the undersigned, do hereby grant a limited power of attorney to [you, the reader], as my attorney. My attorney shall have full power and authority to undertake and perform the following on my behalf:

1. Make deposits and write checks on my account at [name of bank].

2. Form, amend, and cancel limited liability companies in any state.

3. Send and receive letters, instructions, and e-mails in my name.

4. Write letters, make requests, and order and receive merchandise in my name.

5. Accept payments on my behalf and sell and deliver reports on [subject of reports].

6. Engage in any other legitimate business on my behalf—including but not limited to the World Wide Web—and receive payments in my name.

7. Use funds sent to me for any purpose whatsoever.

My attorney agrees to accept this appointment subject to its terms, and agrees to act and perform in the said fiduciary capacity consistent with my best interests as he in his sole discretion deems advisable.

This power of attorney may be revoked by me at any time, provided that any person relying on this power of attorney shall have full rights to accept the authority of my attorney until in receipt of actual notice of revocation.

Signed this_____day of _____, 200_____.

_____

Signature of nominee, with name printed below.

Subscribed and sworn before me on [date] by [nominee], to me known to be the person described in and who executed the foregoing instrument and acknowledged that he executed the same as his free act and deed.

[Notary's signature and stamp.]

QUESTIONS & ANSWERS

Is locating a nominee to act of my behalf something I should consider, even if I am not in business?

Yes, of course, a nominee can help you make a smooth transition to privacy. Imagine, for example, that you decide to move to another location, even if close by. You ask your aunt Bertha from Presque Isle, Maine, to travel to your area and help out. Here is what she can do:

- Sign the new lease
- Get all utilities in her name
- Order a normal telephone, a cell phone, and/or a pager
- Purchase your vehicles, insure them, and name you as principal driver
- Get a new address that is to serve for both you and her (it will actually be yours only)

Where required, a deposit will be paid in lieu of giving out a Social Security number. Have her open a new account and turn the account over to you. From this point forward, you will send all deposits by mail.

If you die before she does, she will own the account. But that's fair, is it not? However, if you are worried about *her* untimely death, then using her as the sole member of a limited liability company may solve any complications that otherwise might arise in such a case, as she could leave the membership to you in her will.

14

BANK ACCOUNTS AND MONEY TRANSFERS

If you can't convince them, confuse them.

—HARRY S. TRUMAN

Did you know that financial institutions are required by the federal government to spy on their customers? The Bank Secrecy Act, which has been around for a long time, authorizes the Treasury Department to require any financial institution to report any "suspicious transaction relevant to a possible violation of law or regulation." These reports, called "Suspicious Activity Reports," are filed with the Treasury Department's Financial Crimes Enforcement Network (FinCEN). *This is done secretly, without your knowledge or consent*, any time a financial institution decides that you have done anything "suspicious."

For example, each deposit, withdrawal, exchange of currency, or other payment transfer that involves a "transaction in currency" (a physical transfer of currency from one person to another) of more than $10,000 will be reported. Reportable currency transactions include:

- Checks or drafts cashed for over $10,000
- Cash deposits over $10,000
- Cashier's checks purchased with cash over $10,000
- New account opened with more than $10,000 in cash
- Exchange of currency—small to large or vice versa; foreign to U.S. or vice versa
- Multiple cash transactions totaling more than $10,000 made in one day by or for the person, if the bank is aware of them.

Does it appear, from the above, that you could safely purchase a $9,000 bank cashier's check with cash and still avoid a Suspicious Activity Report? No, because the BSA also requires all banks to log purchases of *any* monetary instrument involving currency in amounts from $3,000 to $10,000, inclusive. (If you happen to own a sports arena, racetrack, amusement park, restaurant, hotel, licensed check-cashing service, vending-machine company, or theater, you may be exempted.)

What about foreign transactions, for an individual?

Again, a report will be made if $10,000 or more is involved, whether or not it involves cash, traveler's checks, money orders, investment securities, or negotiable instruments in bearer form.

YOUR PERSONAL BANK ACCOUNT

Any bank account you have in your own name (in whatever state), tied in with your Social Security number, can be tracked down by agencies specializing in asset searches for lawyers. This includes Certificates of Deposit as well as IRA accounts.

Robert O'Harrow Jr., writes in the *Washington Post* that ". . . lawyers, debt collectors and private investigators buy the data to help in civil lawsuits, divorces, and other financial matters. Prices range from just over $100 to several thousand dollars for a look at banks nationwide and a report that includes infor-

mation about stocks, mutual funds, and safe-deposit boxes."
O'Harrow relates the account of a security official at BankBoston
". . . who noticed an ad for one of the services and anonymously
ordered a search on himself. When the report came back, the
official, Frederick Tilley, said he learned new details about his
own accounts. 'They came back with the account information,
down to the penny,' said Tilley. 'There are lots of them and it's
freely advertised.' "

Copies of the individual checks themselves may also be
obtained, since all checks are microfilmed front and back. This
reveals not only payees and endorsers but also memos (if any)
and signatures.

If you are the subject of the search, what will the computers
reveal? Do you wish to be identified as one with "deep pockets,"
or would you prefer to be considered "judgment-proof," i.e., with
not enough assets worth suing you for?

Or suppose, with no forewarning, you find yourself under
investigation by someone who wishes to cause you harm. This
could be anyone from an ex-employee to a disgruntled present
or former mate. A private detective may come up with information from so far in the past that you had forgotten it was there.
Imagine that you are forced via *subpoena duces tecum* to turn over
all bank records for the past three years. Are there *any* checks,
any charges, that you would prefer to remain secret? (Think
about this carefully. Consider newsletter subscriptions, contribu-
tions, trips, purchases of alcohol, guns, ammunition, or whatever.
Consider rentals, from autos to motels to videos.)

Yes, I know that small ads run continually in small offbeat
newsletters and magazines, or in direct mail offers, with headings
like "OPEN A BANK ACCOUNT WITHOUT A SOCIAL SECU-
RITY NUMBER." I used to answer these ads, just to be sure that
something new hasn't been discovered. To date, nothing has. The
reports tell you to attempt to open a bank account but to state that
you will not give your Social Security number. The bank representative then refuses to proceed, at which point you threaten to sue

the bank, listing rather generic legal references designed to intimi-
date. To satisfy your curiosity and to save you the cost of a report—
the bank *will* refuse to open such an account.

Nevertheless, all is not lost. Difficult? Yes. Hopeless? No. I
have been involved in the secret use of bank accounts in the
United States and offshore since 1959 and have not experienced
any serious problems.

As I said in the previous section, since we are discussing privacy measures rather than tax evasion, you need not have any
secrets from the IRS. This report is about hiding bank accounts
from your enemies, *not* from the IRS. Some of my suggestions
that follow may be offbeat and perhaps underhanded. I agree,
but they are not currently—nor anticipated to be—*illegal*,
according to the attorney who reviews all my projects.

USE A NOMINEE

This method requires the assistance of a nominee—a third party
who will act on your behalf. Let's call this person Debbie E.
Faith. Debbie will open a bank account in her own name. Here
are the steps:

1. Choose an independent bank in a state where neither you
   nor Debbie lives. This will isolate both of you from routine
   searches and will hide Debbie's possible death (should
   such occur) from the bank authorities long enough for you
   to cash a final check, closing out all but the last $10 from
   the account.

2. Prepare Debbie for obvious questions, such as "Since you
   live in California, why are you opening this account here,
   in Pioche, Nevada?" The answer might be "I'm thinking
   about moving here within the next three months." (She
   should have no problem saying something like that,
   because she can certainly *think* about it . . .)

3. Withdraw cash from your present account(s), perhaps $1,000. Purchase a bank cashier's check from a bank where you are *not* known, made out to Debbie Faith and with a fictitious remitter.

4. Next, Debbie practices, hour after hour, an indecipherable signature, the kind businessmen use all over Europe. She then assembles the necessary identification (a passport is best, if she has one, since it gives far less information than a driver's license), travels to the city where the bank is located, and opens a personal account. She will receive a minimum order of checks from the bank that will have her name and address printed in the upper left-hand corner. This must be a legitimate address, because the checks will be mailed to it later.

5. When the printed checks arrive, tear out the two checks with the highest numbers (so it appears the account has been used), along with a printed deposit slip. You will need these to order new checks from a mail-order company such as Checks Unlimited (800-204-2244; www.Checks Unlimited.com) or Checks in the Mail (877-397-1541; www.checksinthemail.com). Use one of the two checks to pay for the order, and mark the other check (sent as a sample) "VOID." Cross out both the name and address on the sample check, as well as the present number. Write in a starting number of 6001 or higher, so that the account will appear to have been established years ago. Above the deleted name and address, write in Debbie's initials, DEF. Choose a type style such as Old English, that is difficult to read. Add a note somewhere to emphasize that the checks are to have *only* the initials. The mail-order check companies will usually mail only to the address printed on the sample check, so do not try to have them sent to any other address.

6. When the new checks arrive—hopefully enough to last you for years—Debbie sits down and signs them until her

signatures start to vary. Time out for coffee or Dr Pepper, then she continues to sign, with breaks, until finished.

7. You, of course, keep all the checks, either well hidden or under lock and key. From this point on, you use these pre-signed checks in any way you please. (For deposits, order and use a rubber stamp.)

Perhaps you will pay Debbie a flat fee for setting things up. Later, if you need her services again—perhaps for signing more checks—you might offer her $200 for two hours' work. She should be able to sign five or six hundred checks within that time.

PRINT YOUR OWN CHECKS

Although I prefer the printed checks that can be ordered by mail, many of my readers say they use their computer and printer to make their own checks. There are a number of products on the market that enable the user to print the name of the account (leaving out the address), the bank information, the check number and even the special MICR characters that can be printed with magnetic ink. A quick check on the Internet will bring up names like VersaCheck, MySoftware, MyChecks, MyPersonalCheckWriter, MyBusinessCheckWriter, Checknique, CrossCheck, ChecksBy-Now, ChecksByNet, Checker, CheckMAN, and CheckMagic. Or, if you lack access to the Internet, go to Staples, Office Depot, Office-Max, CompUSA, or any other software retailer.

OR NO BANK ACCOUNT AT ALL

Hundreds of thousands of American citizens, as well as a similar number of illegal aliens, manage to live without any bank account at all, and not all are financially disadvantaged. This is one way to ensure that you do not accidentally reveal your home address by writing a check for the rent, the mortgage, utilities, taxes, or home repair.

Worse, there is a real danger if you ever write a check to a lawyer, CPA, or anyone else who—unknown to you—is a crook. When investigating this person—perhaps surreptitiously—government agents will come up with a copy of your check. Might this possibly lead to *your* mail and bank account being examined? Or a tap on *your* telephone?

Therefore, you may decide to pay professionals in cash if you're there in person. If not, you might mail a postal money order, a cashier's check, or a traveler's check. For small payments, I recommend the money orders sold in supermarkets and in convenience stores. They are economical, can be purchased with no ID, and the line for the payee is left blank. You fill in the payee on your own. The issuing office has no record of the sender or the receiver.

For amounts larger than $2,000, you may prefer a bank money order or cashier's check. Many banks do not require ID when you are purchasing the checks with cash. If in doubt, check out a bank beforehand, asking them about their policies. Or test their policy by purchasing a small check to pay for something you are going to order by mail. If asked for ID, tell the absolute truth: "I didn't bring any ID with me; I didn't think I'd need it."

ANOTHER GOOD REASON TO PAY CASH

Frank Abagnale, in his book *The Art of the Steal* (Broadway Books, 2001), says on page 29: "People can get anyone's check. All they have to do is see it. Criminals nowadays will drive around until they find a ritzy neighborhood with million-dollar homes. They'll knock on the door. When someone answers, they'll say, 'Boy, you've got a lot of leaves lying on your lawn . . . I'll tell you what, my buddy and I will clean up your leaves, leave the place immaculate, and it'll cost you just seventy-five dollars.' The guy thinks it's a great deal, the crooks clean up the leaves, and the owner

pays them with a check for seventy-five dollars. That's all they
came for: the check. Then they go to the Internet and order the
checks . . . forge them, and start cashing them. Next time, the
guy will rake his own leaves."

HAWALA BANKING

This is the oldest banking system in existence, used for exchang-
ing money across international borders. Since no money actually
moves anywhere, it cannot be traced. Yes, you read correctly, *it
cannot be traced.*

Although it is widely practiced among Chinese and Indians
(from India), and, to a lesser extent, by Spaniards, the average
American had never heard of it until after 9-11 (Osama was said
to use this system). The easiest way to explain it is to review a
transaction I had in the late 1960s when I flew to Madrid and
then to Boston on business. While in the latter city, I was invited
to a cocktail party, and, when it came up that I lived in Spain, I
was introduced to a short, grossly fat attorney I'll here refer to as
Cabot. After initial pleasantries, I was guided over to a secluded
area where the following conversation took place.

"Jack," he said, "maybe one hand can wash another here. I had
a client from Barcelona who ran out of convertible pesetas.
[Only convertible pesetas—governed by strict rules—can be sent
out of the country.] So this guy paid me by giving me title to an
apartment he had near the beach in Alicante. I had a friend sell it
for me, but it was in normal pesetas, understand?"

"Yes, you can't take the money out. How much, in pesetas?"

"Two million nine," said Cabot, which at that time was equiv-
alent to about $47,000. "Can we do a little trade here, maybe?"

"Well," I answered, stalling, "sometimes I have the same problem myself. Why not just spend the money over there?"

"Listen, not to offend you or anything, but I've been to Spain
twice, and all in one trip. The *first* time and the *last* time. I made

some joke about Franco, and those guys with the triangle hats almost took away my passport! So look, Jack, can we work something out? Like at ten percent?"

"Thirty-two thousand is about all I've got, in dollars."

"C'mon, you got another five somewhere. Thirty-seven K and it's a done deal!"

Because both Cabot and I trusted a mutual acquaintance there, we did the deal in his office the following morning. I gave Cabot a check for $37,000 drawn on a Londonderry, New Hampshire, bank (presigned by a nominee), and received in return his check, drawn on his account in Spain and made out to "Portador" for 2,900,000 pesetas. ("Portador" means "bearer." In those happy days, almost *all* checks in Spain were made out to the bearer!) It cost me an extra day and some travel money to return to the Canaries via Barcelona, but Cabot's check was good. I took the money in cash from Banco Hispano Americano, lugging it back to the airport in a zipper case. This is the procedure known from ancient times as *hawala*, sometimes spelled *hawalah*, and occasionally referred to as *hundi*. Let's review the procedure:

- There are no written documents, the exchanges are based on mutual trust (perhaps for that reason unpopular in the United States?).

- Only local currencies are used. If you are sending money to the UK, for example, you'll pay the U.S. *hawala* banker in dollars and receive pounds in London.

- This exchange cannot be traced—no money crosses a border.

(*Note:* As this is being written, Sen. Orrin Hatch, R-Utah, is about to introduce legislation to further expand federal police powers. Section 201 of his bill (ironically titled the "Victory" Act) states that hawala banking will constitute the crime of money-laundering. The bill may not pass, but check this out before considering the use of hawala banking.)

QUESTIONS & ANSWERS

What do you think about credit unions, as opposed to banks?

In answer, I'll pass along the experience of one of my readers, who, as a college student years ago, worked in the customer service department of "one of the largest banks in the U.S." His job, as a "call center rep," was to respond to phone calls and check account data. "Not only did I have access to the customer's name, address, Social Security number, and date of birth," he writes, but "I saw every financial transaction on the account, including credit card purchases and ATM withdrawal locations." According to my reader, there were thousands of call center reps at the bank with this kind of access. "For fun (and because we were low-paid and unethical), we'd check out the accounts of friends, lovers, coworkers, etc. Further, during late-night calls with angry/rude callers, I occasionally heard a rep reminding a caller to cool it, because we *knew where they lived*. Scary huh?" Hopefully, of course, *your* bank has only your ghost address! Take to heart this warning from one who knows: "Thousands of low-paid workers have access to your personal life and feel no shame in monitoring you. Remember that the next time you open an account at the big bank with the most conveniences. (*Note:* I joined a small credit union after that experience. I like to think things are a bit different there.)"

How should I go about donating money to my church and to my alma mater?

Your church will be happy to accept cash. Send a bank check (or a stack of $1,000 money orders) to your alma mater.

What if a bank requires my fingerprint on the back of a check?

This is an irksome, irritating, and infuriating request, but what if your financial circumstances do not give you the option of just walking away? Keep these two points in mind:

- As long as the check does not bounce, and assuming it is not written on a small bank where the check is returned to the client, the check disappears into the bank archives forever.

- When you give your thumbprint, press hard and slightly twist your thumb. Practice at home first. The goal is to smear the print just a trace. If done right, this will make a match impossible, and yet the clerk may not notice it at all.

There is also such a thing as filling in the grooves of your thumbprint with glue, then allowing it to dry. Then a second coating is given, and, while it's still moist, you press it against the thumb of another person. But I don't think you need to get into all that, unless you are on the FBI's top ten list. (And if you are, better not to cash that check at all!)

Although I do wish to keep my private life private, I am not paranoid. Can't I just keep a normal bank account and a credit card—both in my own name—and get by?

My answer may surprise you. Yes, you can. I do urge you, however, to follow these suggestions:

1. Open a new account in another state, any place where you can give a temporary local address. Perhaps this will be the address of a friend, a relative, or a small mom-and-pop mail-forwarding service. (If the latter, "forget" to add the telltale box number after the street address.) Use your passport rather than your driver's license, because the driver's license will tip them off that you are not local, and many banks will not open an account if you live outside the area.

2. Once the new account is open, close your present account(s) to block the back trail.

3. Choose the smallest possible bank, preferably with no out-of-state branches. This may reduce the number of databases your name will be in.

4. Later, if necessary, you can change the address for the monthly statements to your current ghost address, but let a few months go by first. In a cover letter, give some reason for the change. Perhaps you will be "back and forth," and your ghost address will be more convenient. Or perhaps the new address will be for the accountant who handles your financial matters.

5. Never, ever, as long as you live, reveal your true address and telephone number to anyone at the new bank.

6. Do not use the checks the bank gives you, because they'll include your name and address. Order your own by mail. Either leave the upper-left corner blank, or give one of your initials plus a last name. Do not list any address or phone number. (For detailed information about ordering your checks, review the section "Use a Nominee" in this chapter.)

15

LIMITED LIABILITY
COMPANIES

To have is nothing. To keep is all.

—Unknown

Mary L——— was a schoolteacher who lived with her husband
and four children near Seattle, Washington. In the early 1990s,
Mary purchased a gray Volkswagen Fox. In all innocence, she
titled this car in her own name. Not in her wildest dreams—or
nightmares!—could Mary have foreseen the bitter consequences
of driving a car with plates that would show up in the computer
with her first name, middle initial, and last name.

Years passed. Unexpectedly, Mary fell in love with one of her
students, a thirteen-year-old boy. Despite being married, she was
unable to control her emotions. One thing led to another, and
Mary found herself pregnant. In 1997, the affair became known.
She was arrested, jailed, and sentenced to eighty-nine months
in prison. Given her lack of a criminal record and the fact
that she posed no threat to society, Mary was released on probation. One of the conditions of the probation was that she

would not contact her young lover without permission from the authorities.

Mary carried a pager. The father of her future child, unable—or unwilling—to stay away from Mary, sent her a page with the number of a pay phone. She called him back. That same evening, she picked him up in her little gray Volkswagen Fox.

They went to a late movie, *Wag the Dog*. Then Mary parked her Volkswagen along a street near her home and they talked into the early morning hours. Mary had already packed and had hidden money and her passport in the car. They made plans to flee Seattle together and to make a new life far, far away.

At this point, was there any obstacle to their plans? The boy's mother had no objections—this was, after all, the mother of her future grandchild, and she looked forward to seeing and holding the girl who would be named Audrey Lokelani. The parole board had no idea that Mary was violating parole. She was not wanted by the police. No one else knew of their plans to flee. Nor was society in danger.

From Mary's viewpoint, all was well.

At 2:45 A.M., Seattle policeman Todd Harris was on a routine patrol. He passed a car that was parked along the curb. The parking lights were on. The windows were steamed up but, it appeared, there were two occupants.

There was no sign of misbehavior. Nevertheless, Harris noted the Washington license plate number as he drove by. As he continued on his patrol, he ran the number through his computer to make sure the car had not been reported stolen. Several blocks later, the name of the registered owner came onto the screen. The car was legally registered and was not stolen, but he recognized the name from reading about the case in the newspapers. *Mary K. LeTourneau.*

Officer Harris returned and asked for an ID. The two occupants were Mary and the boy. The boy was taken home. Mary was taken to the station, then arrested for violation of parole. On Friday, February 6, 1997, the judge revoked her parole and sentenced her to serve the full eighty-nine months. Leaving aside the morality of meeting with the father of her child, here is the moral I want you to draw from this story: *At the time Mary titled the car*, there was not—could not have been—the slightest indication of the troubles that lay ahead. But who among us can guarantee that quiet waters will never see a storm?

After the LeTourneau sentencing, I sent a notice to all my clients in the United States and Canada with this headline:

SEVEN YEARS IN JAIL

FOR NOT USING A LIMITED LIABILITY COMPANY!

In neither this chapter nor the next will I be discussing all the various uses to which limited liability companies are being put. They have a vast application in the business, banking, partnership, and asset-protection worlds. Endless dozens of books have been and are being written about obtaining tax identification numbers, writing complex operating agreements, registering them in other states as foreign legal entities, and opening bank accounts here and/or abroad. All these uses are beyond the scope of this book. From now on, when I mention LLCs, I refer specifically to a legal entity that has all of the following characteristics:

1. No one will know who owns it unless the owner tells them.

2. It will be filed in New Mexico—a state that protects privacy.

3. It will be managed by a *single member.*

4. It will be kept in good standing by maintaining a resident agent.

5. It will not have an IRS identification number, such as a TIN or an EIN.

6. It will not require an operating agreement nor the keeping of a set of books.

7. It will list a business address that is not in the state where filed.

8. It will be filed by a specific organizer skilled in the fields of privacy.

9. It will cost less than $100 to form, and less than $100 a year to maintain it.

10. The LLC name will never appear on a state or federal tax return.

WHAT IS AN LLC?

You will often hear that a limited liability company is something "new," but this refers only to the United States. In Europe, LLCs have been used for more than a century. I started using them in Spain more than thirty-five years ago.

Think of an LLC primarily as a partnership, but without the liability and (now hear this!) without the necessity of actually having a partner. Like a corporation, it is a legal entity that stands alone, but it lacks the many onerous bookkeeping details and annual meetings required of a corporation.

A TYPICAL ORDER FOR AN LLC

When this book was first published in 2000, more questions poured in at my Web site about LLCs than about any other subject. As simply as possible, therefore, I will take you through the process, step by step, in the formation of an LLC in the state of New Mexico. I'll start by listing five persons who might be typically involved. (Names and details have been changed.)

* * *

Kathleen is being stalked by an ex-lover and ex-cop Max, who beat her up, which was why she left him. She's about to sell her car, buy a small pickup with tinted windows, and move from Boston to the suburb of Woburn, Massachusetts. (Before moving, she rents a P.O. box in Woburn and lists her *present* address on the form.) Max must be prevented at all costs from finding out about her new purchase by having a buddy run her name through the DMV files.

Olivia Garcia is an experienced LLC organizer from South America. She lives on one of the Canary Islands and receives mail via a ghost address there. Olivia forms LLCs solely for the readers of this book. Her name—but not her address—appears on the New Mexico State Web site for LLCs as "O. Garcia." To all intents and purposes, Olivia works alone, and she is the only one who reads and answers e-mails from clients. She banks by mail with a small branch bank in Alaska under the name of "O. Garcia." No Social Security number ties her to this account, because, as a foreign citizen, she is exempt.

John is the single member of a NM company called "Servicios Residentes LLC." This is the legal entity that serves as the New Mexico Registered Agent for all of Olivia's clients. (A Santa Fe resident is paid well to allow his street address to be used for this company.) John knows almost nothing about LLCs but he doesn't need to. Although he lives in Abbotsford, British Columbia, he maintains a ghost address just across the border, in Sumas, Washington.

Anita is one of three girls who handle incoming corporations and LLC filings in the state of New Mexico's Public Regulation Commission.

Kathleen no longer keeps a land-line telephone where she lives, so she goes to Kinko's (a copy, printing, and Internet service) to log on to the Internet. She goes to *www.howtobeinvisible.com*, clicks on

LIMITED LIABILITY COMPANIES, scrolls down, clicks on LIMITED LIA-
BILITY COMPANY ORDER FORM, and prints it out. She fills out the
following information:

- *Name:* Irish Princess LLC
- *Principal place of business:* 4 Evergreen Villas, Evergreen
  Road, Cork City, Ireland (She has a cousin who works at
  that address and could accept a letter for her if one ever
  came in.)
- *Price:* Three years at $99 per year, plus $99 for the LLC
  itself. Total, $396
- *Mail documents to:* K. O'Donnell, P.O. Box****, Woburn,
  MA 01888

She makes a check out for $396, payable to "O. Garcia," encloses
it in an envelope along with the one-page order form, and mails
it to Sumas, Washington. This is what happens next:

1. John crosses into Washington, picks up the order, returns
   home, runs the application and the enclosed check through
   his scanner, and e-mails the images to Olivia in the Canary
   Islands. She then checks the name on New Mexico's Web
   site. No one has yet filed a company with a name similar to
   "Irish Princess," so she e-mails John to proceed.

2. John—using document papers presigned by Olivia—then
   prepares duplicate Articles of Organization. The Articles
   include a date—usually fifty years in the future—when the
   company will automatically cease to exist. He also prepares,
   and signs before a notary, an AFFIDAVIT OF ACCEPTANCE OF
   APPOINTMENT BY DESIGNATED INITIAL REGISTERED AGENT.
   That same day, he sends a cover letter and a check via Priority Mail to the Public Regulation Commission in Santa
   Fe, New Mexico, along with the two copies of the Articles,
   his original notarized affidavit (plus a photo copy), and a
   stamped, addressed Priority Mail envelope.

3. Anita receives the envelope from John and puts it at the bottom of the stack on her desk. Fifty to seventy orders come in every day, and, as usual, the office is short-handed, thanks to a perennial shortfall in the state's budget. The law requires her to file and return the originals within fifteen days, a law usually—but not always—honored. Normally, Anita would eventually prepare the documents, fold them twice, and stuff them into a normal business envelope. However, since John has enclosed a stiff 9" × 12" Priority Mail envelope (to avoid creases in the documents as well as to speed delivery), she uses that. It goes into her OUT basket twelve days after receipt.

4. Several days later John receives the documents from Anita in Santa Fe. He prepares the order, inserts the documents into the usual Priority Mail envelope, and on that same day mails it from the Washington side of the border to Kathleen. Remember Kathleen's check? That, too, is mailed— for deposit to Olivia's account in Alaska.

5. Kathleen receives (1) a cover letter, (2) a New Mexico Certificate of Organization with a seven-digit identification number, (3) the classy-looking Articles of Organization, printed on 28 lb. bond paper with an engraved border and stamped with the official filing date, (4) a signed "Statement of Resignation and Concluded Participation" to show that Olivia's duties ended with the filing of the Articles, (5) two photocopies of the Articles, and (6) three pages of LLC information prepared by an attorney. The cover letter explains that everything is paid up for the next three years. Beyond that, if Kathleen wishes to maintain her company in good standing, she will be able to do so by paying $99 per year for the resident agent.

How Kathleen can then use *Irish Princess LLC* to buy a car, a house, or a travel trailer will be discussed in the chapter that follows. Later, you'll learn more details about how someone can appear to be running a business in one place whereas they actually live thousands of miles away. Meanwhile, let's examine several areas that many readers have inquired about.

INCOME TAX CONSEQUENCES

Since the IRS treats one-member LLCs as sole proprietorships for tax purposes, there are no income tax consequences. If Kathleen happens to use her LLC for a part-time business, she will merely report earnings and expenses on Schedule C and submit it with her 1040 tax return. Repeat: the income—if any—is listed on her personal tax return. Nowhere on the tax form will the name of her LLC appear. As far as the IRS is concerned, *Kathleen's LLC is invisible.*

PROOF OF OWNERSHIP

"How can I prove I own the company," I'm often asked, "if my name doesn't appear anywhere?"

If ever there were a case where possession was nine-tenths of the law, possession of the Articles of Organization is it. The LLC is owned by whomever you say owns it—who can prove differently? The state does not know. The organizer does not know. *No one* knows unless you tell them! No shares are transferred, because an LLC does not have shares. If ownership is transferred, the state of New Mexico will have no knowledge of this, because no owner was originally listed, and there is no annual report that could add additional information.

Nevertheless, I have sometimes been asked, "What if no one believes me?" I can only say that in twenty-nine years of using LLCs, I have never been asked to prove that I owned one, nor have I ever heard of anyone who had this problem. As far as I am concerned, having the original Certificate of Organization plus the Articles of Organization in my hand is the same as holding a postal money order that leaves the payee line blank. In fact, thinking back, I can't recall a single instance of even showing the original documents at all. Instead, I merely show up at the DMV or the title company with a photocopy of the Articles.

QUESTIONS & ANSWERS

Might an LLC be used as a gift?

If you wish to instill the concept of personal privacy into your children, I can think of no better high school or university graduation gift than an LLC. Think of the privacy that *you* would be enjoying today had you started working on it right after graduation! If you plan to present the actual documents, the LLC will have to have a name. Why not choose a geographical name from your area? For instance, if you live in San Pedro, California, one of these might work: Rolling Hills Associates LLC; Lomita Limited LLC; Point Fermin Enterprises LLC, or Harbor Lake Services LLC.

For real estate, which is better, a trust or an LLC?

Currently, I use an LLC to purchase property, and have our trust own the LLC. Normally, a revocable trust is a permanent arrangement where ownership is locked in until you die. An LLC is more flexible when it comes to making changes in ownership, or dividing ownership between various persons or legal entities. And for privacy, a combination of the two is ideal.

16

HIDDEN OWNERSHIP OF VEHICLES AND REAL ESTATE

"Things are seldom what they seem,
Skim milk masquerades as cream."

—W. S. GILBERT,
H.M.S. PINAFORE (1878)

Several years ago, I swung my black Jaguar sedan down the ramp and into a "24-hr. security" parking garage at Seattle's SeaTac airport, snatched the ticket stub from the attendant, raced for the shuttle bus, and just barely caught my flight to Phoenix. Eight days later, I returned to SeaTac, caught the shuttle back to the garage, and joined the check-in line.

When I presented my ticket stub, the cashier hesitated.

"Sir," he said, "please step to one side. The manager will be right out."

The manager came out, introduced himself, and led me back to his office. I had visions of a scratch in the paint or a ding in a fender.

"The same day you left," he said, "your car disappeared."

"Disappeared? As in *stolen*?" (So much for the twenty-four-hour security . . .)

He explained that the same evening I left, one of the attendants parked a car in the stall where my car had been. When he turned the number in to the cashier, the computer showed the stall was already occupied. They quickly searched the entire building to see if it had been parked in another spot in error. When they failed to find it, they reported it stolen. The next morning, the police spotted it, badly damaged, sitting at home plate on a baseball diamond in a Seattle park.

I have the King County Police Vehicle Impound Report before me, and in the Narrative section, line 4, the officer writes, "*Unable to contact owner.*" Here's why: The car was in the name of an LLC in state A. The address listed for this company was in faraway State B, and a reverse directory failed to show a telephone number at that address.

Although for many years I have been registering my vehicles in the name of limited liability companies, this was the first time my security precautions had been put to the test. No damage would have been done, of course, had the police been able to contact me in this particular case. However, a short time later, my security precautions were to prove worthwhile. As soon as the insurance agent handed me a check for my Jaguar—it was too badly damaged to repair—I bought a year-old dark green Lexus (see first question at the end of this chapter) and headed east.

A few days later, I arrived in Minneapolis and spent Saturday afternoon visiting used bookstores. It was just getting dark that evening when I pulled out of a parking lot onto West Lake Street, in a hurry because I had to meet a friend from Madrid who was about to arrive at the airport. I failed to see an oncoming motorcycle and almost clipped a Harley being ridden by a three hundred-pound bearded bruiser. He screamed something like "$# ⋛@%👁&𖦹!!," waved his fist, and made violent gestures to have me pull over. (If you've ever been on West Lake Street in South Minneapolis after dark, you know this is not a good neighborhood in which to pull over.)

It was too dark for the rider to see any "so-sorry" gestures—had I made them—so I fed more gas to the 290 horses under the hood. The overweight biker followed me right on to 35 W going south, with all the time in the world to memorize my license number. Although I do not scare easily, this time I was seriously alarmed. Enough to set a new Minnesota speed record between West 35th and the I-494 junction, where I cut the lights and peeled off at the exit. Whether he memorized the number or not, and whether he was carrying a gun or not, once I lost the biker I was safe forever—the plates would lead him nowhere. But my heart was still thumping when I pulled into airport parking.

A few Saturdays later, I was in Londonderry, New Hampshire, to meet Carl Prague, an old friend who used to live aboard the *Raider*, a 1912 wooden sailboat with Santa Cruz de Tenerife (Canary Islands) as a home base. A stiff wind was blowing when we stopped at the Country Market on Highway 102 to pick up some wine and snacks, and, when we came out, a few abandoned shopping carts were starting to move. Just as we were putting the groceries in the car, a hard gust sent a cart racing past us and across the parking lot directly toward a parked Honda Civic with a man and a woman in it. There was no way to stop it, and we watched as it struck the driver's door with a resounding clang and bounced back. As we continued to watch, we could see that the woman was obviously screaming at the man to do something, and the "something" turned out to be a trip over to see me. Assuming he wanted some help, I lowered my window halfway as he came around my side, and said hello.

"Your cart hit my car!"

"Excuse me? We didn't have a cart."

"Yes you did, and we saw it come from here."

At least he didn't weigh more than 140 pounds, and my friend Carl is an ex-wrestler, so this time I was just amused, not scared.

"I wrote down your license number," the man muttered, brandishing a scrap of paper, "and you'll hear from my lawyer."

Well, best of luck, buddy, and have a nice day.

PURCHASING A VEHICLE IN THE NAME OF AN LLC

Everything I have to say in this section makes one assumption: *you will pay cash.* I paid cash for the first car I ever bought—a 1931 Chevrolet, and I've been paying cash ever since. As long as you do not finance your purchase, taking title is usually a simple process. Nevertheless, many of my readers have been reluctant to use an LLC, simply because they've never done it before.

One such person was Jim in San Francisco, who asked me to help him purchase a used Lincoln Town Car with almost no miles on it. It was for sale by a private party in Washington, and Jim wanted to title it in that state for personal reasons. He asked for my help because he was not sure he could handle the registration and yet keep his name out of it. Here is the transaction step by step.

1. Since Jim was in a hurry, I pulled a "shelf" LLC from my files that I'll call Golden Gateway LLC. (A shelf LLC is one that has been formed in the past for future use, and just put "on the shelf" until needed. I recommend this procedure to all readers, and personally keep shelf LLCs on hand at all times.) We then flew to Seattle, rented a car, and drove out to Port Angeles to make the deal.

2. The seller, a ninety-seven-year-old (!) woman who had purchased the car in 1991 and then stored it, signed off on the title. She also signed the bill of sale I had prepared beforehand. We filled in "Golden Gateway LLC" as the buyer and gave a ghost address that Jim had already set up through a friend in Cheyenne, Wyoming.

3. Rather than go to the Department of Motor Vehicles in Port Angeles, we went to a private licensing bureau. (They charge a small fee for handling the paperwork, but the lines are shorter and they are sometimes easier to deal with than clerks at the DMV.) Jim went through the line with me, but only as an observer. He wanted to see how I would answer the questions.

> *Clerk:* What's the UBI number for this company? (Washington requires an ID number for all legal entities doing business in their state.)
>
> *I:* Golden Gateway LLC doesn't do business in this state, and Wyoming doesn't require a UBI number.
>
> *Clerk:* Then why not license it in Wyoming?
>
> *I:* For at least six months the car will be in this state, and the law requires we therefore license it here. (100 percent correct, in all states.)

The clerk accepted that and then asked me for an ID. I explained that the car was *not for me* but for the company, and showed her a photocopy of the LLC's Articles of Organization. That ended her questions. (Had she insisted on some sort of an ID number in lieu of the UBI, I'd have given her the seven-digit filing number from the Certificate of Organization.) She then pushed a computer printout over to me and showed me where to sign. I scrawled an illegible signature that matched the one on the bill of sale (although she didn't ask to see it).

> *Clerk:* Print your title after your signature, please.

Since I was neither a member nor a manager of Jim's newly acquired company, I printed "Sales Mgr." (Jim retroactively appointed me "Sales Manager for a Day.") We paid the various license and transfer fees in cash and were on our way. The title arrived at the address I use and was sent on to Jim, as will be the annual registration notifications. What was accomplished?

First and foremost, *total privacy*. Suppose a private investigator sees Jim's car parked in Las Vegas at what he considers a suspicious address. He makes a note of the Washington license plate and obtains whatever information is available with the Department of Motor Vehicles in Olympia. He will get the name "Golden Gateway LLC" and an address in Wyoming, nothing more. If the PI then calls the secretary of state's office in Cheyenne, Wyoming, he will learn that it is not a Wyoming company. He checks back with Olympia. No, not a Washington company, either. That leaves him forty-eight states plus the District of Columbia to check out. The search usually ends right there.

However, assume the PI continues doggedly on and eventually does do a search of New Mexico's database. All he will find there is a principal place of business in Wyoming, plus a Santa Fe address for the registered agent, and no one at that address will have the remotest idea of who owns "Golden Gateway LLC."

INSURING YOUR VEHICLE

The easiest—and recommended—way to obtain insurance is to use your own name, followed by "dba" ("doing business as") and then the name of the company. This will keep your rates low and, when you have multiple vehicles titled in separate LLCs, you should still get the multiple vehicle discounts. You can often get the insurance agent to keep your files under your first or middle initial, plus your last name. Thus, if you own a car, a van, and a pickup, your insurance cards will read something like this:

J. Smith, dba Rey de la Carretera LLC
J. Smith, dba Lake of the Woods LLC
J. Smith, dba Barrington Enterprises LLC

INVISIBLE OWNERSHIP TRANSFER

Going back to Jim in San Francisco, suppose he wishes to transfer ownership of his Lincoln Town Car to his nephew Joe Jones up in Eureka? All he has to do is make out a bill of sale—not for the car, but for the company that owns it—and hand over the original LLC documents. There will be no sales tax nor transfer fees, because the *car* hasn't changed hands—it is still owned by the LLC! As for insurance, Jim would cancel his own, and his nephew would apply for a new policy in the name of "J. Jones, dba Golden Gateway LLC."

The same would be true if Jim decided to transfer ownership to an incorporated business he owns. However, if he sells the car to a third party, or if he trades the car in for a newer model, the sale would go through in the same manner as any other. Jim signs the title by writing "Golden Gateway LLC" and then signing his name below that.

If you have multiple legal entities, such as corporations, trusts, and other LLCs, do you see how easy it is to transfer ownership? If you buy a new pickup and later transfer it to a company you own, you take the Articles out of your personal file and drop them into the company file. Later, if you decide it would be better to have your LLC own it, you switch the Articles to the LLC file. If your brother-in-law wants to buy the car later, you hand him the Articles and take the cash. Here are the only changes that need to be made:

1. insurance company: change the name of the principal driver

2. Department of Motor Vehicles: change of address (for receiving the annual registration notice)

It's often fun for the whole family when it comes to choosing suitable names for the various LLCs that will be used for future purposes.

North Dakota Sodbusters LLC	family home
Victoria's Sea-Crate LLC	SeaSport cabin cruiser
King of the Road LLC	husband's Hummer H2
Her Royal Majesty LLC	wife's Mercury Mountaineer
One Cool Chick LLC	daughter's Mazda Miata
Road Less Traveled LLC	son's Jeep Liberty

All of the above could, of course, be titled in a single LLC to keep costs down. The main problem in having everything in the same LLC—besides losing the fast-and-easy method of transferring ownership—is the protection you lose if a PI is on the trail of your assets. Let's say that in the example above everything is titled in Pacific Partners LLC.

If a PI comes up with the driver of any one of the vehicles and checks the plate, he'll follow this with a search for *Pacific Partners LLC*. What will he find? All the other vehicles, the boat, and— because the home is included—the actual street address. (There is no way to avoid revealing the true address of real estate, of course, so a home should *always* be kept in a separate LLC. All other titles can use a ghost address.)

HIDDEN OWNERSHIP OF YOUR HOME

What I had to say about paying cash for your car goes double when it comes to real estate. Purchasing real estate in the name of an LLC is either very easy . . . or very difficult. If you pay cash, it's easy. Give your attorney—or the title company—a copy of the Articles or Organization, along with clear instructions that your name is to appear only in their office files, and not on any public database. However, if you plan to finance your home, then the mortgage company is going to demand that you do it in your own name. (Until I was in my late fifties, we lacked the cash to buy a home outright, so we always rented . . . and saved some money

as well. As talk show host Bruce Williams—one of the best financial advisers in the nation—constantly preaches, "Renting is
cheaper than buying.")

If you have a living trust, you can, of course, title real estate in
the trust. However, as indicated earlier, you will have an extra
layer of privacy if you take title in the name of an LLC which is,
in turn, owned by your trust.

Note: A trust is not a do-it-yourself project, nor is it something you should order on the Internet. Avoid being scammed—
use an attorney who specializes in this field.

QUESTIONS & ANSWERS

*You mention driving luxury cars, but doesn't that draw
undue attention to yourself?*

Yes. I confess that from an early age I've had a weakness for
upscale cars—Packards in the old days, and, in later years, Lexus,
Mercedes, and Jaguars. However . . . it's never too late for common sense. Thus it was that just one month after the first edition
of this book went to press, your humble servant stepped down to
a Ford Ranger. My wife followed suit by selling her Lincoln and
buying a Mazda. (Top of the line, yes, but who looks twice at a
Mazda?) Now that we've finally set the right example, here are
some reasons why I suggest you follow suit.

- You'll save some serious money. Less initial cost, less
  depreciation, less money at the gas pump, and a lower
  insurance rate. Also, less floor space will be taken up in
  your garage.

- You'll no longer be the subject of envy of your less-
  fortunate neighbors, relatives, and friends.

- You'll no longer be a prime target for carjackers or burglars.
  (Burglars have been known to spot a luxury car and follow

it home. Later, when the owner leaves, they break into the home, assuming that valuables must be there.)

- You will have more privacy as you travel about, blending in with hundreds of similar vehicles on the road.

What about long trips? In our case, we prefer a heavy car with lots of room when we're going to be driving for many hours, so we rent a Lincoln from Hertz. Not only is this cheaper than owning the car, there is an additional advantage. If the car should break down or be involved in a fender-bender far from home, Hertz just delivers another Lincoln, and away we go.

I just moved from Denver to Miami. Since I am keeping my Colorado driver's license, should I also keep my Colorado license plates?

Not unless you also get Florida plates. Leslie L——— is one of my clients. Les works for a well-known electronics company in California's Silicone Valley. He also happens to live there, but he licensed his new Porsche in Texas (for the tax savings) and obtained a Texas driver's license. He does have a ghost address in Texas, and he knows the area around Plano.

One day he was stopped and questioned by the California Highway Patrol. The officer did not accept his story of being from Texas. He was ordered to obtain California plates within thirty days or face a serious penalty. Rather than accept this, Les went to court. "I'm a Texas resident," he said. "The officer made a mistake. Here is my Texas driver's license with my Texas home address." The judge accepted this explanation and Les kept his Texas plates. Two months later, Les was in a commuter parking lot, taking a nap in his car.

"A cop woke me up and was suspicious of the Texas plates and my Texas driver's license. He asked me a lot of questions about what I was doing and how long had I been out here. I simply said, 'I'm a Texas resident working out here temporarily.' He called it in, and everything was okay, so he left me alone."

However, I suspect that with a few more experiences like this, Les will bite the bullet and pay the costly fee for California plates. As for also keeping the Texas plates, see the following question.

Can I have both local and out-of-state license plates for the same car?

Of course. I used to keep dual plates for my Mercedes-Benz, which was originally purchased and registered in New Hampshire. I also licensed it in State B, where I owned a home. I explained to the clerk at the licensing bureau in State B that I was keeping my old registration as well, because I spent half of my time back in New Hampshire.

"But then," said the clerk, "you will have to pay the annual registration fees in *both* states." I assured her that that was no problem. Here is why I kept two plates at that time:

State B plate: This was to avoid problems with curious neighbors or the local cops.

NH plate: I'd get out the screwdriver and switch plates only for short periods of time, such as when I arranged to meet clients and did not want them to know where I really lived. In fact, I called attention to this when I made the appointments: "I'll meet you at Denny's at Exit 34. Watch for a big maroon sedan with New Hampshire plates."

At present, however, I no longer bother with dual plates. If someone wants to have a consultation with me, we usually both fly into some neutral place like Vancouver, British Columbia, or Cabo San Lucas, BCN, so I won't be driving my own vehicle anyway.

I own several very expensive collector cars, and it would cost a fortune to pay the sales tax if I retitled them in the names of LLCs. The registrations are in my name and with my true address. Any suggestions?

In the long term, you may wish to sell your cars. When you buy more, title them with LLCs not only for privacy but for tax-free transfers as explained in chapter 12. Meanwhile, when you next pay your annual fee, turn in a change of address. The new address should not be traceable back to you, and must show on the registration certificate. That way, anyone looking for you will be led astray.

Warning: Learn from a mistake made by Ira G———, one of my newer clients, who is a divorced attorney in a Chicago suburb. His first move was to change the address on the registration for each of his collector cars. One of them was a Triumph stored at a friend's house about an hour's drive from where he lives. He handled the change of address by mail and did not get around to driving over to take the old registration out of the glove compartment. About the same time the new address was registered, his Triumph disappeared. Ira did not discover this fact for about two months and, when he did, the thief appeared to be someone in a dispute with the friend. Ira called the thief, who turned out to be an ex-Hell's Angel, on a first-name basis with local authorities. An argument ensued, in which the thief claimed he took the car from the friend's garage in payment of a debt. He was furious with the lawyer for threatening him. Can you see it coming? This ex-Hell's Angel guy had the car with the old registration in it, which showed *the home address* of the lawyer's ex-wife, where she lived alone with their young son.

Would this be a good time for you to go through the glove compartments of your vehicles, collector-type or otherwise?

What do you think about vanity license plates?

Personally, I prefer not to use vanity plates, because they draw attention to the driver. (If I were to change my mind, I would pick INVSIBL.) If you do decide on a vanity plate, you may wish to copy one of two plates I've seen and liked. The first was seen on a new Jaguar several years ago: 000–000. A month later I saw another one I liked (strangely enough, on *another* new Jaguar): NO NMBR.

Will hiding my true address and having license plates that cannot be traced protect me from stalkers?

You mean, like, "guaranteed"? When it comes to privacy and security, there are few if any guarantees, but the precautions you mention will certainly balance the odds in your favor. However, if someone seems to be able to mysteriously track you down after a "foolproof" move, perhaps he followed your U-Haul trailer or truck when you moved. Some stalkers have trailed their victims from one coast to the other. Or perhaps:

- He found out where your children go to school, and followed them home.
- He followed you home from work, church, or a visit to a relative.
- He followed you home from the airport.
- He requested a hearing, forcing you to show up in court, then followed you home.

The only sure way to avoid being followed is to never be located in the first place. If you have to meet with the stalker for any reason whatsoever, he certainly may attempt to follow you. Then again, ask any private investigator who the toughest person is to follow, and he'll tell you that it's the target who is *aware*. Perhaps not conscious of any specific thing, but just alert in general. Looking around when walking, watching the mirrors when driving, etc.

Carjackers say the same thing—many crimes would have been avoided had the victims been aware of their approach. In my own case, I never allow any specific car to follow me for a period of time in rural areas (where our homes usually are). I drive a few miles over the speed limit, and, if a car comes up behind me, I turn on the right-turn signal, slow down, and force him to pass.

If you live in a city and think a certain car is following you, make four consecutive right or left turns, i.e., go around the block. If the car you've seen in your mirrors follows you, *do not go home*. Drive to the nearest police or fire station or to a well-lighted gas station with a number of cars filling up. Hopefully you have your cell phone with you, in which case you can dial 911.

What precautions can be taken against carjackers?

Privacy and security go together. In the words of the Los Angeles Police Department—referring to carjackings—"Don't give up your privacy." In other words, *never* get into your own car at gunpoint. Just pretend to faint (or maybe faint for real!) and fall down limp.

Here's a scam I hear about from time to time. It's an oldie, but it still works. The latest is a report about a BMW that was parked late at night outside an upscale restaurant in Marin County, California. Someone called the restaurant to report that there was a white BMW 740i in the parking lot and its lights were still on. When the owner showed up (and, of course, the lights were *not* on), he was robbed at gunpoint and his car was taken.

Female drivers, when alone, attract more attention than males. One solution is to tint your windows as dark as—or darker than—the law allows. Then have a male mannequin in the passenger seat. In fact, with dark enough tinting, you may even get by with one of those rubber masks from a novelty store. Just slip it over the headrest—can't hurt, might help. (Don't use this gag for the carpool lane, however. You may stumble across a cop with less than an adequate sense of humor.)

While we're on this subject, I have an article from the *Skagit Valley Herald*, datelined January 10, 1998, and titled "Accused Rapist Had Been Jailed."

> According to police, the man rammed his car into the woman's vehicle about 7 P.M. Wednesday. The woman later told

police she got out and the man then pushed her into his own car, climbed in, and drove south . . . he beat her up and raped her.

Hint to you, husbands: Note the words *"she got out."* Might this be a good time to review security with your wife, and make sure she always keeps her doors locked and has her cell phone with her?

17

PERSONAL COMPUTERS

If you give me six lines written by the most honest man,
I will find something in them to hang him.

—CARDINAL RICHELIEU

I take precautions that many of you readers have never dreamed of, yet never for a moment do I fool myself into thinking that the data on my computer is secure. And, take note—this chapter discusses neither e-mail nor the Internet. It deals only with a personal, non-networked computer that is never, ever connected to any medium outside the four walls of your home.

Perhaps you have a file or a folder that you wish to keep private because it contains personal letters, financial records, business secrets, pictures, a list of confidential names and addresses, or whatever. Here are some of the ways in which such information could be obtained by others:

- A family member or friend (perhaps of your teenaged children) checks out the history, the cookies, and the Recycle Bin.

- A thief breaks into your home, steals the computer, and sells it through a fence who, in turn, sells it to—who knows?

- The local police get a search warrant based on a false complaint and confiscate your computer. Even though you are later proved innocent, they'll check your hard drive in the meantime with a killer program called EnCase.

- A PI will park his van down the street and—thanks to the "van Eck" emissions from your monitor—will read everything on your screen. *Legally.*

- The FBI targets you for some ephemeral reason but does not have hard evidence to obtain a warrant. Instead, they do a "sneak and peek," a surreptitious entry to check out the hard drive on your computer. Before they leave, they'll install a "key logger," which will record every keystroke you make from then on, *including passwords* . . . and you'll never be the wiser.

If you travel with a laptop, the dangers increase a hundredfold. It is estimated that, in the year 2003, more than seven hundred thousand laptops were stolen. Some were left in taxis by mistake. Some disappeared after being left too long at the far end of the airport scanning machines. Others were stolen from hotel rooms, or snatched at the airport when the owner set his laptop down for "just a moment."

ENCRYPTED FILES

If you are willing to put forth the time and the effort, this may keep out family members and the lower class of private investigators. However, if your computer falls into the hands of government agents or the metropolitan police, the hard drive will almost surely talk. I no sooner read about a new encryption system than I read about how it can be cracked. In many cases, secret information has been encrypted, then later overwritten three or four times. It is still not safe, because programs such as Microsoft Word or Lotus 1-2-3 make *temporary* copies that may linger on.

Your best protection will be in *multiple rings of defense.* Multiple overlapping layers are often less expensive than putting everything into one big fancy technology. Further, they seem more secure to me, because you are not subject to a single point of failure.

HIDE THE LOCATION

This is your outer layer. As often mentioned in this book, no one outside the circle of your close friends and (perhaps) relatives should know where you live. If investigators cannot find you, they cannot alter, add to, or confiscate your computer. The same applies if you work in a private office away from home. If you fear surreptitious entry when absent from your home or office, here are two suggestions:

- use a notebook computer only, and take it with you when you leave, or
- use a computer with a removable hard drive and take the hard drive with you when you leave.

FORTIFY THE ROOM

This is your second layer of defense. Gerry L———, a close friend of mine for the past forty years, writes and sells computer programs for small businesses all over Spain. He has a suite of rooms in a high-rise office building on Tenerife Island with a single entrance door. The outside of this door appears normal, but it is backed on the inside with a steel plate. When it's locked, a remote signal slides iron bars across the back. All windows face the open sea, which protects Gerry against being monitored by laser, and he uses only laptops with screens and fonts designed to foil anyone trying to monitor the low-level radiations.

At home, of course, a steel entrance door may be of little help, because of all the windows. However, if your computer is in a room in the basement or on an upper floor, why not install a reinforced door? If you add a keyless electronic access control, you'll be able to thwart PIs and/or government agents despite their lock-picking tools and skills.

Often, however, the computer will be kept in a ground-floor guest bedroom that is being used as a home office. If you have a desktop computer, hooked up to one or more printers and perhaps a scanner as well, you won't want to move it every time you leave the house empty for a short time. In this case, you may wish to install a long narrow table across the back of the closet, and then have a carpenter install secure doors that can lock everything inside.

THE THIRD LAYER FOR DESKTOP COMPUTERS

First, purchase two removable hard-drive trays, along with one hard drive for each tray. (With prices constantly dropping, this is no longer expensive.) Install an operating system in each tray— let's call them A and B. The operating systems can be the same, or different.

When you are working with confidential material, use A. When finished, slide that out and insert B. As long as you hide A in a secure place, you need not worry about having the computer picked up. Since nothing confidential has ever been entered on this hard drive, not even the NSA could find the data. The benefit of this method is that the hard drive in your confiscated machine looks like one that is actually used, so who is to say there is another hard drive and operating system somewhere else? One of my readers takes this a step further and uses three hard drives and trays.

"The first one," she writes, "is for normal day-to-day use. The second one is a decoy, 'hidden' in the same room. The third one is *really* hidden, and well away from the premises." In other words, if an intruder gets into her office, checks out her computer and suspects there may be another hard drive, he'll think the search is over when he finds her second hard drive.

For most of us, using three separate hard drives is overkill. If you go that route, however, I suggest you make it believable. Download a large text file of innocuous material from the Internet and then encrypt it. Tolstoy's *War and Peace* works well, with its more than 600,000 words. Do make sure, however, to remember the password, because, in an extreme case, a judge may order you to either *un*encrypt it or go to jail!

THE THIRD LAYER FOR
LAPTOP COMPUTERS

Instead of multiple hard drives and trays, put only the operating systems and software programs on the hard drive. All else goes on to removable storage units, the kinds that fit into a PCMCIA card slot, a CompactFlash slot (for insertion of cf cards or a Hitachi Microdrive), or in the USB port. Then, when you delete a file, it disappears rather than goes to the Recycle Bin.

When you get ready to enter confidential information, just pop out the everyday storage unit and slip in the clearly marked confidential one. When not in use, keep the latter in a secure hiding place in another room or in the garage. This will keep anyone from seeing the actual files. (Note for the truly paranoid types who worry about experts who can find *anything*: Windows does leave little scraps in unallocated spaces on the hard drive, so if this is a concern, you'll have to swap hard drives that contain the operating system as well as the files. However, that's overkill for most of us.)

WHAT ABOUT THE FOURTH AMENDMENT?

The Fourth Amendment to the U.S. Constitution states, "The right of the people to be secure in their persons, houses, papers, and effects, against unreasonable searches and seizures, shall not be violated, and no Warrants shall issue, but upon probable cause, supported by Oath or affirmation, and particularly describing the place to be searched, and the persons or things to be seized."

With respect to criminal prosecution, the amendment applies solely to "the State" and agents of the state. Therefore, if a non-law-enforcement person sneaks into your home and finds what appears to be incriminating evidence, it can be turned over to the police and will probably be admissible in court. (The court will want to make sure, of course, that the evidence was obtained without a suggestive direction from law enforcement, such as, "We think there might be some evidence but (*wink-wink*) we're not allowed to go get it."

Conclusion: PIs may be more of a threat to you than the authorities, and if they put one of those key-logging devices on your desktop, changing hard drives or PC cards will not protect you.

PASSWORDS

Never store your passwords in your wallet, purse, a sticky-note back on the monitor, or in your PDA. Also, be very careful about those password-hint options at Web sites. Make sure the hint won't be a giveaway to those who know you well.

Here are a few of the most common passwords that should never be used under any circumstances, because even preteens can guess them:

mypass123	administrator	abc123
mypass	patrick	abcd
pw123	alpha	database
admin123	123abc	passwd
mypc123	1234qwer	pass
mypc	123123	88888888
love	121212	11111111
Login	111111	00000000
login	2600	000000
owner	2003	54321
home	2002	654321
zxcv	enable	123456789
yxcv	godblessyou	12345678
qwer	ihavenopass	1234567
secret	123asd	123456
asdf	super	12345
temp123	Internet	1234
temp	computer	Password
test123	server	password
test	123qwe	Admin
foobar	sybase	admin
root	oracle	

However, you should know that computer forensic experts use
password-cracking programs that can pull up any real word *in any
language*. A good friend once used one of these programs to attack
a secret file that was protected by a nine-digit password, author

unknown. When the English program failed, he went to Spanish, then French, then German, then Italian. The seventeenth language he tried was Pakistani, and the password that broke the code turned out to be the name of a relative in Pakistan.

So then, form the habit of never, ever using a real word in any language. Instead, use the first letters of a short sentence you can easily remember. Eight digits should be your minimum. *Example:* The phrase "I was born and raised in North Dakota" translates to "iwbarind."

Next, substitute a symbol for one of the vowels. In the example just given, let's change the "a" to "@." We now have "iwb@rind." Any password formed in this matter should certainly be secure . . . or will it?

RAYMOND V———, a professional paranoid, has a secret office in his home that has triple locks and is protected against CO2 laser-reflective sound being picked up from the window. (He keeps a small massage vibrator on the windowsill, behind the screen, where it can touch the glass.) Two vicious Dobermans patrol the yard behind a chain-link fence.

Raymond—expert in the use of encryption—now compiles a list of names and addresses for a secret mailing list. He protects this list by using PGP encryption that he has compiled himself. He makes sure he's running a clean version, and he chooses as his password **lutl1fml**. He commits this password to memory ("I used to love Ingrid from Muncie, Indiana," substituting the number "1" for the letter "i") so that no one can ever find it even if he's raided. He never encrypts a message while online, so no one can monitor the data line. He even wipes his swap file so there'll be no trace of the password anywhere.

No one, *NO ONE*, he vows, will ever get this password out of him unless they clip wires to his most sensitive parts and crank up the voltage. And, since he lives in the USA instead of some place like Mexico, Paraguay, or North Korea, torture (aka "rubber-hose cryptography") is not an option.

Nevertheless, unless Raymond protects himself against the dreaded "Tempest" as well, his so-called secret password can be plucked from the air without so much as a nod to the Dobermans.

TEMPEST AND VAN ECK

Although these two terms are sometimes used interchangeably, they are not the same thing. "Tempest" is a set of standards used by the government to gauge and reduce electromagnetic emanations from electronic equipment. The radiations themselves are often referred to as "van Eck" radiations, named after Dutch scientist Wim van Eck, who published an unclassified paper on the subject back in 1985.

Tempest frequencies run from commercial AM stations to the upper reaches of 600 MHz, and thus cover transmissions from your TV set, your stereo system, your microwave oven, your wireless alarm system, your cordless phone, *and your computer.* Your desktop monitor acts as a radio transmitter, sending out signals in the 2 to 20 MHz range. (These resemble broadcast TV signals, although various forms of sync will require restoration.) Also, if your computer is attached to a telephone line, that will make an excellent antenna—transmitting signals all over the neighborhood.

So then, your keyboard strokes are transmitted into the air and onto conduit pipes and power lines. Any digital oscilloscope, in the hands of a professional, can detect the leaking signals with ease. Therefore, when Raymond types in his password, the man with the van Eck receiver in the Ford van down the street sees that password magically appear on his screen!

Your printer, too, can betray your privacy. The NSA uses a classified technique called "diagram analysis" to assist in eavesdropping on van Eck emanations from printers. Remember, all monitoring of your equipment is passive, and therefore cannot be detected. Unless you take protective measures, an information

warrior can, with the proper frequency tuning, antenna manipu-
lation, reintroduction of sync, and vehicle location, monitor you
anyplace, anywhere, anytime.

PROTECTIVE MEASURES

1. Use laptop computers only. Laptop screens give off just a
   fraction of the radiation from desktop monitors.

2. Given a choice, live at least two blocks away from your
   nearest neighbor. Check the window from time to time to
   see if a strange van is parked in the street. (If there is any
   doubt, stop using your computer until you check it out.) A
   second choice would be to live in a senior-citizen development, since old folks (like me!) are less likely to have
   expertise—not to mention the desire—to monitor their
   neighbors.

3. Never connect this computer to a telephone line. (If a connection is required for sending and receiving harmless
   e-mails, use a second laptop with a clean hard drive.)

4. Prepare a radio frequency–free room. Two of my readers
   described a similar method. It involves lining the walls and
   doors with overlapping copper mesh screen panels glued to
   the wall. As one reader further describes it: "A ground wire
   connects the mesh to the neutral ground wire of the elec-
   trical socket on each wall. A small copper wire connects
   each aluminum window screen to the wire wall mesh, and
   connects the doors to the wall mesh as well. The neutral
   lead on my house current is grounded in two ways—once
   to the copper pipe that brings water into the house, and
   once outside with a bronze 'grounding plate' used on
   boats, buried 6" underground. *No* RF [radio frequency]
   goes in or out of that room. I covered the wire mesh on
   the walls with wallpaper. *A word of warning, however:* All

the RF protection goes away once you 'plug in' to a tele-phone line."

To see what an ideal secure RF-free computing room looks like, rent the movie *Enemy of the State*. Will Smith and Gene Hackman are on the run, and they head back to a secret lab—"Brill's hideout"—in an abandoned building. This lab was modeled after recommendations from several computer security experts and they got it right.

Warning: If you live in a totalitarian country and are composing a list of freedom fighters, the above solutions will be incomplete. Obtain and study the book *Desktop Witness*, by Michael A. Caloy-annides (reviewed at the end of the next chapter). If you think that mere encryption will solve your problems, Caloyannides will disabuse you of that notion.

MORE ADVANTAGES OF LAPTOP COMPUTERS

I got rid of my last desktop computer eight years ago, and replaced it with an IBM ThinkPad. Since then I've bought five more. The operating systems are on the hard drives, but my files are on removable PC cards. Although I've never built an RF-free room, I know that the van Eck radiations from my laptop screens are far less than those from a normal desktop computer. Also, since we have no close neighbors and I can see for nearly half a mile down the narrow entrance road, I lose no sleep over Tem-pest dangers. Consider these additional advantages:

1. *Travel:* When I go through airport security, and when I leave the hotel, I slip the PC card into a pocket. (According to the fake label on the card, it's a modem.)

2. *Recovery:* Last year the motherboard on my newest ThinkPad suddenly died. I just slipped out the PC card, inserted it into a second ThinkPad, and kept working.

3. **Security:** When I later dropped the dead computer off at a repair shop to see if it could be fixed, there were no personal files on the hard drive.

4. **Invisibility:** Compared to desktop computers, laptops are obviously a snap to hide. I never build a home without including a small, secret room. When the away from home for a day or more, any laptop not with me is resting quietly there.

Note: As I write this, it appears that SanDisk has stopped making the PCMCIA cards—I just had to go to a liquidator for my last order of 350 MB cards ($59 each). However, there are many alternatives out there; one place to start looking is at *www.mobile-planet.com*. They offer CompactFlash to PC card adapters, Type I CompactFlash Memory Cards, Secure Digital Cards, and an all-in-one device called the SanDisk Cruzer that utilizes the USB port on a computer. Another device that also plugs into the USB port is the Targus 64 MB KeyDrive, which clips onto your shirt pocket or keychain. Similar to the Targus is DiskOnKey, designed to work under Windows 2000/ME/XP/NT 4/CE 4, Mac OS 9.0 and higher, and Linux 2.4.0 without software drivers. Sizes run up to 512 MB. Many more brands and types will be on the market by the time you are reading this.

QUESTIONS AND ANSWERS

How can I dispose of an old hard drive?

If possible, do something similar to what they do in the Marine Corps: sand the top off with a belt sander. Or burn it. At the very least, hammer it into bits and pieces and then drop them off a bridge.

Couldn't a PI who secretly enters my home to install a keylogger be prosecuted for trespass?

In theory, yes, but according to both a detective I spoke with and a Harvard-trained prosecutor, since the question is about prosecution criteria, the answer is almost invariably no. Trespass is a minor crime that a prosecutor will seldom mess with, knowing that even if he does file, jurors will seldom convict.

Where should I buy a new computer?

If you are buying a desktop computer, just go to a store and buy a new one in a box. However, I strongly recommend you buy a laptop, and for a good one, you may have to resort to mail order. If at all possible, arrange to make payment by sending in a bank check or money order in advance. Or use someone else's credit card and hand them the money—plus a little extra—up front. (In this case, the computer may have to be shipped to their address, but if not, use your ghost address.) And when you boot up for the first time and must fill in some blanks, don't even think of using your own name. (You can often get by with an "x" or a zero.)

What if I forget my password and thus lose a file I really need?

The protection against losing a password is to use a personal fingerprint reader, such as that found at *www.digitalpersona.com*. These readers convert your print into a unique digital string that becomes your password. Just don't lose that finger!

Is it safe to buy a standard-model wireless keyboard?

Not unless your nearest neighbor lives at least several blocks away. Remember, unlike those operating with beams of infrared light—which are perfectly safe—wireless keyboards transmit radio signals and thus might reveal a password or a credit card number. Logitech reps claim their RF wireless keyboards scramble security codes each time your computer boots up, but that is of little help to those of us who leave our computers running twenty-four hours a day. Microsoft offers Bluetooth, a radio system that encrypts the transmissions—but that system has already been broken by experts. My advice is to avoid this keyboard problem by switching to a laptop. Many notebook computers include Bluetooth for communication with other equipment. I leave Bluetooth turned off and I suggest you do the same.

18

E-MAIL AND
THE INTERNET

Lasciate ogni speranza, voi ch'entrate.
—DANTE ALIGHIERI, *THE DIVINE COMEDY*

The above inscription at the entrance to Hell ("Leave behind all hope, ye who enter!") applies to those who surf the Internet, send and receive e-mails, and imagine that they can avoid all dangers and remain invisible forever. Dante's medieval classic epic is fraught with lust, gluttony, anger, betrayal, sodomy, and things unspeakable. The Internet is fraught with scams, frauds, stalkers, hackers, illegal drugs, hate groups, online gambling, Satanic cults, pornography, cybersex, and pedophiles.

Author Bruce Schneier, speaking of computer "security" on the Internet, says, "The only secure computer is one that's turned off, locked in a safe, and buried twenty feet down in a secret location—and I'm not completely confident about that one, either." Neither am I, and yet I see no other way to run my Web site, keep in daily touch with readers worldwide, and do constant research without entering the scary world of cyberspace. If there were any other way I could do these things, I'd say ¡*Adios para siempre!* to the Internet.

If you are not yet connected to this etherworld and have no pressing need to do so, count yourself fortunate. Otherwise, continue to remind yourself that everything you say, everything you do, every Web site you visit, is being written down in a big black book. It may never be consulted, but who can tell? If you are ever under suspicion, this "book" will be checked out. The pages will come to life from your hard drive, from the records at your ISP, from vendors, from the files of those who have received your e-mails, from government interceptions, and from places not yet revealed.

YOUR HOME COMPUTER

If you already have a computer, and have not previously been security-conscious, then your name is almost certainly inside your computer somewhere. When you connect to the outside world, remember that electronic traffic moves in both directions. Therefore, if you have a computer, your name is probably already in it, along with your address, your telephone number, and other personal details. To purge this information, you must go into the registry—a delicate process indeed—so if you're not 100 percent sure you can do it, call in professional help.

In the future, when you purchase a computer, do not, under any circumstances whatsoever, fill in your true name, address, telephone number, or any other personal data. If the computer will not start up or the software will not load until you fill in the blanks, put in something like Bob or Suzy, with a fake address in Canada or Europe. If a telephone number *must* be entered, use 555 after the area code, as this number will not belong to anyone. Example: 307-555-1234. Only after your computer has been certified as squeaky-clean, should you consider connecting to the Internet.

YOUR INTERNET SERVICE PROVIDER

The moment you sign up for an Internet account, your invisibility begins to fade. At the government's request, every Internet Service Provider (ISP) must furnish—with no advance notice to you—the following information about your account:

- The name you gave them, and the address where bills are sent.

- Records of your Internet sessions (including session times and duration).

- Your telephone number or other subscriber account identifying number(s); including any Internet or network addresses assigned to you.

- The source of your payments, including any credit card or bank account numbers.

- The content of, and other records relating to, your electronic mail messages, including attachments.

Can you get by with a false name, a P.O. box address, and pay the bills by money order? Yes . . . but if the government ever decides to go after you, the ISP will be forced to give up the source of your connections—the telephone line that leads straight to your office or home.

ISP ALTERNATIVE

You might consider setting up an account under another name with a cellular provider that offers wireless Internet access. Then get a national ISP, and have the bills sent to a ghost address in Canada. When you call in, choose a city on the opposite coast from where you are located. This will be expensive, but if money is not a problem, then you will certainly be able to confuse anyone attempting to track you down.

CHAT ROOMS

A "chat room" is a place on the Internet where you can communicate "live" with either an individual person or with a group. At the same moment you type a sentence on the screen, it appears on another screen—or on multiple screens. Neither you, nor your mate, nor your children will know whom you are really dealing with. Teens and preteens are especially attracted to chat rooms, where they can instantly connect with others from around the globe. Your twelve-year-old daughter may think her new pal is a fourteen-year old boy from London, but he *could* be a middle-aged pedophile in your very same state. I consider pornography to be the second worst plague on the Internet. The first is the chat rooms. Would you send your children out to play in the dry woods with a can of gasoline and some matches, or drop them off in a red-light district and let them wander around alone? Then keep them out of chat rooms. (How to do this is beyond the scope of this book, but I've seen it done.)

Keep yourself out of chat rooms as well. I personally know of two families that were broken up by mates who met someone in a chat room. In one case, it was the husband, in the other, the wife. In both instances, they ran off with their new pal and left not only their mate but their children (!) behind. There are thousands of cases like this, and worse—"adventures" that have ended in robbery, rape, torture, and death.

For the record: I have no personal experience with chat rooms. Never been there. Never will. Before you rush in where this author fears to tread, post Dante's warning above your monitor: *Lasciate ogni speranza, voi ch'entrate.*

NEW DANGERS FROM A KEY LOGGER

In the previous chapter, you learned about the danger of this insidious device that could be surreptitiously planted on your desktop (but not laptop) computer. Once you connect to the Internet, however, the information warrior may be able to plant a key logger on your computer—laptop or not!—even if he lives in Nigeria or Bulgaria. The software, such as NetBus or SubSeven, will be downloaded to your computer if and when you click on an unknown attachment or on a Web link embedded in an e-mail message. The protections here are obvious:

1. Never open an attachment from a stranger. Even if it *appears* to come from a friend, if you are not expecting it, check back first to find out what it is and where it came from.

2. Never click on a link in an e-mail that arrives from an unknown person. Not even the ones like *www.whitehouse. com* or *www.teenagegirlsgonewild.com*.

"SAFETY" ON THE INTERNET

Before we left the United States in 1959, we banked at the Liberty State Bank in Powers Lake, North Dakota—a rural community forty miles from the nearest paved road. A few years ago, we took a little trip down memory lane, and one of our stops was at the Liberty State Bank, where we had a chat with one of the officers. I brought up the subject of how hackers and crackers can get into any bank they care to target, and extract whatever information they are after.

"Not in Powers Lake," he said with a smile. "C'mon back." We were led into a room where a young lady sat at a single desktop computer. "This is where we connect to the outside world. For example, suppose we have an incoming wire transfer. The information is saved to a disk. The disk is then removed from the computer, taken across the room, and entered in this computer, which puts it into the mainframe."

Ah hah—the hacker would have to bridge an air gap. I was ready to open an account on the spot, if the requirements for picture ID and the Social Security number could be waived. The answer was no.

"Not even for old times' sake?"

" 'For old times' sake' is not an excuse the *federales* will accept."

This experience, nevertheless, does illustrate one of the better ways to access the Internet without exposing your personal files to those who seek to do you harm.

1. Buy a cheap, used laptop, such as a three-year-old ThinkPad.

2. Enter whatever programs you use, including the Norton SystemWorks, which includes an antivirus. Download a firewall, such as Zone Alarm. This is the computer you will use for Internet access.

3. Save everything that comes in on a removable media, rather than on the hard drive. Transfer the data by taking out the PC card (or whatever you use) and inserting it in what we'll call your "home base" computer. For files to send out, reverse the process.

I make no claim that this method will solve *all* problems—a virus or a Trojan horse can pass from one computer to the other on a disk or a card—but if you've already taken the precautions outlined in the preceding chapter, you'll at least discourage the opposition.

FIREWALLS AND ANTIVIRUS

The firewall I recommend (assuming you have only one computer at home) is the basic Zone Alarm, which can be downloaded free from *www.zonelabs.com*. To quote from their Web site:

> Without a firewall, your computer is operating under an "open door" policy. Bank account information. Passwords. Credit card numbers. Documents and photos that you don't want to share with the world. They are all available to anyone with bad intentions and basic computer skills. Hackers can get in, take what they want, and even leave open a "back door" so they can turn your computer into a "zombie" and use it to attack other computers. Every minute that your computer is connected to the Internet, either through a dial-up (modem) connection or through a broadband (DSL or cable) service, it is at risk.
>
> A firewall is a piece of software that monitors all incoming network traffic and allows in only the connections that are known and trusted. . . . Every time you add a new program that requires Internet access, you would need to determine which port(s) it uses, and reconfigure your computer accordingly. . . . Firewall software takes on this burden for you, allowing access to the ports you need open, and closing off those you don't. It also makes your computer "invisible" on the Internet; if hackers can't find you, they will have a hard time attacking you.

Says computer guru Michael Spaulding: "Zone Alarm is a burglar alarm for ghost intruders but better. In the physical world, a burglar alarm may scare away an intruder but it really does nothing to physically prevent them from intruding. It merely records their presence and/or alerts you, the alarm company, and/or the intruder. Zone Alarm makes you invisible. It hides your presence. When the ghost intruders come knocking on your door (IP address) to see if you exist, Zone Alarm prevents your computer from answering *Here I am and here's who I am!* as it normally would. This eliminates 99.9 percent of your intruder problems. Only if someone knows for sure that your IP address exists, and who you are, and what kind of computer system you have, do they have any chance of successfully targeting you."

Although a firewall should be your very first download, it will not protect you against a virus, and this is a *must-have* when you connect to the Internet. Go to a store like Office Depot or Office-Max and pick up Norton SystemWorks. It includes not only AntiVirus, Utilities, WipeInfo, and CleanSweep (which you can use to clear your cache and cookies every day), but GoBack as well. GoBack lets you restore a crashed system to a previous working state and, when all else fails, GoBack may be your only hope to save the day (as it once saved mine!). For more information, and/or to order Norton SystemWorks, go to *www.symantec.com*.

WHAT ABOUT THOSE "COOKIE" FILES?

A "cookie" is a small piece of information which a Web server can store temporarily on your computer and later retrieve. For example, when you browse through online shopping malls, such as Amazon.com, and add items to your "shopping cart," a list of the items you've picked up is stored by your browser so that you can pay for all of the items at once when you're finished shopping.

Although I've been told by several computer veterans that there is no possible way that a virus could be spread through the use of cookies, the Web sites do use the cookies to track personal information about you. Also, many Web sites still insist on putting IDs and passwords into the cookies. Then, it could be that the next Web site you hit will request and copy down all of your cookies. Now they have an ID and password to another Web site.

On the other hand, if you allow no cookies at all, you will be almost paralyzed on the Internet, but at least you can erase both the cache (which shows the Web sites you've entered) and the cookie files at the end of each day. This should protect your computer against your curious teenagers (or their friends) who are probably knowledgeable enough to know how to look for those files.

USING A COMPUTER AT WORK

Everything I have to say about computers and the Internet applies to using a single computer at home, or in your own private office. None of it applies if you are an employee who has access to a computer at work.

At work, your employer owns all the computers and everything created on them or viewed by them. Do not imagine that you have the level of privilege necessary to clear your cookies and cache, nor that you are skilled enough to locate and defeat a key logger. In fact, expect no privacy of any kind when you work for wages. If you entertain the slightest notion that you are not bare-bottom naked when at work, read *The Naked Employee: How Technology Is Compromising Workplace Privacy*, by Frederick S. Lane (AMACOM, 2003). Some of his chapter headings alone will be enough to scare you:

- Every Paycheck Is a Little Universe of Information
- IDs and Badges
- Microphones and Cameras in the Workplace
- Hardware, Software, and Spyware
- Tracking Employees by Cell: The Electronic Version
- Tracking Employees by Cell: The Biological Version

Zone Alarm will not prevent authorities from finding anything on your computer. Your computer will have exactly the same amount of incriminating evidence, or the lack thereof, regardless of whether Zone Alarm is there or not. It is a firewall—a protective wall that works largely by making you invisible, and logs attempts to intrude. All evidence of your browsing activities, and all your personal files, are the same whether or not you have a product such as Zone Alarm installed.

SCAMS ON THE INTERNET

New Internet extortion techniques arise on a daily basis. Here is a typical example, this one aimed at those of you who use a computer at your place of employment.

1. You receive an unsolicited e-mail containing a link to a seemingly innocuous site, such as a review of the latest SUVs, or a great place to buy laptops at a discount.

2. When you click on the link, a file transfer from a site in Bulgaria is initiated in the background. Files with child pornography are then secretly downloaded to your computer. (Perhaps the extortionists use a malicious Java application that uses reverse tunneling to bypass your company's firewall.)

3. Three days later, you receive an e-mail threat. It accuses you of downloading child pornography and tells you how to find these illegal files on your computer. "Either provide a valid credit card (name, expiration date, and billing address) or we will present this evidence to your boss!"

Unbelievable as it seems, reports show that one out of four employees will actually furnish the credit card details. And only one in twelve will report this threat to his or her employer. Other scams involve opening an attachment instead of clicking on a link. Therefore:

- Never open an incoming attachment unless it is not only from someone you know, but you are either expecting it or there is a valid explanation in the message that accompanies it.

• Never, ever, click on a link that is contained in an unsolicited e-mail from an unknown source.

WHY TO BE EXTREMELY CAREFUL...

Here's an experience that arrived in the mail just as I was preparing this chapter. (Names have been changed.)

Jim and Jane, a young working couple with no children, had long planned a two-week trip to Hawaii. When the time came to leave, they left a key to their home with Jane's brother, Karl. This was to be used only in the case of an emergency.

Upon their return, they picked the key up from Karl and all seemed to be well. Several months passed. One evening, when they returned home from work, they found the computer turned on. Jim was positive it had been off since the previous evening. Alarmed, he checked the history and the cookies and found a sea of child pornography Web sites! He checked all the windows and doors. No trace of a break-in. Jane checked the drawer in her nightstand. The money she kept there had not been touched. This had all the markings of an inside job by someone who had a key.

When contacted, Karl was persuaded to avoid a serious beating by confessing. He'd copied the key they had once left him and had been slipping into their home to use the computer while Jim and Jane were away at work. When an emergency call had come in on his cell phone, in his haste to leave he'd forgotten to clear the history and the cookies and then turn off the computer.

If you are ever caught in such a situation, the first thing to do is to back up the files you need and then destroy the hard drive.

Sand the surface of the disk with a belt sander, melt it down, or hammer it into tiny pieces and then feed them slowly into a fast-moving river. Otherwise, what remains on that drive could some-day be used against you.

As for leaving a key behind, here is how we do it when we plan to be absent for a period of time. A key is hidden outside in such a way that not even the Homeland Security boys will ever find it. If an emergency should ever come up (and so far it never has), our neighbor Maggie has instructions to call my pager number. I will then call her back and describe in detail the hidden location of the key. Maggie is in her eighties and doesn't know a modem from a monitor. In fact, she'll never *see* the computers, because I leave them in an undetectable secret room.

NOTHING ON THE INTERNET IS SECURE

A message itself, when sent over the Internet, can be encrypted with Pretty Good Privacy (PGP), and perhaps the keys can be successfully hidden, but the *senders and receivers can be identified*, as even superhacker Kevin Mitnick learned, to his sorrow. I recently had a chat with Michael Paciello, author of *WEBable* and an international consultant on Internet privacy. For more than two hours, I fired questions at him about making e-mail more private. "What about a fictitious name on a Web-based account? What about PGP encryption? What about putting e-mail on disks and sending them out at Cybersmith? Or with a prepaid phone card? Or mailing the disk to London for resending?"

"Jack," he answered, "nothing you've suggested is secure, as far as hiding who *sends* the message and who *receives* it. If someone gives me a compelling motive, sufficient time, and unlimited expense money, I'll trace your e-mails any time, any place, any-where!"

ANONYMOUS AND PSEUDOANONYMOUS PROXIES

If you wish to send an e-mail to someone and hide the fact it came from you, you might send it to a remailer. This is a service that will strip away your old identity, give you a new one, and then send your e-mail to its final destination. There are many popular remailers, although some have a short life.

A *pseudoanonymous remailer* will know your actual e-mail address. This means that someone could get a court order to force the remailer operator to reveal this address.

An *anonymous remailer* is more secure. Nobody, not even the remailer service, knows who you are. Also, an anonymous remail can be sent via a string of remailers—otherwise known as chain remail—making it even more secure. However, this is quite complicated, and for that reason seldom used. I do not use remailers, because:

1. It is almost a certainty that some of these remailers are sting operations run by the government. They are specifically designed to trap you.

2. There is a PI who runs seminars for other PIs, teaching them how to track down those who send anonymous e-mails. (I sent him an e-mail asking for details and received this reply: "Why would I want to give information to someone writing a book about how to hide assets and identities, when that is the very thing that I investigate? Don't you think it would be rather stupid of me . . . ?")

3. Hackers can and do break into these systems, unknown to the remailer's administrator. They can then read and copy messages at will. (In one well-known case, an unknown hacker worked out a method to send messages via a remailer in such a way that if the recipient answered in a similar fashion, his true name and address would be instantly captured!)

4. Some believe—and I am one of them—that the U.S. government collects, scans, and stores all messages, *including passcodes*, that go into and out of the remailers.

THE SECRET OF MAKING YOUR HARD DRIVE SQUEAKY-CLEAN

Learn from my latest "computer-expert" experience. On my recent trip to one of the biggest cities on the West Coast, my laptop modem suddenly slowed down. I was told that [name deleted] was the place to go. I hurried over to see them, prepared to pay whatever it took to put me first in line. When I entered the modern store, new and used laptops stared out at me from glistening glass display cases all around. The head guru (young, pale complexion, scraggly goatee, pimples, multiple earrings) came out from the back room to see me.

"New hard drives," I asked, "in all the used laptops?"

"No need, my man. Reformatted, every one."

"That's all?"

"You reformat a hard drive, man, that sucker's *clean!* Now what's your problem?"

My problem was that I'd come to the wrong place. I said so, and left. Two weeks later, I came into possession of some details about a homicide investigation in progress. In this case, suspect #1 owns the computer confiscated by the police, and suspect #2 is the young man suspected of murder. The computer forensics examiner writes:

> Don't know if you remember but, a couple of weeks ago I asked for some tips on locating e-mail scraps from a hard drive in a murder investigation. We were joking when we got started, making comments like, "Wouldn't it be great if we just found a Word document that said 'I did it!'" I entered a couple of keyword

searches using one of the suspect's Hotmail addresses. Bam, in like two minutes, after EnCase stopped chewing on the hard drive, we found this scrap of an e-mail where one of the suspects is telling the other one that he is going to do the murder. The scrap contained *both of their e-mail addresses, first names, and a pretty darn good confession.*

The point is that suspect #2, who is the owner of the computer, deleted the [expletive] from the hard drive and wiped it to the point that it wouldn't even boot up without a rescue disk. Still, we nailed it!

Note: When the detective mentions "EnCase," he is referring to Guidance Software's EnCase Forensic Edition, a software program that searches digital storage media for data from deleted files, file slack, and unallocated disk spaces, views TIFF and fax files, and pulls up other bits and pieces that are no longer "supposed" to be in there. It is used by police departments, the CIA, the FBI, NSA, and even the London Metropolitan Police Service. They call it their "standard tool to fight computer crime."

THE ONE SURE WAY TO SEND A SECRET MESSAGE

No, it does not involve e-mail. An e-mail message may linger on backup tapes for years on end—then come back to haunt you. (They are increasingly being used in civil and criminal cases.) Teach your children that a silly or profane e-mail in their youth could come back to bite them many years down the line.

If you or anyone in your family has a confidential message to send, do as I do. Seal it in an envelope, stamp it, and mail it.

ACKNOWLEDGMENTS

For these two chapters about computers and the Internet, I received help from a police detective in a large city who is an expert in both computer forensics and information security, and especially from Michael Spaulding, computer guru extraordinaire. (Michael can be reached at infosecguro@swissinfo.org and usually responds within twenty-four hours.)

RECOMMENDED READING

In the field of protecting private information on your computer, the following two books stand alone. The first shows you how to protect the information on your personal computer. The second warns you about "pretexting" that can make an end run around protective hardware and software.

Desktop Witness: The Do's and Don'ts of Personal Computer Security, by Michael A. Caloyannides (John Wiley & Sons, 2002). Michael—a Senior Fellow at Mitretek Systems in Virginia—is an expert in the fields of information assurance, network security, computer forensics, and other related security areas.

The Art of Deception: Controlling the Human Element of Security, by Kevin D. Mitnick and William L. Simon (John Wiley & Sons, 2002). Mitnick is the most famous computer hacker in the world. According to *Publishers Weekly*, the book "is a tour de force, a series of tales of how some old-fashioned blarney and high-tech skills can pry *any* information from *anyone*." [Italics added.]

QUESTIONS & ANSWERS

Should I worry about file sharing? How about music transfer/ trading programs?

I don't like music/movie sharing, because it draws a great deal of unwanted attention. Also, it doesn't save you much, because it ties up a connection for hours on end. In addition, you are inviting outsiders into your computer. The sharing portion opens your system up to other users, and if something is incorrectly placed into the wrong directory, that information can also be uploaded. (A popular program, Kazaa—similar to Napster—was actually using its software to gather personal information about the users, so that they could sell pop-up information to advertisers.)

What do you think about automatic online bill paying?

Not much. Jeffrey P———, a project leader who develops computer systems for Sharp Electronics Corporation in New Jersey, says that although he must write about forty checks per month, he is concerned about privacy and security. "I work with computer systems," he says, "and know the dangers well. With all that information coming from [the billing companies] to banks, somebody is likely to foul something up."

Computer guru Michael Spaulding adds that "in many cases the providers require certain controls (Java or Active-X) to be downloaded to your machine where they will take information from your system (ISP account name, local time, etc.). This definitely compromises your privacy."

Do you recommend that I install SpectorSoft Spyware on our family computer, so I can check on the kids?

Unfortunately, no. According to some sources, this software is vulnerable to abuse, because *it can send information back to SpectorSoft.* (Reference: *www.interhack.net/pubs/spector/.*)

If I leave my laptop at a repair shop, could they somehow install a key logger?

If you refer to hardware, then this is possible but by no means easy. A repairman might be able to disassemble an existing physical keystroke logger and do the modifications necessary to place it into a laptop. However, the assemblies on laptops are extremely sensitive. The man would have to have significant experience in the disassembly and reassembly of a particular laptop. Actually, if he had your laptop in his possession, he wouldn't need hardware, all he'd have to do would be to install a Trojan horse. He would then wait for you to go online, at which time your preprogrammed computer would send him an e-mail or an instant message, etc. He'd then connect to the Trojan on your computer, at which point he could log your keystrokes (including passwords), view your monitor, even open your microphone (if you have one) so that if you made a phone call, he'd hear your end of the conversation.

However, why would any repairman *want* to do this? The only scenario I can think of is that of a private or federal investigator having you under constant surveillance. In that case, if he saw you drop off a laptop for repair, I can definitely see him bribing or frightening the repairman into doing his bidding. As a general rule, never give the repair guys any personal information, and, if you suspect you are being followed, put the laptop in a brown paper bag and take it to a friend who'll drop it off and pick it up for you. When you leave the house, continue to carry the brown bag (perhaps fluffed up with a sweater you just took off), so that anyone watching you will not realize you made a drop-off.

If I reformat my hard drive, will that get rid of every last file forever?

Bits and pieces may still remain. At the very least, do this: (1) wipe the hard drive with a program like *Norton WipeInfo;* (2) defragment the disk; (3) run a different "wiping" program on the now-defragmented disk. However, a better solution is to just install a new hard drive.

Will Zone Alarm protect my privacy in any way?

No, Zone Alarm is merely a protective wall that works largely by making you invisible, and logs all attempts to intrude. Your hard drive will have exactly the same amount of incriminating evidence—or the lack thereof—regardless of whether the firewall was running or not. All evidence of your browsing activities, and all your personal files, are the same whether or not you have a product such as Zone Alarm installed.

How can I tell if someone is attacking my computer?

You will never know if someone is taking advantage of your systems unless you check the logs. Therefore, go to www. TinySoftware.com and purchase Tiny Firewall for about $40. (It is just as effective as BlackIce, Zone Alarm, or Norton Personal Firewall.) Next, go to www.sawmill.net and get Sawmill for about $100. This will take the logs and put them into an easier-to-read format. Once you have these installed, you must still remember to *check the logs.*

I travel with a notebook computer—how can I slip secret computer files past customs when entering a country with a repressive regime?

First, never enter the files on your hard drive in the first place. (If they are already there, then change hard drives.) Use a notebook that will take a CompactFlash card. Carry a portable CD/MP3 player that takes the same cf card, and keep that card in the player. Have a file in there that will play music (if tested). The rest of the files can be pulled up on your notebook once you are safely at your destination.

Another system—one I once used—was to mix a CD (filled with files, not music) in with other music CDs. It had a label saying it was Elvis's greatest hits, and sailed through with no problem.

How can I access the Internet from my hotel room if I am in a remote area with no local dial-up number?

You can program your laptop to dial out of a hotel room by using a prepaid phone card such as the one sold by Costco. First, go though the process of calling your Internet Service Provider at any of the dial-up numbers in other cities. Carefully note how many seconds are needed to pause after dialing 9, then after calling the toll-free card number, then after pressing 1 for English, and so on.

Next, open Internet Explorer, click on TOOLS, then INTERNET OPTIONS and then CONNECTIONS. When you arrive at the dial-up settings, click to ADD a new number. Give it a name, like COSTCO CARD. Enter the area code (such as 800) in the first box. The second box is where it gets tricky. To allow for pauses, enter a comma for each second.

Here is an example of how the complete number may look: 9,,1-800-555-1234,,,,,,,1,,,,9876543,,,,,1-212-555-1234.   (The last number is for your ISP access.)

What problems might there be in installing a wireless network in our home?

Wireless networks are proliferating because they eliminate the need to run cable through basements and attics. However, wireless systems function as transmitters. Some hacker hobbyists drive or walk around and pick up peoples' network traffic, just for fun. Others, however, may be out to get you, especially if you don't bother to use the built-in encryption option (which, in any case, is not infallible.) I know of two different persons—one an expert in private industry, and the other a police detective—who have picked up these transmissions from more than five miles away!

One of my readers who works in this field recently wrote, "I just wanted to let you know that I've had a significant increase in the number of wireless sites getting broken into, including private homes. You may want to warn others to use their wireless networks with caution or—better yet—just use cables/wire. I am currently consulting with a lawyer about one of his clients who had personal financial and medical info stolen from his home computer by a neighbor."

Am I safe enough in keeping secret files on my home computer, since they are all encrypted?

If your home is ever searched, count on your computer being hauled away. And, when put to the test, it will talk. I no sooner read about a new encryption system than I read about how it can be cracked. In many cases, secret information has been encrypted, then later overwritten three or four times. Pretty safe, eh? Not necessarily. Many programs, such as Microsoft Word or Lotus 1-2-3, make *temporary* copies that may linger on.

Unless you have a truly secret room in your home, I suggest following the advice listed back on page 199, namely:

- use a notebook computer only, and take it with you when you leave, or
- use a computer with a removable hard drive and take the hard drive with you when you leave.

Here's something else to worry about—just in case you and your spouse are not getting along. There are many companies that offer to snoop into any computer you bring them. Prices range from $150 to $250 an hour and they seldom fail to bring up supposedly secret files. In a recent nasty divorce case, the wife suspected her husband was not declaring all his savings or investments. She hired a computer snoop to search her husband's computer. Bingo! Up came a record of his inquiries to an online service that he'd been using to track his unreported stocks. If you still have confidence in your exotic encryption system, consider this. If a lawsuit is filed and you are deposed, you will be asked under oath to explain why you have encrypted these files.

19

HOW TO SECRETLY RUN A HOME-BASED BUSINESS

A little inaccuracy sometimes saves tons of explanation.
—SAKI, *THE SQUARE EGG* (1924)

"Are You Zoned for Business?" That was the title of an article in *Home Office Computing*. The subtitle was "*Registering Your Home Office Is a Difficult but Necessary Evil.*"

In chapter 1, you will recall, I said, ". . . if I mention any procedure which I suspect might be construed as illegal in some states or provinces, I will warn you of that fact beforehand and let you make your own decision." When it comes to working at home without registering for a business license, consider yourself warned.

The authorities seldom if ever send out patrols to search for violators. Rather, they depend upon tips from your competitors or complaints from the neighbors. Further, the usual result of a complaint is merely a warning, so stay cool and keep these tips in mind:

- Never, ever tell your neighbors about your business.

- Do not have your customers or clients come to your home.

- Never receive deliveries at home—but then, you already knew that. The best invisible business is run by mail, phone, e-mail, and/or the Internet. Receipts can be cash and money orders, deposited in various nominee accounts. There will be no bounced checks. No one will know your age, race, background, or if you're a first cousin to the Roswell aliens.

You can sell such a business to someone else in any state or—in some cases—any nation in the world. In 1989, someone I know very well started a mail-order business from the spare bedroom in his cheap tract house in a small town in Nevada. The initial investment was $1,500. The product had to do with a paralegal service that was attractive to Europeans. The first year all he did was break even, so he lived on his savings. Then sales began to grow by word of mouth. In 1992, he withdrew a six-figure bonus (using a convoluted tax-free transaction) and kept working. In 1994, a privacy-oriented entrepreneur from Bellevue, Washington, purchased 100 percent of the stock in the corporation that owned the customer list for $500,000.

Not a single neighbor knew a business had been run from that home, much less that he had been netting up to $20,000 a month before taxes. And the taxes weren't all that much—90 percent of the stock was in a charitable remainder unitrust, not subject to income tax. (A detail beyond the scope of this book.) However, the basic reason for starting the business was *privacy*. The fact that it did better than expected was a bonus.

SHOULD YOU WORK "OFF THE BOOKS?"

Millions do it, and it certainly gives you privacy . . . unless, of course, you are caught. Nothing very private about getting arrested! I have never evaded incomes taxes nor have I ever recommended that course to anyone else. Why cheat and run the risk of a jail sentence when there are so many ways to make money and keep enough for yourself legally?

Loompanics Unlimited (Port Townsend, Washington) publishes a small paperback book titled *How to Do Business "Off the Books"*, by "Adam Cash." There are enough warnings about the IRS in this book to make you more fearful *after* reading it than you were before!

Paladin Press (Boulder, Colorado) publishes a similar book, *Ragnar's Guide to the Underground Economy*. The author lists such occupations as housecleaning, dog-grooming, boat repair, hauling, tree removal, critter control, locksmithing, yard work, window-washing, pet care, house-sitting, photography, carpentry, gunsmithing, chimney-sweeping, roofing, and bookkeeping. An examination of the individual stories told indicates an average annual income of less than $30,000.

Don't even *think* about working "off the books."

ANONYMOUS PROFITS IN REAL ESTATE

Years ago I ran across an aging landlord from Chesapeake, Virginia, named Lonnie Scruggs. For the past ten years, he had been buying old—and I do mean *old*—mobile homes for a few thousand dollars each. He then doubled or tripled the price and financed them at up to 18 percent annual interest. The reason this worked was because his low-income buyers had only two questions: (1) how much down? and (2) how much a month? These deals were easy to sell, because down payments were about $500, and monthly payments were less than $200. (Buyers paid rent to the mobile home park on their own.) Here's why it's so great from the standpoint of privacy:

- You purchase the mobile home for CASH, so no one asks you for credit information.
- You title it in the name of an LLC.
- The renters will either pay cash each month, or make their checks out to whatever name you give them.

Scruggs has two books out on this subject, and although you'll not find them on Amazon.com, several other suppliers on the Internet still stock them. Run a search on Google.com, using "Lonnie Scruggs" and "mobile homes."

INVISIBLE PROFILE

In general, the idea behind running any low-profile business is to keep your name out of the picture, so that you cannot be named in a lawsuit. You will, therefore, run the business in another name. It can be in the name of a nominee only, or with a fictitious business license citing the nominee as the principal. However, a better way is to use an LLC. In fact, some persons use *two* LLCs, with the first one doing business and the second one as the sole member of the first. A totally different method is to use one or more established businesses as a "front," and I just recently dealt with such a business in Boston. Here's some background information.

Thirty-five years ago, I went to the Bombay Bazaar in Las Palmas, Grand Canary, to buy a new watch. At that time, Bulova was at the cutting edge of time-keeping technology, with their electronic Accutron model. Instead of *tick-tick-tick* from a balance movement, the Accutrons emitted a pleasing low-level hum from a tuning fork, and the sweep second hand moved around the dial with silky smoothness rather than by little jerks.

I bought the SkyView model with a transparent dial, and it is still my constant companion. Among other things, it reminds me to "always look for a *second* solution." That is, even when I find a solution for whatever problem, I look for a second one as well. (Bulova failed the test—they neglected to look into quartz movements as a "second solution." Within a few short years, the Japanese, using quartz movements, ran over the Bulova folks like a steamroller.)

I still prefer the tuning-fork technology and am determined to wear my Accutron to the grave. Not long ago, when I was in Dallas on business, the battery in my watch went dead. Thinking there was "no problem," I had a new battery installed. Unknown to me, however, Bulova's 1.35-volt mercuric oxide low-drain battery had been outlawed in the United States because of its mercury content, and jewelers were substituting a different, 1.5-volt battery. The result was that, two weeks later, half of the tuning fork's electronic circuit blew out while I was in a certain city on the East Coast. When I called the Bulova service department at 1-800-233-3350 in Woodside, New York, I was stunned to learn that they refused to carry parts and repair Accutrons any longer. Their miserable excuse was that the 1.35-volt mercury-based batteries were no longer obtainable. But they *are*, in every country of the civilized world, other than the United States. Whoever the guy was at Bulova who first overlooked the quartz movements, he must still be there and is now in charge of public relations!

So where am I going with all this? *I found a solution with a repairman who is I-N-V-I-S-I-B-L-E!*

I started my search by calling jewelers in the Yellow Pages that listed "Bulova" as one of the brands they sold. The first three assured me that Bulova Accutrons could no longer be repaired, but the fourth jeweler was my kind of man. If I'd drop off the watch, he'd see to it that an independent repairman would fix it, and put in a new Eveready #387 1.35-volt mercuric oxide low-drain battery (purchased in Canada).

"May I talk to the repairman, please?"

"No, he doesn't have any contact with the public."

At first I thought the jeweler was just trying to protect a commission, but further investigation showed this was not the case. Whoever the repairman was he dealt only through established dealers, with all checks being made out to the jewelry store. And— listen to this!—the actual repairman had never been seen, and no one had a clue as to his name, address, or telephone number.

The only contact between the stores and the repairman was a courier known as "Tony." Every Friday, Tony, who appeared to be in his late seventies and walked with a limp, made the rounds in this city, picking up and delivering Bulova Accutrons and similar models, receiving payment *in cash.* The storeowners were happy, because they got a commission and rendered a needed service to their customers, and we Bulova Accutron owners were happy to keep our watches running. Could this repair guy be tracked down? Without a subpoena, some industrial-strength threats, or a PI who successfully trailed Tony, I don't think so. And who would want to? Why would anyone care?

Suppose, then, that you wish to set up an invisible, untraceable business, and, for whatever reason, do not want to use a corporation, an LLC, or a nominee. Okay, why not copy the Bulova repairman?

1. Locate retail businesses or public offices where the owners are willing to act on your behalf in return for a commission. Contact them in person or via a representative. Your business could be in repair, replacement, software, small products, information, reports, or any other kind of business where *the customer would contact the store or office.*

2. Checks will be made out to your dealers, and the dealers will pay you or your rep in cash. They will want a receipt for their tax records, but this can be in any business name you like. Who cares; who would ever check?

3. You keep good records with QuickBooks (no audit trail when you correct errors), list the income on your personal tax return (Schedule C), and all's well with your world.

A REVIEW FROM CHAPTER 15

Go back and read the subsection A Typical Order for an LLC. Did you notice the references to a ghost address in Sumas, presigned documents in John's possession, letters and checks first scanned and then sent by e-mail, and order blanks downloaded from the Internet? To Olivia's clients, John is invisible. If he drops dead, Olivia will find someone else to take his place, and none will be the wiser. As for Olivia, she answers e-mails from her clients at any hour, with not a clue as to where she is at the moment. Did you notice that she can work via e-mail almost anywhere in the world? As for those pesky work permits required in foreign lands, think about it. Who needs a permit just to send or receive an e-mail?

QUESTIONS & ANSWERS

What is a "fictitious" business name, something fraudulent?

No, it has nothing to do with anything shady or illegal. State laws require any person who regularly transacts business for profit in the state, under a "fictitious name," to register that business name with the Secretary of State's Office. For a sole proprietorship or partnership, a business name is generally considered "fictitious" unless it contains the full name (first and last name) of the owner or all of the general partners and does not suggest the existence of additional owners. Use of a name that includes words like "company," "associates," "brothers," or "sons," will suggest additional owners and will make it necessary for the business to file and publish the fictitious business name on company letterhead, business cards, in advertising, or on its product.

The problem with a fictitious name is that the owner of the business and the street address will be matters of public record. Although sometimes useful, I seldom recommend a fictitious name.

20

SECRET SPACES, HIDDEN PLACES

Do not put us to death, for there exist in our possession hidden treasures . . .

—JEREMIAH 41:8

Don't laugh when I tell you this, but, after hiding it, be sure you can some day still *remember* wherever it was you hid the machine pistols/ammunition/jewelry and precious stones/ chemical products/clippings/videos/photographs/silver dollars/ negotiable securities/secret maps/compromising documents/ forbidden books/red-hot love letters/whatever.

From 1959 until General Franco ordered Spain's laws to be changed in 1970, my companions and I were hiding small boxes in all of Spain's fifty provinces, and, with the advent of legality, a plaintive cry was heard across the land: "*I can't remember all the places where I hid things!*"

And now, with that warning out of the way, let's discuss how you can hide items of varying sizes and values. Here are the categories:

Small: Valuable stamps, bills, rare coins, diamonds, and other items up to the size of a miniature pistol.

Medium: Documents, books, stacks of letters, and guns up to the size of a rifle.

Large: From computers and file cabinets up to you yourself, your mate, your mother, or your mistress.

In your home, with one exception (a secret alcove, which I'll mention later), do not hide anything in the master bedroom. Burglars, sneaky visitors, police, private investigators, U.S. marshals, agents for the Drug Enforcement Administration (DEA), and members of the Bureau of Alcohol, Tobacco and Firearms (ATF) will look there first. Here are a few suggestions for hiding small items in your home or yard:

- Interior of hollow doors, or inside rolled-up window shades.
- Inside a doghouse or a rabbit hutch, or in the crawl space under the house.
- Under the insulation in the attic (one of my favorites).
- Behind wall phones or cold air return vents.
- In the bottom of dog food or kitty litter bag.
- In the bottom half of double boiler, or a box of sanitary napkins.
- Inside zippered cushions, hollow canes, or umbrellas.
- Inside a guitar or other musical instrument, or in the empty case of an old portable radio.
- In file cabinets (with innocuous file names).
- Inside an old stereo or TV set in the garage.

In any of our various homes, it would seem to be no problem to leave cash and other valuables out in plain view. After all, the addresses are secret, and if the bad guys *can't find* the house, they can't raid it! However, we do keep valuables well hidden, and so should you. Can you guess why?

If a burglar is attracted to your home, it doesn't matter what arrangements have been made for privacy, because it's not *you* he's after, it's the house. On the other hand, since the burglar has (hopefully) never attended a DEA seminar, nor will he have the time for that kind of a search, many of the hiding places on the DEA list are worth considering.

Here are typical ways to hide small, medium, and large items in your home.

Small: Save old junk-mail envelopes. Put a few hundred-dollar bills in each one, and hide them in such places as:

- Sheet music in a piano bench.
- In a hollowed-out section of an out-of-date computer manual.
- In the box of old tax receipts in a storage unit.
- In one of the hanging files in a file cabinet. Slip the envelopes into a file marked "Tax receipts" or some other uninteresting subject.
- Rolled up and inserted into a "foot powder" spray can with a removable bottom.

When my car was stolen from SeaTac airport, the thieves broke open the glove compartment searching, I assume, for a gun. All they found were stacks of what appeared to be junk mail, so they tossed all those envelopes on the floor, and the envelopes were still there when the police recovered the car. The *police* didn't notice, *either*, that two of those so-called junk mail envelopes each had five $50 bills in them.

When I travel, I use a slim dress belt with two sections, each of which will hold three bills folded lengthwise four times. I used to carry six Canadian $1,000 bills, but, in 2001, the Canadian government pulled them off the market. However, about that time euro notes appeared, so I switched to them. The 500 note is *very* popular in Europe and becoming more so in the United States and Canada.

As for outdoor mildew and rustproof storage, nothing beats silver or gold. Although I am not a fan of gold, some readers do like the new Canadian Maple Leafs. These one-ounce gold coins currently sell for about $35 over the spot price of gold, and can be scattered about in very small hiding places indeed. A hundred thousand dollars worth of Maple Leaf coins can be stuffed into a coffee can, in which case you'd have a "medium" sized item to hide. However, since gold pays no interest, and there are dealer commissions in both buying and selling, holding a large quantity of coins has its disadvantages.

Medium: My principal items in this category are reference books in the fields of scanning, hacking, vanishing, and doing business in the underground economy. Should my wife and I both die in an accident, I do not care to have these come to light. It's a nuisance, but I keep these—plus tax records—off the premises in private storage. (In case of death, a friend of total confidence will clean out the unit and destroy all contents.)

Large: A three-drawer fireproof file cabinet is best stored in a secret room that will hopefully be large enough to hold one or two persons as well. A room such as this will give you added security, especially if you are the wife of a traveling man who leaves you home alone. We discovered one new home with an unusual "extra" purely by accident while traveling from Las Vegas to Portland in 1994. On the way (I won't say where, for a reason that will become obvious), my wife wanted to check out a certain rural upscale holiday home development. The builder included an astonishing list of electronic items as "standard," not the least of which was a soundproof room with a complete home movie-theater system with seating for twenty. But there was something more, not shown in the brochures. The agent showing us the model home saved the master bedroom for last. After showing us the "his" and "hers" bathrooms (à la Harrah's at Lake Tahoe), we were shown "his" walk-in closet, then "hers." At this point, the agent asked us if we'd seen the *entire* home.

"Yes," said my wife, "we've seen it all."

"Actually, you haven't," she said, and with that she gave a firm push to the door-sized shoe rack at the far end of the closet.

The shoe rack swung back on oiled offset hinges to reveal a secret room. It was about nine feet square and lined on two sides with storage shelves. There were no windows, but I noticed a vent for the heating system, and a telephone jack on one wall.

"Would you care to comment," I asked her, "on the purpose of this room?"

"No, we call this our *'don't ask, don't tell'* room."

I pass this idea on to you as worthy of consideration when you plan your next new home. The only hesitation I'd have would be that the secret room (more often called a "panic" room) would be common knowledge among the architect, the contractor, and the workers. Also, the building plans would be on file with the city or county. Gone are the days when pirates buried treasures in deep holes, then murdered the men who'd done the digging.

When you make the house plans, therefore, list the secret room as "storage." Whether finished or unfinished, give some excuse for including at least one outlet in the room, along with an overhead light and a telephone connection.

To close this section, I'll mention an unusual way to bury something that has only been possible since the days of satellites and GPS units:

1. Put some film in your camera, borrow a 50' or 100' tape measure, and purchase a handheld Global Positioning System (GPS) and a compass at any marine store.

2. Go to a "trackless," state-owned, desert wilderness (first choice: central Nevada), and look for a distinctive rock in a slightly raised area, to avoid any problem with a flash flood.

3. Carefully take a reading on the rock itself, using the GPS receiver. Write down the precise latitude and longitude. Take pictures of the rock.

4. Bury your container a certain distance away, and note the distance and the magnetic compass direction.

5. With your will, leave instructions. For extra security, give the latitude to your sister Josie, without telling her what the number represents. Then, in your will, you can describe the rock, the exact container location, and the precise longitude. Tell the executor, "Ask my sister Josie for the secret number I gave her. This is the latitude. (And without the latitude, your cache will be safe. Wouldn't Captain Kidd have liked to have a working GPS!)

The GPS will put the finder right next to the rock, the picture will identify the rock, the compass will indicate the correct magnetic direction, and the tape measure will bring the searcher to the "X" that marks the spot.

By the way, neglecting to put these instructions in your will and then getting Alzheimer's would be uncool.

AND SPEAKING OF NEGLECT...

From the Associated Press: " 'A worker preparing a forested site in DuPont (Washington) for a park-and-ride lot unearthed a plastic garbage can containing as much as $10,000 in coins and bills . . . Sound Transit bought the 4-acre property just weeks before the buried cash turned up,' said agency spokesman Lee Somerstein. . . . 'It was a bulldozer operator . . . whose machine ripped the top off a 32-gallon Rubbermaid trash can, exposed the buried money and unearthed a mystery,' Somerstein said . . ."

As this book goes to press, no one has yet come forward to claim the money.

QUESTIONS & ANSWERS

You mentioned keeping a radio in your secret or "panic" room, but aren't such rooms horrendously expensive? (I saw the movie.)

After the movie *Panic Room*, with Jodie Foster, was released, there was an item on CNN's *Headline News* about the increasing number of homes that have such rooms, with costs often running up to $75,000. Any home we ever build does include such a room, but at a minimal cost. *You don't need steel walls if the room is invisible.* If you are short of space, even a hall closet will do. The trick is that the door must not come down to the floor level. Enclose the bottom two feet and lower the top as well. Repaint or repaper the wall. Cover the opening with a mirror or a display case.

In addition to a pager and a cell phone, keep a bucket in there, along with a few candy bars, a jug of water, and a sleeping bag. A .12-gauge shotgun is optional.

What do you think about buying gold coins and burying them?

Before I answer that, note this gem from *California Lawyer*: "Texas attorney Scott Erikson pleaded guilty to laundering nearly $3.4 million from two Resolution Trust institutions after authorities found a hand-drawn treasure map in his home that led them to $1 million in buried gold coins bought with some of the stolen money."

He knew enough to hide the coins, but not enough to hide the map. This reminds me of those with secret overseas bank accounts who keep the bank statements at home. By the way, a million in gold weighs about 250 pounds. That alone would discourage me from trading cash for gold. But if you want to bury just a few dozen gold coins, well, why not? Just make sure you hide the map as well as you hide the coins.

What if a criminal breaks into my home and threatens to torture and kill me if I don't lead him to a hidden stash?

Hopefully this will never happen, because (a) you have never told a soul that you had *anything* hidden, and (b) you have serious layers of protection in your home. Nevertheless, some homeowners have two major hiding places, the first of which they are willing to give up. This could consist of a thousand or so in cash, plus some apparently rare coins and a few expensive-looking zircons that appear to be diamonds. Order the zircons on the Internet. Then go to a local jeweler and buy a luxurious, blue-velvet signature box in which to keep them.

You mentioned having a fake can with a removable bottom. Where can I buy one?

If you have access to the Internet, do a search for "diversion safes." (Include the quotation marks.) They cost from $15 to $25, plus shipping. Or contact Spy Yard, 12 The Arcade, Nashville, TN 37219. The phone number is 866-269-7007 and the Web site is *www.spyyard.com/personal_safes.htm.*

21

COOL STUFF THAT DID NOT FIT IN EARLIER

Come, Watson, come! The game is afoot. Not a word!
Into your clothes and come!

—ARTHUR CONAN DOYLE,
THE ADVENTURE OF THE ABBEY GRANGE

If Sherlock Holmes were alive today and on the trail of a terrorist, he would not have to leave his rented first-floor flat at 221B Baker Street, London. Instead, he would be hacking into confidential databases on his computer, making "pretext" telephone calls on his untraceable cell phone, and squeezing information from his Muslim informants in the Arab world.

Contrast that with the average private investigator. Even other PIs lament the fact that there are so many incompetent and/or shady characters in their field.

ARE MOST PIS COMPETENT?

No more than all lawyers are competent. As in any other profession, there are a few experts, but many more barely plod through. To illustrate, consider the famous Barbara Kurth Fagan case:

Stephen and Barbara Fagan had been married for five years, eloping to Haiti on the day that Stephen divorced Leah, his first wife. Then came a venomous divorce. He got the house. She got the kids. He didn't like that, and on October 28, 1979, he snatched the children, then only two and five, from his ex-wife's home in suburban Boston. He fled with the girls to Palm Beach County, Florida, where his parents and a sister already lived. He changed the girls' names to Rachael and Lisa and his own to William Stephen Martin.

Back in Massachusetts, Barbara regained her maiden name of Kurth and filed a criminal complaint. Over the years, she hired various private investigators but they came up blank. Finally, she gave up. She pressed ahead with her own life, remarried, and became a noted expert in cell biology.

Meanwhile, her ex-husband fashioned a good life for himself in South Florida: big houses, fast cars, and very rich wives. Nearly twenty years passed before someone in his or his latest wife's family decided Fagan's days of high living should come to an end. A tip to the authorities was all it took. Police nabbed him at his $2.2 million oceanfront estate, bought by wife number four, and he was returned to Massachusetts to face felony charges of kidnapping.

Why couldn't Stephen Fagan's wife track him down? One reason was given in the May 25, 1998, issue of *Newsweek:*

> Fagan and his daughters insist Kurth should have been able to find them if she'd really searched. Kurth's family says she spent more than $10,000 on lawyers and private investigators—to

no avail. A 1982 report from one PI warns her that staking out Fagan's sister's home in Florida would be an expensive long shot.

Others say she spent triple that, but whatever it was, either it was not enough, or—more likely!—she hired the wrong investigators.

TRAVEL

BEFORE YOU LEAVE

Private home. Before you leave on a long trip, do you leave a key with a neighbor? I suggest you not only not leave a key, but do not even say you are leaving. (Use timers that turn on lights, TV, stereo, sprinklers, etc. at varying times.) Louis R. Mitzell Jr., in his book *Invasion of Privacy*, tells the story of a Maryland couple who, before leaving on a vacation in August 1994, left a key with a neighbor. When they returned from their trip, they picked up the key, thanked the neighbor, and thought no more about it.

"Then," writes Mitzell, "in January 1995, the couple was adjusting a heating vent in their bathroom when they discovered a camera. Later that night, the couple found a second camera behind a heating vent in a dressing room and followed cables leading through their attic, down a drainpipe and underground into their neighbor's home. The neighbor had been watching the couple in the bathroom and dressing room for months—and it wasn't against the law."

Apartment: The problem here is that even if you do not leave a key with anyone when going on vacation, the landlord *does* have a key. Landlords surreptitiously enter apartments more often than you might think—in fact, it once happened to me. That was forty-five years ago, but there were such serious consequences that I haven't forgotten it yet.

Anthony Herbert, in his book *Complete Security Handbook*, has this to say in the section about locks: "Change them without the management's knowledge. (Remove the cylinder, take it to a locksmith, and get combination changed.) If the manager or janitor later complains, ask why he was attempting to enter your apartment while you were not present. Better to incur a minor lease violation than to be dead!"

No one should be permitted to visit your apartment unaccompanied, except in a life-and-death emergency!

OVERSEAS

If you travel to the United Kingdom and carry a laptop with sensitive information, beware of random checks. An agent might ask, "Do you have any pornography on your hard drive?" Even though you have no such thing there and tell him so, he'll say, "Well then, you won't mind if we turn it on and have a look, right?" If a password is needed, he will ask for it. If a file is encrypted, he will tell you to unencrypt it. It appears this is beginning to happen in other countries, and it may soon be coming to an airport near you. The remedy, of course—if you must get a secret file through customs—is to mail it ahead on a PC card, a CompactFlash, or on a CD. (See chapters 17 and 18.)

PRESCREENING

The Computer Assisted Passenger Prescreening System II (CAPPS II) scans multiple public and private databases for information on individuals traveling into and out of the United States. The system feeds the results to an analysis application that mathematically ranks travelers' potential as security threats. If you prefer not to be screened, head north to Canada by train, bus, or car. Then fly out of—and return to—Canada. Perfectly legal.

CROSSING INTO MEXICO OR CANADA

In an emergency, you may be forced to journey north or south. If so, and if you are a native-born U.S. citizen, there should normally be no problem when crossing a border in either direction, as long as neither you nor your vehicle look suspicious.

You should know, however, that there are two types of border inspections, primary and secondary. You do not want secondary, not ever, because then your name will go into the computer and, to paraphrase the ads for the Roach Motel, travelers who check *in* to the computer never check out. Suggestions:

- Dress like a tourist. Clean and neat, but no tie.
- Do not cross with anything to declare, or with any item even remotely suspicious. No fruit, no weapons, no drugs. Best way to cross is on a tour bus. Next best way is on foot, at a busy crossing, during the busiest hours, but taking a car is certainly more convenient, despite the fact that your license plate may go into a computer. (Here's where it pays off to have your car registered in the name of an LLC.)
- Do not cross into Mexico with an RV if you can avoid it. Some Americans have been arrested in Mexico and held under false pretenses, with the goal of allowing the American to go free if he leaves his motor home behind. (An RV is okay for Canada.)
- If there are several lines leading to multiple booths at the crossing, pick your lane and then stick with it. If you change lanes, the inspector from the original lane may spot you, think you're trying to avoid him, and make you get back in line. Then, when your turn comes, you'll get more attention than you really wanted to receive.

Never cross in either direction with a flippant attitude, because both customs inspectors (CIs) and immigration inspectors (IIs) have you in their total power. They can search you, your vehicle, and your belongings for whatever reason, or for no reason at all. Therefore, before you approach the border, first check your wallet or purse, and then the glove compartment and the trunk. (If you carry my book with you, put on a different dust jacket!) Be prepared to answer any questions whatsoever, no matter how personal or insulting. Lawyers (and some egocentric businessmen) have been known to say, "Do I *have* to answer that?" The response, as given by Customs Inspector Ned Beaumont in his book *Beat the Border* is:

> "You don't have to answer. But then again, you don't have to cross the border. And you're not going to cross the border until you answer that question and *any others I see fit to ask*. Understand?"

CIs and IIs are skilled at deception, aka lying. If they preface something by saying "You don't need to worry about thus-and-so. . . ." *start worrying!* They may try the good cop/bad cop routine, like in the movies. Remember that it's really bad cop/worse cop. These folks are not your buddies. Keep cool and collected on the outside, skeptical and cynical on the inside. Beaumont makes this point in his "People Smarts" section:

> An inspector talks to more liars in a month than the layman does in a lifetime. How good at spotting liars do you think that inspector is going to be in a year? Or five? Or ten? I've worked with inspectors who'd been on the job for 20 years. They could detect a lie . . . *without fail*, in the first five seconds of the inspection.

When you are asked for the purpose of your trip, do not just answer "business" or "pleasure," the inspectors hear that all the time. Be specific: "We're going up to Abbotsford to buy a Clipper canoe," or "we're going to the boat show at the Winnipeg Convention Centre."

A final word of warning: Don't even *think* of using a false ID.

Even if it's perfect, *you'll* know it's not, and the inspector will sense that fact.

HOW TO DEAL WITH CLERKS AND TELLERS

First of all, dress like they do, or just a bit better. (Source: John J. Molloy, *Dress for Success.*) No matter how convinced you are that clothes make the man or woman, reading Molloy's best-seller will make you even more of a true believer. To Molloy's book, I add the following: If you are a woman, dress and act like a woman, emphasis on "dress," as in the noun. If you are a man, and if getting others to accept your requests for privacy is high on your list of priorities, show up freshly shaved and with a recent, short haircut. Source: Me. Right or wrong, I often refuse requests from anyone who draws attention to himself or herself by outward appearance rather than by inward qualities of honesty, integrity, loyalty, and virtue. (I wish they'd teach that in grade schools.)

Next, when at all possible, *deal with the opposite sex*. This applies to trips to the bank, the county courthouse, the utility companies, and to any other location where low-level clerks deal with the public. If you are a woman, seek out a man. If you are a man, talk to a woman. Source: innumerable private investigators.

HOW TO DELAY THE SERVING OF A SUBPOENA

A subpoena is an order, usually signed by a notary public, to attend a legal proceeding, such as a trial or deposition. A subpoena *duces tecum*—Latin for "bring with you"—means you are ordered to bring certain documents with you, which can be anything from bank statements to old love letters. The purpose of a subpoena is to force you to produce something you do not want to produce, and/or to appear in a civil or criminal court case when that is on the very bottom of your "things-I-like-to-do" list. Although it is not correct to say that if they can't find you they can't serve you, this process certainly can, and often should be, delayed as long as possible, which will give you time to think things out.

(At this late date, don't do a Nixon and erase tapes, nor an Ollie North and shred documents. If your tape, document, or photo files need work, stop reading NOW and start erasing, burning, flushing, burying, encrypting, and shredding *before* the storm clouds gather.)

In a civil case, a subpoena can be delivered by a law-firm employee, a professional process server, peace officer, or anyone else of legal age (in some counties, registered and bonded) capable of making multiple attempts, able to correctly fill out the proof or certificate of service, and who can testify as a credible witness if the service is challenged.

In a criminal case, service will be achieved if you acknowledge receipt of the subpoena by telephone or mail, as well as in person. The way you identify yourself (should you ever want to . . .) is by name, date of birth, and driver's license number.

Delaying service of a subpoena is not for amateurs. Beyond a certain point, if it can be shown that you *willfully* disobeyed it, the court can issue a bench warrant for your arrest. Now is the time to call in an experienced shark, preferably of the species great white, bull, tiger, or oceanic whitetip. This lawyer will know many sneaky tricks about *serving* subpoenas and will thus be able to tell you how and up to what point you can delay service.

Now then, if service appears to be inevitable, at least take control of *where* and *when* this is to happen. Don't get caught unaware like Franklin K——— from Cleveland. He owed his lawyer money, but he had a daughter's wedding coming up, so he chose to stall the lawyer and throw an elaborate wedding reception. The lawyer learned about this and decided to cause the most possible humiliation to his delinquent client.

At the precise moment Franklin stood up to propose a toast to the new bride and groom, the sheriff barged in and served Franklin with a subpoena! Learn from this and, if you fear you will be served with a subpoena, do not attend a public gathering where you may be known, and do not admit your identity to a stranger.

If you *are* served have your legal beagle bring a motion to quash. (You may have heard that the process server must touch your face or body with the papers. Not true; he can just toss the papers at your feet, or whatever.) Have him claim that service was improper and statutory requirements were not met.

When all else fails, follow the advice of the anonymous writer who penned these words:

When uncertain,
Or in doubt,
Run in circles!
Scream and shout!

LAST-MINUTE BITS AND PIECES

FACIAL RECOGNITION SOFTWARE IS HERE TO STAY

As you have heard by now, facial recognition is now being used to find "prospective criminals" at sporting events and at busy intersections where foot traffic is prevalent. So far, some errors have been made, but the software is being improved as I write this. It appears that once you are targeted, neither sunglasses nor facial hair can protect you. However, unless you are known to have associated with international terrorists, and/or are wanted for serious crimes, this should not be a problem for you.

Incidentally, facial recognition can also be used to add another layer of security to your computer. Visionics has software called FaceIt!, which uses your face as a password for the screensaver on your computer. Only a person with the same facial structure as yourself will be allowed to gain access to your system. (It makes you blink, to show that you are still alive!)

CREDIT CARD SECURITY MEASURE

Restaurants and other businesses sometimes toss out credit card receipts without shredding them. To protect yourself against this possibility, as soon as you sign the slip, *cross out the last four digits of the number* (both on the original, and on your copy.). If anyone protests, assure him or her that you absolutely positively have this legal right.

FAKE IDS

As I've said before, it is useless to order fake IDs on the Internet. Either you won't get anything at all, or what you do get will be worthless. Here is an additional reason: Sooner or later these companies get busted. When they do, the authorities will, of course, grab the customer list. Would you like them to spot *your* name and address on that list?

TIPS ON MAINTAINING A <u>REALLY</u> LOW PROFILE

Consider the methods of Kate M———, one of my readers, who takes her privacy very seriously indeed. She has found the people she meets uninterested in privacy, and skeptical about her concerns, but that hasn't stopped her. "I've mostly quit telling others about it and just quietly go about the business of protecting myself without telling anyone what I'm doing," says Kate. She's chosen to work from home for maximum flexibility and privacy, staying in control of her own schedule and managing to avoid the crowds. "Often, I go grocery-shopping late at night (eleven P.M.) or even at two or three A.M., at the store that's open twenty-four hours. Advantages include no traffic; parking right at the front door of the supermarket; no lines. . . . I can do my shopping in 30 percent less time. Plus, I see almost no one. Also, I can check my P.O. box and drive by my ghost address (a lockable mailbox on a rural road.) Even without tinted windows, driving at night means fewer people can recognize me. Even my nondescript old car and its color are harder to recognize at night. When I park the car out in public in the daytime, I'm now very sensitive to making sure there are no identifying items inside (letters or anything with my name on it). But I've also discovered that when I shop in the daytime, if I park in an out-of-the-way place at the outer edge of the parking lot, there are fewer people who will walk past my car on their way into the store/mall. So fewer people to notice my car."

However, I do not necessarily recommend Kate's use of the dark to enhance privacy. In many areas, it would be dangerous for a lone woman to be out so late at night.

THE "LAST FOUR" DIGITS

Does it sound innocent enough when you are asked for "the last four digits" of your Social Security number? For example, cable TV operators ask that question when you order their service (assuming you wisely decline to read off the number of your driver's license). This number can identify you, because who else with your same name would also have the same last four digits of the Social Security number? The easy solution is to have some other four-digit number ready to use. Think about it ahead of time. Perhaps it will be a date in history, or the house number where you once lived long ago.

TRACKING THE CAR YOU RENT

An increasing number of national car-rental chains are using a tracking device on each car. For some scary information about what these devices can do, go to *http://aircept.com/products.asp.*

BEWARE THIS PHONY PHONE CALL

Suppose a bounty hunter wants to track you down. If he can locate your girl- or boyfriend or a family member, he may put an illegal tap on that person's telephone. Let's say it's your mother. The bounty hunter calls your mother and says he is calling from the scene of a multiple car accident. Would she please check to see if you are alive and well? Because one of the casualties *may* have been you!

When this person immediately calls you, the bounty hunter will be listening in.

SERIOUS WARNING ABOUT RÉSUMÉS!

A lead article in the newsletter *Bottom Line Personal*, based on an interview with me, brought some excellent advice. Writing to me as "a public service," a reader of the interview warned:

> "You neglected to point out how dangerous it is to put one's résumé on the Internet. I am a professional recruiter and I can tell you more harm can come from this one action than anything else. There are malevolent people out there who are profiling everybody who has a résumé on the 'Net. It is by far the most dangerous thing you can do." Quite rightly, this expert cautions against allowing untold thousands of people to view some of your most personal data: "Please let people know they must *never ever* put a resume on the Internet. *NEVER EVER!*"

THE LATEST ON "LO-JACK"

A reader in New York recently posed this question: "Several years ago, trying to save money on car insurance, I purchased a Lo-Jack system and had it installed in my car. The insurance savings are great, but after reading your book, I wonder if this was a smart move. The system allows the police to locate the car, if it is ever stolen, by emitting a tracking-signal. I don't quite understand the technology, but do you know if it's possible for a PI to use it to track my movements? Can they get access to the Lo-Jack frequencies? Should I get rid of it?"

"Lo-Jack," said a PI friend, "just like anything else committed to paper or a computer, can be compromised. For example, I just handled a case where a client wanted her husband tracked in New York. I developed a source in the EZ-Pass system that gave me his whereabouts at any given time without having to use physical surveillance. I'm sure that with a few phone calls and the proper amount of cash spread around, I'd find someone in the local police department who uses Lo-Jack who would supply me with information. It hasn't failed yet."

FILLING OUT FORMS

A recent documentary on TV showed how private information is picked up and sold to criminals involved in identity theft. *Tens of thousands of businesses toss out application forms without shredding them.* This includes applications for employment, for loans, and for credit cards. If you have *any* family members currently filling out such forms, make sure that they never list your home address, and specifically ask how such information is later disposed of.

RECORDED MUSIC ON HOLD

When some large corporations—especially the telephone companies—put you on hold with recorded music, the company operator does *not* hear the music. Instead, he or she is listening to what you may be saying to another person while waiting to come back online.

ARE YOU UNDER SURVEILLANCE?

In days gone by, an unfamiliar van parked across the street from your house or apartment might have been a signal that a PI was inside. However, the public is getting wise to this, so the latest ploy is to use a generic sports utility vehicle (SUV). The tip-off in this case may be a darkened window where the *driver* sits. In most states, it is against the law to put a dark tint on the driver and passenger door windows. Therefore, the PI carries a piece of darkened Plexiglas, cut out in the shape of the window, and puts it in place only when he is parked and doing surveillance work.

TEXT MESSAGES VIA CELL PHONES

"I just spoke with a person who works for InphoMatch, Inc., Chantilly, Virginia," wrote one of my readers. "InphoMatch contracts to cellular telephone companies to handle their SMS (Simple Messaging System) messages (text messages sent via cellular phones). He told me that when someone sends a text message, the following is recorded: message content, the sender's cell number, the recipient's cell number, and the time and date of the message. Federal law mandates that all 'billable information' (pretty broad term) be maintained for ten or fifteen years."

MAGNETIC LOCKS

To quote from the Web site *www.rev-a-shelf.com:* "Rev-A-Lock is an ultrasecure, magnetically operated cabinet and drawer lock designed to make it virtually impossible for children to break into cabinets and drawers containing unsafe items. Only the extremely powerful magnetic key, which is supplied with the product, can open the lock. Refrigerator and other magnets won't work. . . . Rev-A-Lock can be seen in the hardware and security departments."

These locks are also marketed under the trade name Tot-Lok. They are extremely useful for purposes of privacy. There is no keyhole to give away private hiding spaces. Suppose, for example, that you slip your laptop into such a place whenever you are away from home. If an agent slips into your home on a "sneak and peek" warrant, he will almost certainly not find your computer. However, if he does, he will have had to break into the space, and this means that at least you now *know* what has happened!

YOUR MEDICAL RECORDS

The dreaded Federal Medical Privacy Rule took effect on April 14, 2003. Although the government claims the new rule *enhances* your medical privacy, the opposite is actually the case. It eliminates your freedom to give or withhold consent regarding the release of your personal health information to many persons for many purposes. *Without your knowledge or consent*, your records can be released to public-health authorities; to a governmental authority investigating an incident of domestic violence; for health oversight and regulatory activities; for judicial and administrative proceedings pursuant to court orders and subpoenas; to law enforcement officials for crime prevention purposes; for organ donation purposes; for medical research under specific guidelines; and to "avert a serious threat to health or safety."

Do any PIs have informants who will obtain a medical file for a price? Of course they do. In fact, there are investigators who—in return for a substantial fee—will have someone hack into your doctor's computer system or bribe an employee to see your file, or—if there is no other way—have an accomplice break into the office at night and steal it.

Is there anything that can be done, other than using a false name and paying cash? My only suggestion is that when you are asked to sign a waiver for the release of your medical records, do not sign the "blanket waiver." The blanket waiver may read something like this (italics added): "I authorize *any* physician, hospital, or other medical provider to release to [insurer] *any* information regarding my medical history, symptoms, treatment, exam results, or diagnosis." Cross this waiver out and write in something more specific, such as, "I authorize my records to be released from [name of hospital, clinic, or doctor] for the [date of treatment] as relates to [the condition treated]."

ELECTRONIC GREETING CARDS

If you receive an e-card from someone you do not know, think seriously about deleting it *without first opening it*. It may contain a Trojan horse that will record your keystrokes or steal your passwords.

PUBLIC SCHOOLS

If you have children in a public school, have you taught them how *not* to answer questions that invade their—and often your—privacy? Here's a typical question, taken from a Minnesota's Basic Skills Writing Test. Each student was asked the following essay question: "Your teacher has asked you to write about one thing you would like to change about yourself. Name one thing about yourself and give specific reasons why you would like to change it. Give enough details so your teacher will understand your ideas."

Explain to your children that their answers may become a part of their student file . . . and come back years later to haunt them.

MAGAZINE LABELS

A good practice is to tear off the labels *as soon as the magazines arrive*. You may not want the labels left on when you toss the magazines in the trash, even though they have your ghost address rather than your real address. I suggest that you especially may not want the labels on when you'll be reading the magazines on the plane or in your hotel room.

VEHICLE SEARCHES

In two cases that the Supreme Court has refused to review, police searched cars after those involved refused (or were unable) to produce their driver's license and car registration. This means that warrantless searches are allowed anywhere documents "reasonably may be expected to be found." Therefore, if an officer stops you for a traffic violation, he can look pretty much anywhere in your car, even the trunk. (If you use a ghost address or a P.O. box instead of your true address, would today be a good day to review the contents of your vehicle?)

ACTIVATING A PHONE VIA THE INTERNET

Rather than do this from home, use a public access terminal at a library, or try a Kinko's in another town. Wipe the browser's cache and history when you're done.

UNWANTED MAIL?

Order a rubber stamp with one of these three messages:

- MOVED. NO FORWARDING ADDRESS
- NOT DELIVERABLE AS ADDRESSED. UNABLE TO FORWARD
- DECEASED

INFORMATION-SHARING

Airline passengers are not the only ones being profiled to determine if they are a danger to flight safety or for any other reason. Since 9-11, the private sector has also been sharing information with the government. Many supermarkets, of course, make this information available, but so do clubs you might not think of, such as the National Association of Scuba Divers. Libraries and bookstores are under pressure as well.

And, by the way, did you know that some national hotel chains share lists of movie titles—including pornos—rented by their customers? While the name of the movie isn't on the bill, it *is* included in the customer profile. This information is shared with their many affiliates, including other hotels and restaurants.

INSTANT-MESSAGING (IM)

Until now, many of the five million users of IM have assumed that these messages were hard to track. Not so. Software maker Ascentive sells a program called BeAware that grabs and stores screen shots of IM sessions. A similar program is sold by San Diego–based Akonix. A reader who has seen these programs work says about IM, "At every stop along the road from person A to person B, the mail employees can read the card. *No one should ever use IM for any confidential matters.*"

22

AN EXAM, A SECRET, AND AN INVITATION

Heaven has no rage like love to hatred turned,
Nor hell a fury like a woman scorned.

—WILLIAM CONGREVE,
"THE MOURNING RIDE"

In the manner of Earl Stanley Gardner, I call this account "The Case of the Supernatural Stalker." It all started the night David N———, depressed after an acrimonious breakup with a girlfriend, stopped in a bar in downtown Seattle, ordered a boilermaker, and struck up a conversation with a woman on the stool next to him. One thing led to another and the woman—her name was Mimi—ended up in his bed. She was back in his bed the next night, and the day after that she moved in. David was twenty-nine at the time, and although Mimi claimed to be a year younger, he began to have doubts. The next evening, he pulled her driver's license from her purse while she was taking a shower. Not only was her true age thirty-seven, but her last name was not the one she had given him. When he confronted her about the discrepancies, a screaming match followed, after which she packed up and left.

He returned home from work the following day to find his best suits scattered over the bedroom floor, sprayed with red paint. Personal papers from his desk were strewn about, and his address book was missing. The telephone rang at three o'clock the next morning, but no one spoke when he picked up the receiver. Twenty minutes later, it rang again, with the same result, so he left it off the hook for the rest of the night. The next day he skipped work to get a new, unlisted telephone number and to have a locksmith come in and change the locks. At some time the following night, all four of the tires on his car were slashed. Although Mimi was obviously responsible, he didn't go to the police because he had no proof.

Within a week, unable to concentrate on his work with the continual harassment, he quit his job, rented a U-Haul trailer, and headed south. On the way through Portland, he stopped off to see his mother (Edna N———) just long enough to say that he'd had his mail forwarded to her address. Once he had a new address, he'd have her send it on to him.

His travels ended in Redwood, California, where he got a job on a commission basis and was able to rent a small cabin on a temporary basis. He gave the owner a false name, and arranged to leave both the telephone and the utilities in the owner's name. For the first week, all went well, and he was slowly starting to relax. Then, late one evening, the telephone rang. A wrong number? He picked up the receiver.

"Better not start your car in the morning!" screamed Mimi.

AN EXAM

How was Mimi able to call him, when nothing at this location was in his name? Here is a list of the things she did *not* do:

- She did not follow him when he left Seattle.
- She did not use a private investigator, nor any other accomplice.

- She did not use a computer in any way.

- She did not call any of his friends.

- She did not find out his mail-forwarding arrangements.

The rest of this page is blank. Can you guess the answer, before you turn the page?

Since Mimi had David's address book, it was a simple matter of going through it until she found "Mom," followed by an address in Portland and a telephone number. Two weeks later she showed up at that address and waited until she saw a woman—obviously David's mother—back a Volkswagen out of the garage. The garage door closed behind her. Mimi then followed her to a self-service gas station and watched her fill the tank. When Edna headed in to pay for the gas, Mimi snatched the garage-opener from the Volkswagen, raced back to the house, opened the garage, entered the home, and grabbed the address book from a drawer on the telephone stand. When she went through it later, she found David's old number. A line had been drawn through it and the new number in California was penciled in.

The case of David N——— is not unique. I cite this particular example to demonstrate the length to which some stalkers will go. When the stalking becomes an obsession, their entire life revolves around their target, to the point that nothing else matters. They will quit their jobs, sell their belongings, travel any distance, and go to any length to track their quarry down.

A SECRET

None of the information in this book will be of assistance to you unless you put the suggestions into practice. I urge you to start *now*. Do not wait until you can find the time—you may never find it. Do not wait until you can "do it right," because that day may never come.

All successful persons can list one or more secrets for their success. My entrepreneurial father passed his own two secrets of success on to me when I left home to seek my way in the world. ("To make money, you must go where the money is" and "Never take a partner.") Earl Nightingale wrote an entire best-selling book with a single theme, *The Strangest Secret*. ("We become what we think about.")

Well, *my* secret isn't very strange. In fact, it's so obvious that I fear you will disregard it:

> *For every desired action, set a date, and when the date arrives,*
> *just go ahead and do it, NO MATTER WHAT.*

My rule does not have any rhythm to it, it doesn't even rhyme, but it works for me and it will work for you. Here is the application: Make a list of what you wish to accomplish and set a date to complete each item. And, when the time comes, just do it. Decide on your level of privacy, then write down the suggestions you plan to follow and set a date for their completion. Your goal—at the very least—is to never again have your true name coupled with your true address. Here is a short review:

- Obtain at least one new address and give this ghost address to your out-of-town relatives (including your parents!), friends, banks, insurance companies, utility companies, IRS, DMV, and everyone else.

- Disconnect your present telephone. Then have it reconnected in another name. Get a cell phone in another name.

- Open an out-of-state bank account and obtain checks that show neither your full name nor your address. Start with a high number.

- For sensitive e-mail, use one of the Web accounts such as Yahoo, Zipmail, or Hushmail. (None are totally secure, but they are usually a big step up from your local Internet service provider.) Use discernment when filling in the "personal" information.

- If you are renting, move. If you are a homeowner, sell, then start over.

- Order one or more LLCs so they will be on hand when you suddenly need them.

- Start an invisible home-based business if you have not already done so.

- Look at every challenge to your privacy as an adventure. Get a life, have fun, and sleep soundly at night.

AN INVITATION

As this book goes to press, it is as up-to-date as I can make it. However, some changes may have taken place before you have this book in your hands. If you have access to the Internet, check *www.howtobeinvisible.com* for updated information. The password is "ssndob," short for Social Security number and date of birth. (Note that the password is in lowercase letters.)

If you have any comments or suggestions, I invite you to contact me. If you have Internet access, leave a message on my Web site. Otherwise, a letter will be fine. When you address it, please do not start it with "J. J. Luna." Rather, address it using four lines in this exact order:

Marrero & Luna
Apartado de Correos, 2
35626 Morro del Jable, LP de GC
Canary Islands, Spain

If, after putting some of my suggestions into practice, you have an interesting anecdote to relate, by all means, send it along. Perhaps it can be included in the next edition of this book. All messages and letters will be read, and, when time permits, I'll do my best to answer those that are pertinent.

CLOSING REMARKS

Remember Eddie Burke, the forty-eight-year-old handyman who was arrested in connection with the 1998 murder of seventy-five-year-old Irene Kennedy of Foxborough, Massachusetts? As I wrote in chapter 1, although Burke was known to be innocent, he was locked up for forty-one days, demonized in newspapers and on TV, and his entire life was put under a microscope.

Years passed without any clue as to the real killer. Then, at six A.M. on June 28, 2003, I pulled into the Waterhouse Country Store along New Hampshire's Highway 111 to pick up a coffee to go. Among the newspapers displayed on the counter next to the cashier was the *Boston Herald*. The front page headline was "BITE MARK LINKS KILLER TO 1998 SLAYING," and I took a closer look. Yes, this was the Eddie Burke case! I bought the paper, took my coffee to a booth, and started to read. According to Norfolk District Attorney William Keating, DNA taken from a bite mark on Irene Kennedy's breast matched convicted killer Martin G. Guy, who was serving a life sentence for another crime. A secondary article was titled "Vindication Bittersweet for Ex-Suspect," and quoted Burke as saying, "My mother died, my life has been ruined, and I've been in hell for four years. And half of this pinhead town still thinks I'm a murderer."

As you will recall, even though Burke was the wrong man, the contents of his house were published by the media, and for years to come he was branded by many as a murderer. Good reason, is it not, to keep your private address private? And, if you have any secrets to hide, hide them in a secret place or in a secret room.

As I was preparing this final chapter, I received a letter from one of my readers who lives in a southern state. Duane is a young single man who has a job that keeps him on the road for up to six weeks at a stretch, and he claims a ghost address saved his life. Here's his story:

Over a period of time he got to know Araceli, an attractive

Mexican girl who worked at one of the hardware stores on his route. On his last trip through, he took this girl out to a country dance. On his return trip, when he stopped in the same town for gas, a secretary from the hardware store spotted him and came running up.

"What are you doing here? Araceli's boyfriend is looking for you with a gun and he says he's going to kill you!" It turned out that the boyfriend worked at a used-car lot where he had access to DMV records. "Was he ever mad," said the secretary, "when he found out your car tags were registered to some company in Alaska!"

Remember, no matter how many laws there are against revealing private information, there are always employees in the DMV, in the utility, cable TV, and telephone companies, as well as in car dealerships, that not only have access to the information but will sell it to others. Even the police have been known to pass information on to friends—or to the highest bidder. In a recent case, informants inside the LAPD were found to be on the payroll of one of the tabloids, furnishing inside information about calls from and investigations of prominent entertainment personalities.

This book would not be complete without a passing mention of the USA PATRIOT ACT (officially, "Uniting and Strengthening America by Providing Appropriate Tools Required to Intercept and Obstruct Terrorism Act of 2001"). On October 26, 2001, this Act, often referred to as USAPA, was signed into law, giving sweeping new powers to both domestic law enforcement and international intelligence agencies. It expands all four traditional tools of surveillance: wiretaps, search warrants, subpoenas, and pen registers. (A pen register collects the outgoing phone numbers placed from a specific telephone line.) Government agents can now go from phone to phone and computer to computer without demonstrating that either is even being used by a suspect or target of an order, nor is the attorney general required to report to the court what it is doing. In practical terms:

- It allows law enforcement to obtain the telephone numbers of all calls made to or from a specific phone.

- It is now easier to obtain surreptitious or "sneak and peek" warrants under which notice can be delayed.

- It removes many of the checks and balances that prevented both police and the foreign intelligence agencies from improperly conducting surveillance on U.S. citizens who are not involved in criminal or terrorist activity.

- It allows the FBI to check bookstore purchases, medical information, and public libraries, and includes a gag order threatening librarians with criminal prosecution if they tell anyone of such visits.

As this book goes to press, additional acts are being proposed. Although details are lacking, it seems evident that the government will receive sweeping new powers to increase domestic intelligence-gathering, surveillance, and law-enforcement prerogatives. Does this mean the sky is really falling?

For anyone remotely connected with terrorists or terrorism, the answer may be yes. For the rest of us, however, personal privacy can still be maintained. If you truly put the suggestions in this book into practice, especially the one about never again allowing your real name to be coupled with your home address, you will be far ahead of the pack when it comes to making yourself invisible.

Since this book was first published, thousands of readers have faded from view. So can you.

Yours faithfully,

J. J. Luna

Fuerteventura Island
December 2003

GLOSSARY

aka: "also known as."

CMRA: commercial mail-receiving agency, Also known as a "mail drop."

CPA: Certified Public Accountant.

DEA: Drug Enforcement Administration.

DOB: date of birth.

Ghost address: a private mail drop address to be used in lieu of your own.

IRS: Internal Revenue Service.

LLC: limited liability company.

Mail drop: an address (other than where you live) used for incoming mail, package, and courier deliveries.

NSA: National Security Agency.

PI: private investigator or private eye. Sometimes used to refer to a "private detective," although some states prohibit PIs from calling themselves detectives.

SSN: Social Security number.

APPENDIX

COMPUTER SECURITY

Michael Spaulding, the owner of InfoSecGuru, specializes in Information Security & Assurance. His expertise is across all data protection spectrums, including application development, network security, Internet voice, security assessment services, and data privacy. He has consulted Global Fortune 500 corporations, domestic and foreign government intelligence, services, and has spoken at numerous security conferences. Spaulding can be reached at *www.infosecguru.com* or infosecguru@swissinfo.org.

GHOST ADDRESSES

Two addresses are available to those who prefer to receive mail in any name they choose, and without furnishing identification. The first is a private street address in a small city in Alberta, Canada, available to all readers. The second—limited to a private club consisting of owners of New Mexico LLCs—is in Alaska's Aleutian Islands.

If this information is not posted at *www.howtobeinvisible.com*, then direct your inquiry to canaryislands@hushmail.com or write to:

M. M. Martin
Benito Perez Armas, 12
35500 Arrecife de Lanzarote
Canary Islands, Spain

NEW MEXICO LIMITED LIABILITY COMPANIES

Letters addressed to the box number below will be sent on to a young woman who has been forming legal entities for the author since 1990. She forms New Mexico LLCs for $99, plus $99 per year (three-year minimum) for the New Mexico registered agent. (For details, go to *www. howtobeinvisible.com* and click on the LLC link.) If you have any questions, direct them to *senorita@swissinfo.org* or mail aletter to:

Tenerife Trust
P.O. Box 466
Burlington, WA 98233

PRIVATE INVESTIGATOR

Condor Investigations, Inc. specializes in locating hidden assets and finding individuals. In business since 1988, Condor has worldwide affiliates and is owned and operated by Patrick Picciarelli, former NYPD lieutenant and author of several true-crime books. Condor can be reached at 724-684-8184 or e-mail pat@lifename.com.

CONSULTATIONS WITH THE AUTHOR

Although Jack Luna is available for private consultations, these are limited to readers who are willing to identify themselves and give references to prove that they are law-abiding citizens with legitimate reasons for protecting their privacy. The consultations are normally held in Las Palmas de Gran Canaria (Spain) or in Vancouver, British Columbia (Canada).

However, *a personal consultation may not be necessary*. "I have no additional secrets," says Luna. "Everything I know about privacy, I've put into this book." If you are nevertheless interested in contacting the author, direct your inquiry to canaryman@swissinfo. org or write to the Morro del Jable, Canary Islands address listed on page 271.

INDEX